Lloyd C. Gardner is the
History at Rutgers University.
policy, Gardner is the author
foreign policy, including *The Lo*

...ghdad and ... ...gs.

The Road to Tahrir Square

*Egypt and the United States from the
Rise of Nasser to the Fall of Mubarak*

LLOYD C. GARDNER

SAQI

*To the memory of four great teachers: Doris Evans,
Dorothy Whitted, Ben Spencer, and Dave Jennings.
In the past we are found.*

*

ISBN 978-0-86356-875-6

Published in the United Kingdom by Saqi Books 2011
Published by arrangement with The New Press, New York

A full CIP record for this book is available from the
British Library.

A full CIP record for this book is available from the
Library of Congress.

Printed and bound by CPI Group (UK), Croydon, CR0 4YY

SAQI
26 Westbourne Grove, London W2 5RH
www.saqibooks.com

CONTENTS

INTRODUCTION

Clinton, in Cairo's Tahrir Square, Embraces a Revolt She Once Discouraged

—Headline on a story by Steven Lee Myers,
New York Times, March 16, 2011

Secretary of State Hillary Clinton was the first high-level Obama administration figure to go to Cairo after the popular uprising that toppled Hosni Mubarak, Washington's most reliable ally in the Middle East for over a generation. "To see where this revolution happened," she exulted on a walk through Tahrir Square, "and all that it has meant to the world, is extraordinary for me." The *New York Times* headlined her "stroll," however, as something more like catch-up with a racing series of events that had left the United States unsure of where it stood now that a pillar of its Middle East policy had disappeared.

The initial wavering in the Obama administration when the protests began on January 25, 2011, reflected uncertainty and fear about the future. Secretary Clinton said on that first day of protests, "Our assessment is that the Egyptian government is stable and is looking for ways to respond to the legitimate needs and interests of the Egyptian people." One implication of that statement was that the United States felt able to judge what was legitimate and what was not. The president then spoke with Mubarak on the telephone, urging him not to resort to force, while Vice President Joe Biden, in an effort to encourage a peaceful solution, refused initially on American television to call the Egyptian president a dictator. Many more telephone calls over the next two weeks were made by Secretary of Defense Robert Gates and the chairman of the Joint Chiefs of Staff, Admiral Mike Mullen, to their Cairo counterparts, at first in an attempt to learn what the Egyptian armed forces believed about the protestors, and then, when it became clear that Mubarak would not step down, to prevent the military from taking sides.

While the Pentagon's main concern was not to lose touch with an army in which it had invested over $50 billion since the time Mubarak had come to power, two of America's other allies, Israel and Saudi Arabia, fretted about U.S. policy in "abandoning" the aging dictator who had controlled Egyptian politics with unquestioning support from the military. Americans had paid little attention, on the other hand, to the policies their government had followed during the Mubarak era, let alone to the background story of how Washington had finally developed such a close relationship after a series of missteps in the years since the 1952 Egyptian Revolution. Now more than ever, with the revolutionary spirit inspiring protestors in country after country, the debate over future policies required a historical grounding. This book opens a door on that past.

At first there had been Gamal Abdel Nasser, whose determination to lead the Arab world away from reliance on the United States and the West at the height of the Cold War forced an unhappy Eisenhower administration to make difficult choices opposed to its European allies during the 1956 Suez Crisis. Then there had been Anwar el-Sadat's audacious initiatives beginning with the October War in 1973 that surprised Nixon and Kissinger as well as Jimmy Carter. Finally, after Sadat's assassination, Hosni Mubarak had emerged, a man whose enormous ambition to rule matched perfectly Washington's desire to make Egypt into what it had always wanted it to be: a loyal ally who held the line against radical nationalism in the Arab world.

Mubarak had kept Sadat's peace with Israel (negotiated over the heads of other Arab countries) and provided public support for America's policies elsewhere in the Middle East (especially Iran and Iraq). And, notably, Mubarak provided pivotal support to the George W. Bush administration's War on Terror, cooperating with the CIA's "rendition" program by accepting suspects sent to Egypt for "questioning" using methods that could not be approved elsewhere after they became known, including waterboarding and other forceful interrogation techniques.

Of course, Mubarak expected to be paid, and paid handsomely. In exchange for these "services," the United States provided Egypt with military aid totaling nearly $1.5 billion a year—second only to Israel's subsidy—and hoped for the best as far as Mubarak's internal policies. Generally speaking, such hopes took the same form as the Clinton administration's attitude toward gays in the U.S. military: "don't ask, don't tell."

After the attacks of September 11, 2001, when the supposed weapons of mass destruction (WMDs) that Iraq's Saddam Hussein had hidden away could not be discovered and indeed were found not to exist, the Bush administration turned to the rhetoric of spreading democracy as the motive for war against Saddam's regime. Wilsonian idealism of this sort is often invoked to cover embarrassing gaps (like the missing WMDs) and to couch the protection of such material interests as oil wells on a higher plane of motivation. But it is a risky ploy, for ideas can take on their own momentum.

The events at Tahrir Square would likely have occurred without American rhetoric after 9/11, of course. Yet whether they would have occurred without years of unstinting American support to Mubarak is a far more interesting question. Would Mubarak have felt able to pursue his repressive policies had he not enjoyed full American backing across nearly three decades?

However one thinks about those questions, the history of U.S.–Egyptian relations provides the essential missing factor if we are to understand where and why the new government in Cairo, even in its interim form, has already departed significantly from Mubarak's agenda of satisfying Washington above all other things. The new government has signaled its intention to reestablish diplomatic relations with Iran, to end cooperation with Israel in blocking the border with Gaza, and has already brokered an agreement between rival Palestinian factions, one of whom, Hamas, is regarded as a terrorist organization by Israel and the United States. Egypt, said a representative of the government, intends to keep its commitment to the peace treaty with Israel—adding a comment obviously directed at Mubarak's cooperation on rendition, among other secret acts, that it also hoped to do a better job complying with some human rights protocols it had signed. "We are opening a new page," said Ambassador Menha Bakhoum, spokeswoman for the Foreign Ministry. "Egypt is resuming its role that was once abdicated."[1]

Without the proper historical background, it would be hard to understand what Ambassador Bakhoum was talking about—abdication to whom? And why? Hillary Clinton, in a bright red blazer, walked "the fine diplomatic line" on her stroll through Tahrir Square. She announced millions of dollars in economic aid for Egypt while being careful not to inject herself into other questions about whether the interim government was moving too fast, or not fast enough. She appeared to be enjoying the moment, greeting those who approached to take pictures with cell phones—a reminder of how the new revolution spread on Twitter inside and outside Egypt so fast it left American policymakers without time to draft position papers.

"Wonderful to be here," Clinton said, waving and shaking hands. One of those she greeted shouted back, "Thank you for walking the streets of Tahrir."[2]

In this book we walk back to 1952 in order to get to Tahrir Square in 2011.

*

Thanks to Rebecca, who pointed the way to some key sources; to Marc, who plotted this adventure; and to Nancy, for being there all the way.

1

PRELUDE: SEARCHING FOR A POLICY

Great Britain is endeavoring to use the Near Eastern Area as a great dam which serves both to hold back the flow of Russia toward the south and to maintain an avenue of communications with India and other British possessions. . . . The Soviet Union seems to be determined to break down the structure which Great Britain has maintained so that Russian power can sweep unimpeded across Turkey and through the Mediterranean. . . . The United States has been pursuing a policy of the open door in the Near East. It has taken the position that the independent countries of the Near East . . . should not be considered as lying within the sphere of influence of any Great Power.

—Loy Henderson, director of the Office of Near Eastern and African Affairs, "The Present Situation in the Near East—A Danger to World Peace," December 28, 1945

When President Roosevelt hosted King Farouk on board the USS *Quincy* anchored in the Great Bitter Lake of the Suez Canal on February 13, 1945, he offered the Egyptian monarch some advice. FDR suggested breaking up "many of the large landed estates in Egypt." They should be made available, he said, "for ownership by the fellaheen [agricultural laborers] who worked them, and that at least 100,000 additional acres be placed under irrigation annually as a continuing program."[1] It was bold, even presumptuous, to offer such advice to a king who had come aboard an American warship for a friendly chat. But Roosevelt had similar things to say during the war about what other Middle Eastern rulers had to do to meet the postwar expectations of their peoples. At the 1943 Tehran Conference, for example, where the final plans for D-Day were agreed upon with Churchill and Stalin, the president had discussed reports from advisers about what American ingenuity could do to bring Iran's economy into the modern world. He was "rather thrilled with the idea of using Iran as an example of what we could do by an unselfish American policy." "Iran," he wrote Secretary of State Cordell Hull, "is definitely a very, very backward nation." It consisted of tribes with 99 percent of the population in bondage to the other 1 percent. "The real difficulty is to get the right kind of American experts who would be loyal to their ideals, not fight among themselves[,] and be absolutely honest financially."[2]

American forces had entered Iran during the war to ensure that Lend-Lease supplies reached the Soviet Union. Along with the military came a corps of economic experts and others who had ideas about how to accelerate development of Iran's economy after the war. In contrast, in Egypt the United States had neither a large troop presence nor the advisers on hand eager to take on the country's very similar problems. But during his brief chat with Farouk two days after the close of the Yalta "Big Three" conference in the Crimea, the president enthused about prospects for increased trade between the countries. When peace came, he said, he hoped American purchases of long-staple cotton, a vital Egyptian export, would increase, along with trade in other commodities. Tourist travel to Egypt, he felt sure, was certain to become greater after the war. Thousands of Americans, Roosevelt predicted, would visit Egypt and the Nile region, both by ship and air.

Trade with Egypt had in fact increased eightfold during the war. The American minister in Cairo, Alexander Kirk, had advocated extending Lend-Lease aid in order to solidify the two nations' relations after the war. After deliberation in Washington over possible ramifications in Anglo-American relations, such aid was granted, followed by diplomatic efforts to secure favorable investment laws to encourage joint-stock companies with American firms. Washington also sought permission for American commercial airliners to carry passengers from Cairo to the principal cities of Europe. As one policy planner put it, "Cairo is vital to air navigation, just as Suez is to shipping."[3]

The implication here was that the wartime British occupation of Suez belonged to the passing era of European imperialism, now in an accelerated decline caused by the war, while the new age of commerce depended on secure air routes, just as the original industrial age had hit its peak with projects like the Suez Canal. "Freedom of the seas" had been the catchphrase of the dominant powers of the time; now it was all about "freedom of the air"—a phrase that well matched the postcolonial age.

Roosevelt's New Deal–like ideas and his zeal for far-reaching land reform were not shared by many of his foreign policy advisers, but there was a consensus that the American mission in the postwar era would be to help the British "out"—in both senses of the word— from predicaments such as the vexed matter of Suez and similar situations elsewhere tied to a defunct colonial ideology. During the war Secretary of State Hull warned that the United States could not work *with* the colonial powers in Europe and *against* them in the rest of the world. But in the full blush of victory at war's end, Washington imagined things would now go more smoothly as its influence would spread even to areas Joseph Conrad had called the "Heart of Darkness." But Roosevelt's successors found that "whittling down" the British Empire, as one policy adviser cautioned— complicated as it was by domestic politics on related issues like the contest over the future of the British mandate in Palestine—risked a disaster.

The Need for Commitment

Making a safe transition would depend, American policymakers agreed, on Washington's ability to convince Farouk and other Middle Eastern leaders that the United States would not allow the old colonial powers, Great Britain and France, to reclaim the privileged positions they held before the war, and was, in fact, ready to offer economic and, if carefully managed, military aid to insure the independence and internal security of those countries. All this had to be handled so as to ease the transition from the old colonial order to a new global politics led by the United States, without permitting extreme nationalists or

Communists to take advantage of the situation to gain a foothold in the area. In this regard, the onset of the Cold War presented both an opportunity to shift the subject to common defense against a military threat that obscured old arguments, and the challenge of Communist penetration of reform movements.

Roosevelt's comments to the Egyptian king and his later guests, Emperor Haile Selassie of Ethiopia and, especially, King Ibn Saud of Saudi Arabia, were designed to promote a postwar vision of the Middle East following such a safe path to prosperity. Saud remained skeptical: "What am I to believe when the British tell me that my future is with them and not with America?" The British told him that America's interest in his country was transitory. Once the wartime emergency was over, Lend-Lease aid would end and the Americans would return to the Western Hemisphere—leaving Saudi Arabia behind within the pound sterling area economically and defended by the Royal Navy and British army. "On the strength of this argument they seek a priority for Britain in Saudi Arabia," Saud said. "What am I to believe?"

That was not going to be the future, insisted Roosevelt. America's postwar plans envisaged "a decline of spheres of influence in favor of the Open Door." He hoped the door of Saudi Arabia would be open to all nations, for only by free exchange of goods, services, and opportunities "can prosperity circulate to the advantage of free peoples." That was all very well, replied Saud, but the British would continue as before to claim a sphere of influence around and over his country. Roosevelt's adviser William Eddy warned the president that words would not be enough. Ibn Saud's well-grounded fears could be dispelled only when the United States acted to implement a long-range plan to secure the Open Door.[4]

The American minister in Cairo, S. Pinckney Tuck, had escorted King Farouk to the meeting with Roosevelt—a small gesture that pleased the Egyptian ruler. Instead of going aboard the warship with the king, Tuck had stepped back and did not accompany him to where the president sat waiting. Farouk told the American diplomat afterward that the British ambassador, Lord Killearn, to his great annoyance, always insisted on being present when he met with Prime Minister Churchill. It was a little thing, but Farouk appreciated Tuck's display of respect.

In the waning days of World War II, one of the key questions was whether or how the United States would supplant the United Kingdom in the British Empire's former possessions. Egypt was never a formal colony, but the history of Anglo-Egyptian relations revolved around the issue of continued British control of the Suez Canal and the military base and garrison that had protected the canal since the late nineteenth century. Opened to shipping in 1869, the Suez Canal had been built by a French company operating under a concession granted by the Egyptian khedive, Sa'id Pasha. The British had not even been in the picture originally and had, in fact, opposed the canal's construction. When the canal revolutionized global commerce, however, and the Egyptian government sought to sell its shares of the company to pay off international debts for four million pounds, the British leapt in with both feet. Although the Constantinople Convention of 1888 declared the Suez Canal a neutral area, Sa'id's successor invited British troops in to suppress a rebellion against his government. There they stayed through World War I and World War II. During those years the British high commissioner became, in effect, a viceroy, who according to the 1936 Anglo-Egyptian Treaty of Friendship and Alliance had to be given preference at the Egyptian court over representatives of any other nation.

London regarded its Suez base as a strongpoint from which to defend all its interests in the Mediterranean and North Africa and was loath to give it up, even in the face of rising nationalist sentiments. These had manifested themselves in different ways. During World War II, King Farouk was known to be pro-Axis and had even written Hitler a letter saying he would welcome an invasion. Rommel's Afrika Korps never got to Cairo, but the British demanded that Farouk dismiss pro-German ministers or be turned out of the palace. Born in 1920, Farouk was the great-grandson of the famous Muhammad Ali Pasha, Egypt's longest-ruling figure until Hosni Mubarak. Farouk had gone to school in Britain and began his reign in 1937. He had been very popular at first, but his lavish lifestyle soon began to alienate not only ordinary Egyptians, but important figures in the so-called Free Officers Movement as well.

American policymakers were fully aware that undermining the British in the Middle East was not a way to achieve American objectives in the region. The head of the State Department's policy planning staff, George F. Kennan, the author of the famous 1947 "X" article, "The Sources of Soviet Conduct," which summarized the rationale for a Cold War "containment" policy, insisted it would be not desirable to attempt to duplicate British strategic facilities in the Middle East such as the base at Suez, because, for one thing, British facilities would be available to the United States in the event of a war with the Soviet Union. Any attempt to take bases away from the British was an even worse option to contemplate, involving a host of problems that would weaken Western influence and only embolden enemies. "This means that we must do what we can to support the maintenance of the British in their strategic position in that area."[5] Kennan had put his finger on a pressure point in emerging American policy toward Egypt: if supporting the Open Door policy meant straining British relations with Arab countries, where was the benefit for the United States? The United States still needed British military support to defend its strategic interests, and yet siding with a colonial power risked alienating powerful anticolonial forces stirring across Africa and Asia.

Kennan was quite clear about what America's interests were in this regard, and they did not involve "sentimentality and day-dreaming": "We have about 50% of the world's wealth but only 6.3% of its population. . . . In this situation, we cannot fail to be the object of envy and resentment. Our real task in the coming period is to devise a pattern of relationships which will permit us to maintain this position of disparity without positive detriment to our national security."[6]

Unfortunately, the U.S. government was now subject to pressures that "impel us toward a position where we would shoulder major responsibility for the maintenance, and even the expansion, of a Jewish state in Palestine," Kennan wrote. To the extent that policy moves in this direction, the United States "will be operating directly counter to our major security interests" in the Arab world.

Kennan had no real answer for dealing with this problem, nor did any of his successors find a way to get around the Arab-Israeli imbroglio.

At the time Kennan wrote, the Truman administration was trying to find a solution to please Congress and public opinion, and indeed was caught in a bind that brought it into precisely the sort of conflict with Great Britain that Kennan and many in the State Department feared would destroy the influence of the West across the whole region. Whenever envoys of Middle Eastern states— with the exception of Israel—appeared at the State Department to argue their grievances over American policy and Palestine's fate, the Egyptian ambassador served as their spokesman. The Arab League was seated in Cairo, and King Farouk liked to think that his championing of resistance to Jewish plans for a state carved out of Palestine and his responsiveness to resentment at British military policy could be combined into a program that would save his monarchy.

But there was another distressing problem confronting U.S. policymakers as they attempted to act as a friend to both London and Cairo in resolving the growing disputes over the British military garrison at Suez and revision of the 1936 Anglo-Egyptian Treaty. Before the war these were matters that would not have involved the United States, but the war had changed the world—ideologically by the discrediting of European imperialism, and materially by the exhaustion of the military capabilities of the colonial powers. American policymakers saw themselves in a race, moreover, facing the challenge of what a later secretary of state, John Foster Dulles, would call "International Communism."

In the spring of 1947, with the "Truman Doctrine" (which called for the support of the "free peoples" of the world against totalitarian regimes) in newspaper headlines, the Anglo-Egyptian dispute over continued British occupation of the Suez neared a flashpoint. Foreign Secretary Ernest Bevin called in the American ambassador, Lewis Douglas, to caution him against an American attempt to mediate the crisis. London had offered to withdraw all troops by September 1949, but that was apparently not enough for the Egyptians, who were seeking to take the dispute to the United Nations. This was an unwelcome development for London and Washington, obviously, quite a turnaround from the Anglo-American cheerleading when the Iranians had brought the issue of Russian troops to the Security Council a year earlier. While Bevin was prepared to negotiate changes to the 1936 treaty with Cairo, he would not countenance intervention by the United Nations, or by any country that attempted to compel his government "to breach the terms of a treaty entered into in good faith."[7]

No one in Washington desired to force London into mediation, but neither did the administration expect to stand by and watch while the British risked losing everything. The most that could be done in the short term, it seemed, was to support London's desire for a right of return in the case of an emergency at Suez, as well as its interests in establishing other military bases in nearby Libya to take the pressure off talks about revision of the treaty. Matters took a turn for the better in 1948 when the British proposed Anglo-Egyptian staff talks on military defense of the Suez Canal, and the Egyptians responded with suggestions that they would not oppose British military bases in Libya or the Sudan. These talks broke down, but there seemed to be a clue here for a possible way of meeting the Egyptian demands for arms aid by incorporating it within a political arrangement that would not be opposed by Israel and its friends in Congress—a powerful and, indeed, growing force in American domestic politics.

On the day before the United States recognized the new provisional government of Israel, on May 14, 1948, Ambassador Tuck reported from Cairo that Egypt was making a "determined effort" to obtain arms "from any source available, including Czechoslovakia." Policymakers now had multiple worries, including fears that the Anglo-Egyptian dispute over Suez and Sudan's future offered the Soviets an opportunity in the United Nations to drive a wedge deeper between the West and Middle Eastern countries as Moscow championed Cairo's demands for a British evacuation from the military base and recognition of the Sudan as part of Egypt. Farouk complained bitterly to the new American ambassador, Jefferson Caffery, that Washington, by its Palestine policy and refusal to sell

Egypt arms, was making good relations impossible. "You have re-fused everything we have asked for."[8]

Farouk's complaints anticipated and were hardly different from those of later Egyptian leaders over the years, until Anwar Sadat traveled from Cairo and made a separate peace with Israel. Then the arms flowed into Egypt in a steady stream, as Egypt became a regional stabilizing power for American policy and relieved at least part of the burden on Washington for having been Israel's original sponsor and its most loyal backer over the years. But there was an-other aspect to Farouk's failure that his successors did not over-come. Roosevelt had warned the king that he must move to relieve the conditions of the poor and landless fellaheen. While Egypt's national pride was at stake in the Palestine and Suez questions, the underlying economic problem proved in the end to be the most cor-rosive challenge to leaders in Cairo.

Reporting on a conversation with a British diplomat in 1949, an American counterpart warned Washington that the feeling in Lon-don was that a revolution in Egypt was looming just ahead. It might be stopped by an "enlightened intervention by Farouk, but this young man appears to share the outlook of the reactionary landowners and other vested interests." The situation was worse than in other Arab countries because of population pressure and land shortage. "The [British] official did not know how long the patient 'have-not don-key' would support the heavy burden of the unenlightened 'haves' but he 'imagined that it would kick before long.'"[9]

The British diplomat added that he thought Farouk would go out feet first, after having been killed by revolutionaries. However, when the "revolution" came in 1952, the military simply escorted him out of the country. Otherwise the diplomat's prediction came true, including his opinion that this time it would not lead to sig-nificant change for most Egyptians. Instead, political objectives would emerge, he said, "from the men who 'took over' the revolu-tion and turned it to their own purposes." The challenge for Amer-ican policymakers was to make sure that those "objectives" meshed with Washington's goals.

Palestine and Israel

In the 1944 U.S. presidential campaign, both political parties at their national conventions had offered encouragement to the Zionist movement. Against the background of mounting political pressure in Congress for a commitment to the idea of a "national homeland" for Jewish refugees in Palestine, the State Department hoisted warning signals about Saudi Arabia's expected reactions. "The king is first a Moslem," asserted a pre-Yalta State Department memo, "and secondarily an Arab. . . . He considers himself the world's foremost Moslem and assumes the defense of Moslem rights. Hence his opposition to Zionism." Any alteration in his position would involve a loss of the respect of his co-religionists, and possibly the overthrow of his dynasty. Secretary of State Edward R. Stettinius Jr., who succeeded Cordell Hull in 1944, added in a note to Roosevelt that the king could not be moved this side of the grave. "Ibn Saud's statement that he regards himself as a champion of the Arabs of Palestine and would himself feel it an honor to die in battle in their cause is, of course, of the greatest significance."[10]

When the king came aboard the *Quincy*, however, the day after Farouk's visit, Roosevelt saw a man unlikely to fight anyone on the battlefield—at least not personally. Ibn Saud's crippled condition gave the president a chance to commiserate about their mutual problems getting around—and to offer to send him one of his specially designed wheelchairs. But neither gifts nor Roosevelt's sympathy could get Ibn Saud to change his position a single degree. The Jewish people had been driven from their homelands, began Roosevelt, and the world had a humanitarian obligation to these refugees. That might be so, Saud replied, but they should be given lands within the Axis countries, not lands belonging to the Arab peoples. Roosevelt tried other arguments—he argued up one side and down the other, he reported to his aides—but it was no use. Nothing for it, then, but to retreat to an old delaying tactic. In a mutually agreed memorandum of their talks, Roosevelt offered the standard formula. He promised the king "he would do nothing to assist the Jews against the Arabs and would make no move hostile to the Arab people." Satisfied with the promise, the king thanked Roosevelt for his statement and indicated he would send an Arab mission to the United States and Great Britain "to expound the case of the Arabs and Palestine." Whatever Roosevelt really thought about that proposal he kept to himself, saying only that would be a very good idea.[11]

As soon as Roosevelt returned to the White House from Yalta, Rabbi Steven S. Wise, chairman of the American Zionist Emergency Council, was on his doorstep. Wise emerged from a forty-five-minute meeting with an important announcement for waiting reporters. The president had assured him that he had *not* changed his position about favoring unrestricted immigration into a free and democratic Jewish commonwealth in Palestine. Wise then read a statement Roosevelt had approved: "I have made my position on Zionism clear. . . . I have not changed and shall continue to seek to bring about its earliest realization."[12]

Now it was the Arab leaders who wanted to know where American policy was heading. Roosevelt maintained until the hour of his death a studied ambiguity. On the day of his fatal stroke in Warm Springs, Georgia, April 12, 1945, the president signed a letter to the prince regent of Iraq assuring him that "no decision affecting the basic situation in Palestine should be reached without full consultation with both Arabs and Jews." Close readers of the minutes of his meeting with King Saud and this letter to the prince regent could, however, perceive shading toward the Zionist position.[13]

As in so many other questions, Roosevelt's successor Harry S. Truman was left to deal with the dilemma of satisfying both sides, something that was beyond the reach even of an atomic-powered White House. Less than a week after Roosevelt's death, Secretary of State Stettinius warned the new president of the peril presented by the Palestine question and any indications that the United States would succumb to Zionist pressures: "There is continual tenseness in the situation in the Near East largely as a result of the Palestine question and as we have interests in that area which are vital to the United States, we feel that this whole subject is one that should be handled with the greatest care and with a view to the long-range interests of this country."[14]

Truman had just learned that scientists had been working on a weapon that could revolutionize warfare and put the United States in a dominant position amid the wave of postwar questions about to sweep across the world. He could not figure out, and no one could, how possessing an atomic bomb would help him with the Palestine problem, which, his advisers told him, threatened American interests in vital oil-producing areas and, they argued, the future peace of the Middle East and the world. On August 17, 1945, hardly more than a week after the United States dropped atomic bombs on Hiroshima and Nagasaki, Egypt's chief representative in Washington, Mahmoud Fawzi, met with Loy Henderson, head of the Near Eastern desk in the State Department. Like other Arab diplomats in Washington, Fawzi pressed for information about the Palestine issue and a more concrete definition of what had been meant by Roosevelt's assurances he would consult with both Arabs and Jews over the fate of Palestine, particularly in light of Truman's pointed comment at a news conference the day before.

The comment had come after a reporter's question about whether a Jewish national state had been discussed at Potsdam with Stalin and Churchill. Truman responded in what would soon become a characteristic prickly, self-confident attitude, with a generalization about not needing to consult with the Soviet Union—even about a potential problem that, in this case, could unravel relations with Moscow as well as Arab countries. He had discussed the question with Churchill, he said, and was still discussing it with Clement Attlee, the new British prime minister; but when the reporter pressed him on whether that discussion also included Stalin, Truman responded that it had not, but there was "nothing Stalin could do about it." He went on to add, "We want to let as many Jews into Palestine as is possible." Of course this would have to be worked out diplomatically with the Arabs and the British, but it would have to be on a peaceful basis, "as he had no desire to send half a million American soldiers to keep the peace in Palestine."[15]

Truman's disregard for Stalin's help in solving the problem also had to do with the emerging debate with the British over how to end the mandate that had brought London into the position of a very troubled overseer of what would soon be an area in "civil war" as clashes between Palestinians and Jewish newcomers spread over the land. Fawzi told Henderson on October 1, 1945, that Egypt was "extremely anxious" to have close and friendly relations with the United States, but Cairo had an obligation to "discharge its responsibilities for assisting in maintaining peace in the Near East." If Cairo was to be successful, he went on, it had to possess the confidence of the Arab nations. He hoped, therefore, that Washington would have consideration for the "delicate position of Egypt." Under the apparently quiet surface of the Arab world, there was intense feeling regarding Palestine. As Henderson put it, "A sudden move on the part of the great powers prejudicial to Arab interests in Palestine, might well set the Arab world in motion and result in violence on a wide scale."[16]

Henderson promised to bring Fawzi's views to the attention "of the appropriate officials of the Department." He needed no warning from Fawzi, however, or any other Arab representative to convince him that Truman was moving headlong down a very dangerous path. A month later Cairo and other Arab capitals were rocked with the news that Truman had pressed Attlee to allow one hundred thousand Jewish emigrants from displaced person camps in Europe to enter Palestine as soon as possible. Henderson made sure that Acting Secretary of State Dean Acheson knew about these repercussions, quoting an American diplomat's question to Washington: "Press has featured the announcement sensationally. In view of this and the publicity given recent American Congressional visitors . . . does Department authorize me to make any statement to attenuate the shocking effect which the Presidential declaration is having in Arab countries?"

There was not much to be said, however, as Truman's political advisers and the State Department were now at odds. Henderson added in his memo that the situation had become critical in terms of saving American prestige, so carefully built up over the years in order to offer protection to American material interests. Mere resentment that the United States had decided to disregard Arab opinion was bad enough, but it would be much more serious "if we should give them ground to believe that we do not live up to our firm promises already given . . . assurances . . . given in writing by both President Roosevelt and President Truman."[17]

Two days later Fawzi and other Arab diplomats met with Acheson and Henderson. The Egyptian expressed astonishment that the United States was actually pressing Great Britain to open up Palestine to one hundred thousand Jewish immigrants, citing the promises given by the two American presidents that nothing would be done to change the situation without prior consultation with both concerned parties, the Arabs and the Jews. Fawzi said that Roosevelt had also told him personally at the time he met with King Farouk that he would do nothing without consultation with Egypt and other Arab states. Besides that, if the United States was urging Great Britain to make such a change, with such a great impact on the people of Palestine, it would be encouraging violation of international law, specifically the conditions of the Palestine mandate, which prohibited such action without the consent of the inhabitants. "Certainly," he concluded, "a mandated country like Palestine was entitled to more rights than a protectorate."[18]

In an effort to damp down the Arab protests, Truman's new secretary of state, James F. Byrnes, met with the diplomats a few days later. He tried to assure them that no change had been made. "The United States continued to adhere to the policy that it would give no support to any changes in what it would consider to be the basic situation in Palestine until after such change had previously been fully discussed with Arabs and Jews." This, of course, was like closing the barn door after the horses had already bolted.[19]

Over the next several weeks and months Truman dueled publicly and acrimoniously with British foreign secretary Ernest Bevin over the president's insistence that one hundred thousand refugees be admitted to Palestine as soon as possible. On one occasion a reporter asked if perhaps we would "get along better with England if we made some gesture toward welcoming a few of these immigrants to the United States?" Truman made an irritable reply, as if to dismiss the matter; the reporter knew what the immigration laws were, didn't he? "We have to comply with them." But that opened him up to a follow-up question. Did the president intend recommending any change in the laws? "I do not."[20]

Bevin—frustrated and angry at worldwide criticism of the British refusal to allow shiploads of Jewish immigrants to land—lashed out at a Labour Party conference, "I hope I will not be misunderstood in America if I say that this [one hundred thousand] was proposed with the purest of motives. They do not want too many Jews in New York." Bevin's Labour colleagues were embarrassed by this ugly display, but Truman somewhat surprisingly told a correspondent he understood the pressure on the foreign secretary, because he was often tempted to blow up himself at the pressure and agitation from New York, a remark it was not possible to misinterpret.[21]

Even so, Truman did not back down from his demand that one hundred thousand refugees be admitted to Palestine. And he knew what the game was. Bevin's objective, the president always believed, was simply to draw the United States into joint responsibility for whatever happened, so that the Arabs would have someone else to blame. The Americans had used World War II to gain the upper hand and were now all over the Middle East, but they could ruin things for everyone. Truman's affirmative statements about the refugees were picked up by the Saudi Arabian government, however, which promptly demanded the letters exchanged by Roosevelt and Ibn Saud be made public. The request left Secretary Byrnes in a quandary, forcing him to tell the British ambassador, on the one hand, that FDR was really too ill at that time to be transacting such important business, and reconfirm to the representatives of Middle Eastern countries, on the other, that American policy had not changed since Roosevelt's letters. It was still the intention of the United States to "consult" with both Arabs and Jews before anything was done about Palestine's future. "Consult" was obviously a weaker expression than the impression conveyed in FDR's correspondence, especially his letter of April 5, 1945, which said that "no decision" would be taken without "full consultation" with both Arabs and Jews, and that he would "take no action . . . which might prove hostile to the Arab people."[22]

Even though Roosevelt's letters contained no binding commitment—as Truman rightly said—Arab leaders complained of being nuanced to death. It was not an unfair accusation. Secretary Byrnes tried to explain to the British ambassador, Lord Halifax, how Truman understood the situation. "The problem now," he informed a nonplussed Halifax, "is . . . to determine the number that could be absorbed into the population. He could not join in a plan to divert from that." William Eddy, Roosevelt's specialist on Saudi Arabia, had returned home in the fall of 1945 for a chiefs-of-mission conference hoping to head off any action that would commit Washington to the Zionist cause. Ibn Saud had made it clear to him before he left, Eddy said, that promises of "consultation" were not enough. The king expected that the publication of Roosevelt's correspondence would put an end to Zionist demands for unilateral action. If it did not, the implications for American policy in the Middle East were serious. The independence and survival of the Arab state of Palestine, the king said, was a matter for the nations of the region to determine, not one for Americans—Jew or gentile—living five thousand miles away. Saud had not said he would take retaliatory action against Aramco, the American oil company in his country, if Washington went ahead with plans to put Jewish refugees into Palestine, but there were other dangers, specifically to the future of the planned Dhahran air base. "The more fanatic" Arabs, reported Eddy, had already called Dhahran a "base for political aggression and foreign occupation."[23]

The president agreed to meet those attending the chiefs-of-mission conference and hear their arguments—but only for half an hour, on November 10, 1945. The attendees made the case that the Arab world deserved the central place in foreign-policy thinking, not only as a "counterpoise" to Zionist ambitions, or because it was at the center of British strategic concerns, or athwart the great air routes of the future, or even because it happened to contain both "the two cradles of civilization and the greatest known undeveloped oil reserves of the world." The Arabs deserved attention because of the revolutionary ferment spreading across the region, which posed the greatest challenge. "If the United States fails them, they will turn to Russia and will be lost to our civilization; of that we feel certain." Above all, the diplomats asked, what could they tell these governments about American policy toward "political Zionism"? Truman smiled at his own nascent Cold War rhetoric being thrown back at him. "That *is* the sixty-four dollar question," Truman quipped. It had caused him more trouble already, he admitted, than almost any issue facing the United States. He latched onto their phrase "political Zionism," however, to fashion his answer. He hoped that admitting "some refugees from Europe" would "alleviate" the situation at least long enough to work on a compromise with "humanitarian" Zionists, but confessed he was not at all confident, because Palestine was a "burning issue" in domestic politics and would no doubt continue to be one in 1946 and 1948.[24]

Agreement of Sorts on Israel

Truman received support from another source, however: former prime minister Winston Churchill. A pro-Zionist from years past, Churchill was above all an advocate of Anglo-American teamwork—as Britain's best and only way to maintain its position in the Middle East, particularly against nationalist challenges in Iran and Egypt. He spoke of the challenge in very similar ways to the outline George Kennan had given about sharing military facilities. As Churchill saw the situation, Great Britain was caught in a vise geographically and otherwise between Palestine and Egypt, with Suez squeezed from both sides. It can be argued, indeed, that protecting Suez and the military base was a major underlying theme of the famous "Iron Curtain" speech Churchill delivered at Westminster College in Fulton, Missouri, with Truman sitting on the stage behind him. Rightly enough, most attention has gone to his description of postwar Europe as divided between East and West by an Iron Curtain; but after that he turned to the Middle East and offered to share with Washington something that could prove invaluable as a counter to the Soviet Union—military bases to double the strength of the United States. Suez was certainly one of the most important in any such calculation.

"Turkey and Persia are both profoundly alarmed and disturbed at the claims which are being made upon them and at the pressure being exerted by the Moscow government," Churchill noted. Confronted by these challenges, general and specific, the United States and Britain must develop a common strategy. "Would a special relationship between the United States and the British Commonwealth be inconsistent with our overriding loyalties to the World Organization? I reply that, on the contrary, it is probably the only means by which that organization will achieve its full stature and strength." The British Empire had much to offer; it had bases all over the world. "This would perhaps double the mobility of the American Navy and Air Force. It would greatly expand that of the British Empire Forces and it might well lead, if and as the world calms down, to important financial savings. Already we use together a large number of islands; more may well be entrusted to our joint care in the near future."

Churchill's pro-Zionist stance, so out of tune with Labour, was his vision for saving the empire, or as much of it as possible, and yet it certainly helped Truman with critics. The British wartime leader and imperial defender-in-chief put his own government on the defensive on that issue, by implying that a united Anglo-American front would check the Arab "fanatics" so many talked about and who were, in any event, less of a problem than keeping the Russians out. While it was certainly possible that the Palestine issue could unravel the "special relationship" into separate threads, building up the Soviet threat as a way of encouraging Americans to take seriously the general situation in the Middle East had become a central concern of British policymakers. Churchill's assertions were in tune with that objective, while taking a tack different from that of Attlee and Bevin on Palestine. The British purpose all along, wrote historian John Keay, was to draw the United States into defending the periphery, Greece and Turkey, as vital to their common purposes.[25]

In early summer 1946 a special Anglo-American committee reported favorably on the proposal to allow one hundred thousand immigrants into Palestine. The committee had been boycotted by the Arab nations invited to give their views, which gave the Truman administration an opening to say that the commitment to consult made by Roosevelt and Truman had been discharged. "However, we remain open for consultation by any and all interested parties whenever they desire."[26] After that disclaimer, American policy moved toward a plan for dividing Palestine between Arabs and Jews, with an attempt to set boundaries for a partitioned state. In Cairo the head of the Arab League, Abdul Rahman Azzam, flew into a rage denouncing American policy, but an Egyptian diplomat told an American embassy official privately that his government would accept an invitation to a London conference on the question of how to deal with the immigration question "without conditions."[27]

Truman and his advisers had taken a British appeal in early 1947 for help in providing military and other aid to Greece and Turkey and transformed it into what was quickly labeled a "doctrine" for resisting supposed Soviet subversion anywhere. Once the so-called Truman Doctrine was put in place, and the Marshall Plan announced for rehabilitating European economies under American direction, "containment" became the general rubric under which all American policies were shaped, so as to define the Cold War as a struggle between the "free world" and the Soviet bloc. Inevitably, the Palestine question became a part of Cold War maneuvering, with the Soviet Union happy to increase tension between the United States and Great Britain by throwing its influence behind Egyptian demands that Suez be evacuated, and also supporting both sides in the emerging Arab-Israeli dispute.

Truman's successors would keep expanding the doctrine to fit the needs of policy elsewhere, especially in the Middle East and the Far East. Long after the Soviet Union collapsed, moreover, the term "free world" was still used to explain American policies in the Second Gulf War (the Iraq War) and in Afghanistan. But all that was in the distant future. The immediate problem was to get around the argument with London over Palestine and Zionist aspirations. Finally, Foreign Secretary Bevin threw up his hands, delivered some very ugly comments about Truman's political pandering, and tossed the question to the United Nations, as if to say to Washington, "You made the crisis, now you solve it."

The United Nations actually tried pretty hard. It created a special committee, UNSCOP, to review all the proposals. As might be expected, the committee came back with a divided report. The majority favored partition—the division of Palestine into an Arab state and a Jewish state—and making Jerusalem a protected international city. Truman had privately favored this approach, and when the report came before the General Assembly in the fall of 1947, the United States voted for partition. Behind the scenes, however, the White House brought pressure on several governments to fall in line. It was no secret the State Department opposed these backdoor maneuvers, seeing them as a too-clever-by-half attempt by pro-Zionist aides in the presidential mansion to avoid sole responsibility for an imposed "solution" sure to alienate the Arab countries.

At the United Nations, Secretary of State George C. Marshall met with Arab diplomats to try to calm down their reactions to the vote for partition. Once again a bevy of Arab spokesmen took turns delivering the warnings. One said that the Zionist experiment would have failed at the beginning if it had not been for outside financial support; another argued that once lodged in Palestine, the Jewish immigrants would eventually try to gain more and more lands, that what was happening was only the beginning. "Faris Bey el-Khouri [of Syria] reinforced the thesis of failure by pointing out that although a thousand years ago the Crusaders had attempted to establish their dominance in the Holy Land, they had finally been ejected with disaster to themselves." Marshall listened to these complaints without comment, keeping to himself his doubts about the White House determination to find a way out that would meet domestic demands on Truman without damning him forever in the Arab world.[28]

The British meanwhile continued to suffer the blame for keeping Jewish refugees from landing in Palestine, without gaining very much sympathy from the Arab countries. Contributing to the final decision of UNSCOP was the infamous *Exodus* affair in the summer of 1947 when British authorities turned back a ship carrying Jewish refugees from Germany. The episode was a nightmare for British authorities, as most of the would-be immigrants to Palestine were Holocaust survivors, whose fate drew worldwide attention when Foreign Secretary Bevin insisted they were illegal and must be sent back to French ports. Later, the *Exodus* was called "the ship that launched a state." Had the British understood the power of this image better, wrote historian Ilan Pappé, they would have made this highly symbolic journey from the land of the Holocaust into a special exception. But they did not, while the Americans remained aloof from any responsibility. The upshot was that the insensitive British decision "prompted UNSCOP to discuss the fate of European Jewish survivors instead of the Arab demand to determine the future of Palestine according to the demographic reality of 1947."[29]

As early as 1946, however, Truman had acknowledged what seemed inevitable: that a Jewish homeland in Palestine "would command the support of public opinion in the United States." And that was the way he played it from that time to the creation of Israel in 1948, hoping the one hundred thousand refugees could be settled, allowing for more time to work out the way the immigrants and Palestinians could somehow live together in a divided state. American maneuvering room was curtailed, however, by a surprising development: the Soviet Union, which had shown no interest in supporting a Jewish state, turned around during the partition debate in the fall of 1947 to declare its support for dividing Palestine—with the potential, Americans suspected, for dividing Arabs from the Anglo-American condominium. State Department experts, already in despair about the White House's pro-Zionist bent, thought the Russians had devised a clever move to penetrate the Middle East by cultivating relations with Israel after being blocked elsewhere by the Truman Doctrine. Over the long term, even if Israel did not become a political outpost for the Soviet Union, American-Arab relations would suffer as a result of the creation of a Jewish state.

Frustrated and hard-pressed for money to maintain overseas bases, the British announced they would end their Palestine mandate—part of the settlement after World War I that parceled out the Ottoman Empire to the victors—on May 15, 1948. With nearly one hundred thousand troops and police stationed in Palestine, not even the prospect of losing military bases could change the raw economics of the situation. The only alternative—a last-ditch one—was to support King Abdullah of what was then known as Trans-Jordan, who lusted after the area of Palestine known as the

West Bank and imagined himself the ruler of vast territories that would include the "realms" of Syria and Lebanon. Abdullah had good contacts with the Jewish Agency, the forerunner of an Israeli provisional government, and in a secret meeting with some of its leaders at the time of the partition vote assured them he would not attack a Jewish state, "but that he would annex Arab Palestine."[30]

Abdullah's ambitions were well understood in Cairo. Such intra-Arab rivalries seriously damaged any united front against a newly created state of Israel. Back on December 3, 1947, U.S. ambassador Pinkney Tuck had reported from the Egyptian capital that King Farouk, in accord with other Arab countries, pledged to resist partition "by force of arms." Farouk had two divisions on the Palestine frontier, but they would not go into action until the British mandate ended. Meanwhile, they were also there to prevent the "infiltration of Russian Jewish saboteurs into Egypt." Several had already been apprehended, and documents found on them left no doubt about their intentions.

Farouk had absolutely no doubts either that, in the end, after some initial reverses, the combined Arab force would succeed in driving the Jews out of Palestine. Many of the Jews, he acknowledged, had experience of one kind or another in World War II, but that advantage would ultimately disappear as the Arab armies fought on. As Tuck reported it, "King Ibn Saud, Farouk said, had pledged him his word he would 'follow Egypt' and Farouk expressed the belief that despite the great financial advantages which Ibn Saud derived from American ventures in Saudi Arabia, the 'old man would rather destroy his oil wells than break his word.'" Tuck thought this boasting was a little too much, but he did not doubt that Farouk intended to try to play a lead role in resisting the creation of Israel by military force.[31]

War and the Egyptian Dilemma

Tuck was right in thinking that Farouk's dream of an Arab victory behind his leadership was overly optimistic—way too optimistic—as there was no real accord among the Arab forces when the fighting started.

The war began immediately after the British ended the mandate in May, with an Arab invasion of the areas allotted by the 1947 UN partition plan for a Jewish state. Egypt had sent the most troops, but their logistical support, let alone any idea of a coordinated campaign, quickly faded. War continued for about a month, until the first truce on June 11, by which time the Israelis had stopped the invasion cold. Even so, Egypt and Syria refused to continue the truce, and war resumed on July 6 and lasted for two more weeks. The result was a crushing defeat for the Arab countries on all fronts. Palestinians fled or were driven out in large numbers, forming a refuge problem that would bedevil efforts to reach any final settlement over the next six decades. In this second war, the United Nations attempted to impose an arms blockade, but the embargo mostly affected the Arab countries, for the Israelis stepped up purchases from Czechoslovakia and shipped stockpiled arms from Europe and the United States. The Arabs fought with weapons left over from the colonial era, and without any real coordinated plan of battle. At the end of the war, then, the Israelis enjoyed an arms superiority they have never since given up.

And even after the second truce of July 19, the Israeli advance did not end. By October 1948, Israeli forces had driven through the Negev Desert to the Gulf of Aqaba on the Egyptian border. Farouk's boasting proved fatal for his imagined position as historic Egyptian leader and was a trigger to the military coup that drove him off the throne and into exile in 1952.

The State Department, led by Secretary Marshall, had continued to oppose the White House's "haste" to extend de facto recognition to Israel before there was a real state with internationally recognized borders. More than anything, Marshall feared a conflict that could spread and involve the entire Arab world, jeopardizing American oil interests and the internal stability of the nearby governments. But when Truman's White House advisers, led by Clark Clifford, pointed out that the creation of a Jewish state could only be halted by American military intervention, and that the Soviet

Union would be ready to grant almost immediate recognition, Marshall and his chief aide, Robert Lovett, were thrown on the defensive. In the White House, Lovett produced a file of intelligence telegrams and read from them about Soviet activity "in sending Jews and Communist agents from Black Sea areas to Palestine." It was shortly after this display that Marshall made his famous statement that if Truman followed Clifford's advice, and if he were to vote, "I would vote against the President."[32]

However, a separate Jewish state now looked inevitable; the effectiveness of the Jewish paramilitary forces in Palestine had already determined the outcome. The very day the mandate ended, the Provisional Government of Israel was announced. Truman granted immediate de facto recognition, to be followed some months later by de jure recognition and the first of the almost constant loans and aid grants that have since become a given. On November 29, 1948, Truman wrote a warm letter to the new Israeli president, Chaim Weizmann, acknowledging the latter's own letter of congratulations on Truman's election. They both had much to celebrate, Truman said, but "it does not take long for bitter and resourceful opponents to regroup their forces after they have been shattered." He had interpreted his election, Truman went on in this vein, as a mandate for the Democratic platform, including the plank on support for Israel. Still more, he assured Weizmann that the United States would "oppose any territorial changes in the November 29th Resolution which are not acceptable to the State of Israel." It would be hard to improve upon such an oath of fealty.[33]

Trying to make the shock to Arab sensibilities a little less devastating, Clifford had drafted a statement for the president at the time he recognized Israel, expressing the hope that "when the peoples in the portion of Palestine assigned for an Arab state have set up a State in accordance with the provisions of the Resolution of the Assembly on November 29, 1947, similar recognition will be granted to that State by the United States and by the other members of the United Nations."[34] It was not to be. As Dean Rusk had feared, the violence accompanying the birth of Israel seemed to settle once and for all that those "bitter and resourceful opponents" of the new state were on the wrong side of history. And it would be more than a half century until an American president spoke of such a Palestinian state in anything like a serious manner. Abdullah had his deal, moreover, annexing the West Bank, which made another Palestinian state moot. He seemed to be on the verge of bringing Syria and Lebanon under his sway as well when a Palestinian extremist shot and killed him at the Dome of the Rock in Jerusalem on July 21, 1951.

At the conclusion of the first Arab-Israeli War (actually a series of short wars) in 1949, the odd people out were the Palestinians. Historian Ritchie Ovendale notes that the Anglo-American Commission on Palestine estimated there were 226,000 Jewish refugees in Europe when Germany surrendered in 1945. By 1949, the wars in Palestine had created almost one million Arab refugees, living in various countries. Their numbers would double in the next two decades. The war had not united the Arab world; indeed it led instead to upheavals in individual Arab countries, "often fomented by a new, young and disillusioned generation which had been nurtured on what was considered the injustice of Zionist dispossession of Arab land with the assistance of the Western powers."[35]

Although skirmishes would continue into 1949, there was also a serious appeal by Egypt to make a new beginning with the United States. On December 17, 1948, a newly appointed ambassador, Mohamed Kamil Abdul Rahim, met with Acting Secretary of State Robert Lovett. The ambassador said he had been chosen especially by Cairo because of his long-held feelings that there should be close relations with America. He then launched into a familiar litany about how Israel had made the Arab people feel gravely endangered by an "alien group with aggressive intent." Lovett had himself pressed the case against recognizing Israel in the White House, of course, but now he called for an "unemotional recognition of fact." Israel was there to stay. It was time to try to resolve questions that would endanger the future and to stop concentrating on the past. The nature of the conversation about what the United States could do in the way of economic investment in the region, aid for the refugees, and settling of border disputes indicated that Washington had taken over management of the old mandate's—now Israel's—relations with the rest of the Middle East. Egypt would do well to recognize that fact as well, Lovett implied, and set goals for its future relations with the United States that would benefit both Cairo and Washington. The ambassador left without committing himself to the American position, but an Egyptian-Israeli armistice was signed on February 24, 1949.[36]

What made the Palestine-Israel question so bedeviling was that the Egyptians wished to pursue a twin policy of opposing a Jewish state and demanding a complete withdrawal of British troops from Suez—both in the name of anti-imperialism. The problem for Washington was that while it agreed London needed to get out of the way of Egyptian nationalism in order to preserve both British and American influence in the area, there was no reason to imagine that the Egyptian military could substitute for British arms if Middle Eastern stability was threatened in any way. Policymakers in London and Washington pondered how to achieve a common approach to the problem, holding lengthy talks in the Pentagon in 1947 with many position papers discussed in an effort to clarify the issues.

Both Israel and Egypt continued to appeal for direct arms aid from the United States. In response to these appeals, Secretary of State Dean Acheson would often refer to the statement made by America's ambassador to the United Nations, Warren R. Austin, on August 4, 1949: "So far as the United States is concerned, it does not intend to allow the export of arms which would permit a competitive arms race in that area. Export of arms to this area of the world should be strictly limited to such arms as are within the scope of the [various nations'] legitimate security requirements."[37]

At best this was a stopgap measure, because, one way or another, arms from Eastern Europe or one of the Western powers would be secured by Middle Eastern nations. In an assessment of the situation, the newly created National Security Council issued a remarkably candid report on October 17, 1949. Compared to the progress of the Israeli military, the Arabs were light years behind. Israel had its own nascent arms industry, while the equipment and training of the Arab militaries were inadequate to any serious task. This imbalance created a temptation for Tel Aviv to renew its wars with neighbors in order to improve its position, and posed "the danger of Israeli extremist pressure to resort to military action." In other words, Arab weakness could lead to unending instability and exacerbate both internal problems and old rivalries. Should that happen, American interests across the region would be constantly in danger from waves of nationalist protest.[38]

An arms race of sorts had already begun. Israel complained to Washington that Britain was supplying weapons to the Arabs intended for use in a renewed war. The Israeli ambassador argued that the weapons were not meant to repel an attack by the Soviet Union, but for the purpose of attacking his country. "I completely agreed with the Ambassador," Secretary Acheson noted in a memorandum, "that the arms being supplied to the Arab States would not enable them to stand off an attack by the Soviet Union. For that matter, the arms we were furnishing the Western European states would not enable them to do this either. But I thought that I could understand the desire on the part of the Arab states to restore their self-confidence by strengthening their arms, and the necessity from the British point of view of having this self-confidence restored to strategic nations in the Near East."[39]

The argument continued for some time, with the ambassador at last warning that Israel had no choice, then, but to buy weapons from Czechoslovakia. "My government has no alternative but to take all steps necessary for its protection." Five years later, ironically, an Egyptian arms deal with Czechoslovakia would set in motion a series of events that would lead to the Suez Crisis—but for the moment it still seemed possible to control the situation. Acheson hoped, for example, that it might be possible to start a peace process in some other country besides Egypt—for example, Saudi Arabia, where American influence might be greater because of the oil concession run by Aramco. When Acheson's emissary, George McGhee, broached the question of a possible treaty in Riyadh, the Saudi foreign minister instead took the opportunity to warn against any move by Israel to impinge on Jordanian territory. Jordan was part of the wall separating the Arab countries from Israel, he said, and any attempt to expand beyond that barrier would be met by force. "We shall never admit a Jew in Saudi Arabia and we shall never admit anyone traveling with an Israeli visa."[40]

If there was to be no way to halt arms shipments to the Middle East, and, in fact, no desire to give up a real avenue to increased political influence, the answer was to incorporate the arms within some larger scheme, as Acheson had implied in his statements to the Israeli ambassador about American arms for NATO. At a Cabinet meeting on April 14, 1950, the secretary of state said the United States was not doing what it could to see that the Arab countries and Israel were "properly armed." The solution might be to get the British and French, as the primary suppliers for the Arab countries, to join with the United States in a nonaggression statement, committing the three to send only "defensive" arms to their Middle Eastern customers, and pledging they would come to the aid of any country attacked in violation of the armistice agreements that had ended the 1948 Arab-Israeli War.[41]

Truman thought that was a grand idea, and such a tripartite declaration was duly made on May 25, 1950. But, again, declarations needed to be followed up with deeds. From the time Israel first appeared with such galelike political force in the 1948 election, the split between the White House and the State Department had never been mended. Acheson, more circumspect than George C. Marshall, who had once threatened to resign, tried to work around Truman. In late 1951, according to one of those who participated in the planning, the secretary of state "borrowed" Kermit Roosevelt Jr. from the Central Intelligence Agency to head up a highly secret committee of specialists to study the Arab world, with special emphasis on the Arab-Israeli conflict and to "work out solutions, *any* solutions, whether or not they fitted orthodox notions of proper governmental behavior." Among the ideas put forward was one for promoting a "Moslem Billy Graham," who would be used to mobilize religious fervor in a great move against Communism.[42]

Here was a very good example of the timeworn dictum, be careful what you wish for, because you may get it. While no Moslem, Billy Graham actually came to power in Cairo, religious radicalism was a constant worry for American policymakers in later years. Egypt's proposed role was crucial, Acheson's special committee concluded. "Egypt was a country worth high priority on its own merit, and its influence on other Arab states was such that a turn for the better there would be felt throughout the Arab world." The defense of the Middle East, as Acheson had already insisted in earlier talks with the Israeli ambassador, was not a matter of large armies or big air forces, but rather of bases and political positions.

From an American viewpoint, the case for sending arms to Egypt was divided into several competing questions. There was always the question of how such a policy could survive the scrutiny of Israel's allies in Congress, who were constantly on the lookout for the presumed "Arabist"-minded State Department's maneuvers. On the other side was the National Security Council's warning that Arab military defects could be dangerous for American interests. And this problem had two further interconnected aspects: if the United States did not come up with a solution, the Arab countries might turn to the Soviet bloc for arms, or, the mounting frustrations of defeat could help to spark an internal upheaval in one or more of the countries. At the moment, with the Suez issue simmering, Egypt was the most likely place to explode.

Some American policymakers believed—or hoped—that Egyptian defeat in the first Arab-Israeli War would convince Cairo that it needed the support of the two English-speaking powers for its own safety. The war opened up an opportunity "for us to continue to give friendly advice and counsel which would serve to temper Egyptian tendencies toward extreme nationalism," according to one memo; it was hoped as well that enticing Egypt into three-party talks on Egyptian defense problems would contribute to similar moderation of nationalist demands. But whatever the doubts American officials had about British policy, Egypt was still considered primarily London's area of responsibility. The U.S. ambassador to Egypt, Jefferson Caffery, had looked at all the alternatives and concluded, once again, that any effort to force a British "evacuation" would not advance American interests. The United States still had to rely on London's political and military support; but given Egypt's nationalist fever, perhaps it would be possible to "sell" the Egyptian government on the idea of a tripartite arrangement as elevating Cairo to an equal position in the defense of Suez—as an actual sign that its demands had been met. "We must, in exploring alternatives, consider only those which would permit British and perhaps ourselves to have bases in Egypt," Caffery wrote. The Korean War, which began in June 1950, no doubt colored Caffery's opinion about the likelihood the Pentagon would demand new American military bases, but his ideas were only a natural progression from wartime thinking about how the nation's interests had moved forward in several Middle Eastern countries. His proposal needed careful handling, Caffery continued, "so as to be acceptable [to] present Egyptian thinking." The price "would undoubtedly be high and would include arms and at least a façade of military consultation which would give [an] outside appearance of a full exchange of views on a sovereign basis." It would be costly as well in terms of domestic politics, for, of course, the administration had to overcome the usual skepticism in Congress.[43]

Caffery's frank discussion about the advantages of and requirement for "at least a façade of military consultation" to give the appearance of "a full exchange of views" and the equality of tasks and assignments to satisfy Egyptian nationalism ran somewhat along the lines that Acheson, and later John Foster Dulles, would try to promote. At one end of such an extended line of thinking was NATO, with its mutual, Three-Musketeer-like obligations ("One for all, and all for one"), and at the other end a not-yet-blueprinted Middle East alliance. NATO was a perfect model in important ways, for, as Dean Acheson would say in congressional testimony, it worked in all directions: it served as a military alliance against the Soviet Union, but it also brought together two ancient enemies, France and Germany, while engaging London on the European continent so that it would no longer be tempted to play the Victorian-era role of splendid isolation.

In April 1951, the Truman administration sent an ace diplomatic troubleshooter, George McGhee, to Cairo to sell the idea of a tripartite defense system. He met with Egyptian foreign minister Muhammad Salah-al-Din Bey and began by telling him that the United States had no desire to become a party to the negotiations over Suez, but wished to continue to discuss the question with both Cairo and London in a friendly vein. The United States well understood the positions of each, Egypt's legitimate nationalistic aspirations, and Britain's belief that it had been guaranteed certain rights under the 1936 treaty. There was a third consideration in the debate, he continued—the defense of the Middle East, which had always been an area problem involving many countries. Salah-al-Din Bey responded that his country felt that defense was first of all a national problem, but that "all others come in as allies when war actually breaks out." Cairo had further promised the British that it would maintain the base in good order "so they may depend on it at the outbreak of war." Egypt was desirous of participating along with other "free nations of the world" in case of aggression, but it insisted on having the "first say in their own territory," while "the help and assistance of other countries comes secondary when it is needed."[44]

Salah-al-Din Bey wanted to talk about another issue. The British insisted on independence for the Sudan, but Cairo would never agree to separating the "unity of Egypt and Sudan." His government could not understand why the United States sided with the British, "when they are violating our rights." Beyond all these questions, however, was the core question of real support for the Egyptian army and economic assistance. Indeed, the final result of almost every question in U.S.–Egyptian relations down to the present day would depend on Washington's support of the army.

Egypt was not the only Middle Eastern nation to raise the question of economic aid in line with what was being offered to European countries under the Marshall Plan and military support for NATO members. The shah of Iran had come to Washington to plead the case for his country's right to receive American aid based on promises made by the Allied occupying powers in the 1943 Declaration of Tehran, only to be told there were limits to what the United States could do.

McGhee responded to these comments by saying that he could not believe that any grievances against the British could be regarded in the same light as the menace of a new type of imperialism far worse than anything London had imposed. The British, he went on, were extricating themselves from a colonial past. But because of the international emergency now—presumably the need to rearm because of the Korean War—they found themselves in an awkward position. "They have given up most of the countries in the world which they had under the old colonialism." Then he summed up:

> We entirely approve of the development of the indigenous defensive forces of the Middle East and feel that the British themselves fully accept that principle even though they may not appear to do so at times. One of the purposes of the tripartite declaration [of May 1950] was to furnish the Middle East with an opportunity to play a part in Middle East defenses. We took that decision in the face of considerable criticism in our own country. We took that position in order to make it clear that the furnishing of arms to Egypt for defense purposes was a good thing from the standpoint of our own foreign policy. . . .
>
> We can assure you that we [could] never revert to colonialism which the world has known in the past. We feel that this calls for an evolutionary type of action for nations who find themselves in a position [sic] which have a certain aura of colonialism.[45]

After McGhee finished, the foreign minister said he well understood the analogy the American had made about Russian imperialism, but the Egyptian masses did not. He then asked one question: what would the U.S. attitude be in case of a break with Britain over the Suez and Sudan? Taken aback, McGhee replied that he could not possibly answer such a question "at this time."

Washington was concentrating on not having to answer that question at any time. A few months later, at a NATO council meeting in September 1951, membership in the defense organization was extended to Greece and Turkey. President Truman immediately cabled the Turkish president proposing preliminary conversations about a "Middle East Command" that would include the United States and the United Kingdom, along with Turkey and Egypt. By the time arrangements had been made to discuss the language of the proposal, however, the Egyptian government had formally abrogated the treaties of 1899 and 1936 regarding the Sudan and Suez. The break had come.

In a speech to the Egyptian parliament on October 8, 1951, Prime Minister Mustafa al-Nahhas Pasha ended with a ringing statement: "For the sake of Egypt I signed the 1936 Treaty and for the sake of Egypt I call on you today to abrogate it." Ambassador Caffery reported that bedlam broke out. Speakers from all parties vied in expressing support for "irrational" actions, according to Caffery. "But there was no doubt then, and there has not been since, that regardless of the consequences and with no heed to the future, articulate Egypt was behind the Prime Minister to a man."[46]

Even had the invitation to join the Middle East Command arrived before the prime minister gave his speech, it was hardly likely it would have made the slightest difference. Based on a meeting afterward with a group of prominent Egyptians, Caffery reported that some said this was not the end of Anglo-Egyptian negotiations on a new Suez regime, but a new beginning. The group maintained, said Caffery, "that the Egyptian people would now feel free to negotiate from strength rather than weakness with anyone whom they choose." It was an interesting phrase, one that Dean Acheson had used to describe the only position the United States could take in dealing with Russia: "negotiation from strength."

When asked in later years about criticisms of his use of the phrase, Acheson made a clever side-step that avoided an obvious pitfall. "One could argue," he said, "that if both sides always sought to negotiate from strength, they would constantly be getting stronger but their relative positions would never change and you would never have negotiations."[47] What the United States worried about was that the Egyptian side would constantly seek to get stronger, and the British side could not meet the challenge, forcing the United States deeper into an already ambiguous role. Just a few days later, moreover, Cairo turned down the Turkish invitation to become a founding member of the Middle East Command, seeing it for what it really was, a façade that promoted the fiction of an equal role for Egypt in defense consultations and actions.

A week after the action of the Egyptian parliament, Secretary Acheson expressed regrets to an Egyptian diplomat that the invitation to join a Middle East Command had been turned down, especially as it seemed to him to offer a means for revising the 1936 Anglo-Egyptian Treaty "in a manner wholly consistent with Egypt's position as an independent and sovereign nation." As for the abrogation of the treaty, "The US Govt considers that the recent action of the Egypt Govt with respect to the abrogation of the Anglo-Egypt Treaty of 1936 and the 1899 Agreements concerning the Sudan is not in accord with proper respect for international obligations and for its part believes it to be without validity. This action must be regarded as a serious retrograde step in the endeavors of the free world to develop systems of cooperative defense and in efforts to promote world law and order."[48]

Acheson's reprimands did not halt the march of events in Egypt. On July 23, 1952, the military staged a coup d'état and insisted Farouk leave the country. The next day, demonstrators flooded the streets leading to Ismailia Square, carrying flags and banners proclaiming "Long Live Nahhas, Hero of Independence," and, more ominously, "Get Out of Our Country!" Egypt was declared a republic, and Ismailia Square was renamed Tahrir (Liberation) Square.

Among slogans heard was "Long Live Mossadegh," the prime minister of Iran who had nationalized the British oil company, Anglo-Persian, in his country and was considered a hero in Egypt. In fact, after a visit by Mohammad Mossadegh to Washington, where once again the Truman administration had tried to make peace between an old ally and a nationalist challenge—this one about oil—the disappointed Iranian prime minister had traveled home via Cairo. A crowd of two thousand met his airplane, and ten times that many gathered at the square in front of the palace. On placards he was greeted as the "Destroyer of Britain" and the "Enemy of Imperialism." "For good measure," said a newspaper account, "anti-American slogans were heard, apparently because the United States was charged with refusing Dr. Mossadegh a loan to get the oil fields and the Abadan refinery going." The prime minister's aides thanked the crowd, as he was not feeling well and had to be carried into his hotel in a "bath chair," but sent a message that Iranians would support Egypt's demands that Britain quit Egypt. In response the crowd shouted, "Revolution!" and "Give us arms!" His visit to King Farouk, it was reported, would be highlighted with a documentary film on "British atrocities."[49]

Plainly, it was not going to be easy for the United States to find a safe path through the tangle of old and new issues that overlay Washington's efforts to convert Egyptian nationalism into an asset for containing the Middle East within the boundaries of the "free world."

2

THE NASSER GAMBLE FAILS

We have an opportunity to do business with a group of men who will not easily give commitments because they believe in keeping their word. If we are going to do business with them, we shall have to take this into account and we shall have to move quickly. Admittedly such a course of action will involve a considerable gamble.
—Ambassador Jefferson Caffery, June 1, 1953

Only a few weeks after Secretary Acheson expressed his disappointment that Egypt had not accepted a bid to become part of a hookup with NATO in a Middle East Defense Organization, a fight broke out on January 25, 1952, between British troops and a battalion of Egyptian auxiliary police at Ismailia, the halfway point along the Suez Canal. The incident marked the beginning of the endgame for yet another of the British strongholds that had kept the empire together. It also upset Washington's hope that—at least for a few years—the United States could count on the British to hold the line in that area while the postwar order took shape under its guidance.

In early 1947, the British had called for help in funding Greece and Turkey to enable those countries to resist, in the Greek case, Communist-led guerrillas who threatened to win a civil war against a royalist regime supported by London, and, in the Turkish case, external pressure by the Soviet Union to change the regime that had allowed Ankara to govern access to the Black Sea. Moscow's postwar ambitions seemed clear. It desired a new opening onto the Mediterranean and what that involved for protecting the burgeoning Soviet empire's lifelines up to the Suez Canal and beyond.

Throughout the nineteenth century, Greece and Turkey had been integral to British "containment" of Czarist Russia. Now, London was saying, the United States would have to come into the arena and do its part in keeping the bear from raising havoc either through Communist agitators or diplomacy backed by military threats. Washington policymakers were thrilled by the opportunity to step in at the historic "crossroads" of empire; yet they were alarmed by evidence of how ill-prepared Congress and the public were to understand and accept the stakes of the contest already under way and gaining momentum with each day.

President Truman and his foreign policy aides did not fear a confrontation with the Red Army. Assessing the Soviet military capabilities, policymakers downgraded the likelihood of such a confrontation. The Russians would not attack, Dean Acheson would often say, unless they were out of their minds. Truman agreed—and said so privately. Talking with reporters on board the presidential yacht *Williamsburg*, as he stirred a bourbon highball, Truman shrugged off the possibility of war in the near future. "No," he said, "I don't think we'll ever have any real trouble with Russia—not for a long time to come anyway. Russia is afraid to death of having to fight anybody right now and they know it would be over pretty quickly if they got into war with us. We's [sic] got too much stuff for them, too many thing[s] that they haven't got."[1]

The president had been told by Arthur Vandenberg, however, a Republican senator, that if he wanted to get action out of Congress, he would have to "scare hell" out of his fellow lawmakers about the Soviet threat. Before the Truman Doctrine speech on March 12, 1947, asking $500 million in military and economic aid to Greece and Turkey, favored journalists received inside information (in what would become a time-honored tradition over the next decades) about what was brewing, in order to build up support for administration positions. They became, in effect, part of the campaign. In the *New York Times*, columnist James Reston dutifully reported that there had been a top-secret meeting at the White House where Truman revealed that the British were unable to continue bearing the costs of aiding Greece. The objective of American policy over the past two years, Reston said, had been to take "a firm position vis-à-vis the Soviet Union along a line running from Stettin on the Baltic down through Germany and Austria to Trieste. . . . The British have in effect asked whether the United States was prepared to assume a great part of the responsibility for world peace and stability assumed by Britain in the nineteenth century. That is what is at issue rather than the appropriation of a loan to a small Mediterranean country."[2]

The Truman Doctrine did, indeed, foretell a serious course. The president's speechwriters crafted an appeal that neatly cornered the legislators. He strengthened the speech's draft from it "should" be American policy to aid countries resisting subversion backed by outside pressures—a neat linking of the different threats to Greece and Turkey—to it "must" be, in the final version delivered to Congress. The legislators had little choice but to sign on, if only because they could not leave Truman out on a limb. This maneuver also became the technique of choice in the Cold War: a presidential vow to stand up in some corner of the world where American "national security" seemed threatened, followed by a pivot toward Congress to supply the means.

But it would prove more difficult to get King Farouk's successors to sign on for their parts in defending the "free world." The Suez military base and the canal were seen as strongpoints for launching strikes against the Soviet Union in case of a war in Europe or Asia, and—most especially—for keeping a base for military action elsewhere in the Middle East should it be impossible to prevent a Communist takeover of radical nationalist movements in, for example, Iran in 1953. Linking Egypt with a Western defense organization, finally, would provide a way for channeling intra-Arab rivalries into a common cause, and, eventually, offering some hope for solving the Arab-Israeli impasse. Egypt was thus thought to be the key to a special Middle Eastern "containment" policy, which like the NATO policy in Europe would work in several directions. NATO would not only be a bulwark against the Soviet Union, but, as Acheson and others said, would resolve the Franco-German rivalry of the past century. For all these reasons the outbreak of violence between British troops and Egyptian police at Ismailia on January 25, 1952, sent a warning to Washington that the United States was at risk of being put into a situation that could easily end badly, with an

Egyptian refusal to play any role in the American-led "free world" commonwealth of nations designed to replace the imperial order.

The bottom line for American policymakers, therefore, was that under no circumstances would any American forces, including even a token force to show the flag, be sent to Egypt to back up British soldiers resisting an Egyptian uprising along the Suez. "The British gambit in Egypt has been played out," read a State Department recommendation to Secretary Acheson in May 1952 about London's efforts to maintain full control over Suez in negotiations about troop evacuations. "The result is stalemate. We see the situation this way. . . . As in Indo-China [where the French clung to power] these problems always come back to weaken the combined strength we are all trying to create. And they come back also, as in Iran, Tunisia and Morocco, to weaken an asset, which is not ours alone but belongs to all the West—the belief that the interests of the U.S. are broad enough to include those of other peoples."[3]

Suez After World War II

From the time of the opening of the Suez Canal in 1869, its value as the lifeline to India had been paramount in British strategic thinking. British troops had first occupied the Suez Canal area in 1882 to put down a rebellion, promising to retire, said generations of foreign office secretaries, "as soon as the state of the country" permitted. "Egyptian nationalists spent the next 72 years trying to get the British to act on their expressed desire to withdraw."[4]

Instead of withdrawing, however, the British grip around Suez tightened as the years went by. In December 1914, the fifth month of World War I, London declared the Ottoman suzerainty had been terminated, proclaimed a protectorate over Egypt, and transferred all foreign policy functions to its chief representative in Cairo, now called the high commissioner. Foreign Secretary Lord Curzon declared, "The welfare and integrity of Egypt are necessary to the peace and safety of the British Empire, which will therefore always maintain as an essential British interest the special relations between itself and Egypt."[5]

The 1936 treaty imposed on Cairo permitted the British to house ten thousand troops and four hundred pilots there along with all necessary support personnel for twenty years. In 1942, as Field Marshal Erwin Rommel's Afrika Korps approached the Egyptian capital, student demonstrators cheered. Fearing rioting and insurrection, British high commissioner Sir Miles Lampson ordered three tanks and a company of soldiers to smash through the palace gates to King Farouk's chambers. Either appoint pro-British Mustafa al-Nahhas premier, he declared, or be thrown out himself. Farouk had been toying with the idea of appointing a pro-Axis premier in case the Germans actually reached Cairo. It took him less than an hour to decide he wanted to stay. The episode marked Egypt's worst humiliation, said a young army officer, Gamal Abdel Nasser. "Hearts were full of fire and sorrow."[6]

By the war's end the British had eighty thousand troops in and around their Suez base, along with a storehouse of supplies worth over $1 billion. Suez also incorporated a huge air base by which those supplies could be moved to trouble spots without interference from, or even the knowledge of, Egyptian authorities. And the British were seeking to expand their military presence in the area with bases in the former Italian colony of Libya, and to keep a strong military presence south of Egypt in the Sudan. Suez was thus the linchpin for Great Britain's postwar vision of preserving a world role even as Britain's formal empire started to disappear. Yet it became an unwanted source of tension with Washington, where London's delaying actions in coming to terms with Egyptian nationalism were not viewed with great favor, but as a test of wills the West was bound to lose. The problem was the British no longer had much to offer. Asking them to step aside, however, was out of the question—at least for now. As it turned out, "now" lasted quite a long time before it suddenly came to an end in the 1956 crisis.

Churchill and his successor, Clement Attlee, had sought to damp down the smoldering coals of Egyptian resentment before Suez flamed up into a demand that the British remove all troops not just reduce the force to the number permitted under the 1936 treaty. And although both sides agreed that a final evacuation agreement should provide for a cadre of workers inside the military base and rapid reoccupation by regular military should an emergency arise, who was to determine just what was an "emergency"? Leaving aside that question, the entire atmosphere for serious negotiations had been compromised by Egypt's humiliation in the first Arab-Israeli War. That defeat was seen not merely as a military fiasco, but as a final judgment on Farouk's years of prolificacy and misrule. He had led the country into a morass of corruption, poverty, and—the war had shown—near-fatal weakness.

"Farouk was in his palace," wrote Mohamed Heikal about Egypt's turmoil, "and one half per cent of the population was getting 50 per cent of the national income. . . . The political parties had collapsed with no sense of direction and no sense of purpose. There was nothing to be proud of and there was no dignity."[7] A newspaper editor, Heikal had become a confidant of Colonel Gamal Abdel Nasser, the leader who emerged in the Free Officers Movement after the coup that swept Farouk and his family out of his palaces and into exile.

Nasser was one of the few who had fought with distinction in the 1948 war against the Israelis. He returned from the battlefront "convinced that the real enemy was in Cairo." Born in 1918 to a middle-class family, Nasser was already involved in anti-British demonstrations as a teenager. After several false starts, he finally gained admission to a military academy just before World War II and was stationed in the Sudan during that time, when he, like many others, exhibited sympathies for the Axis (in this case Italians in Africa) as allies in a common struggle against the British. Egypt was officially neutral in the war until 1945, however, when it made an opportunistic decision to join the Allies. Nasser first saw military action in the 1948 invasion of Palestine. The Free Officers Movement offered him and others the chance to come together to discuss what had gone so terribly wrong—and what must be done.

Farouk's days were numbered in the aftermath of the "Battle of Ismailia," in which forty-one Egyptian police were killed and another seventy-two wounded. The next day mobs surged through downtown Cairo, setting fires and attacking the symbols of British power and prestige: the Shepheard's Hotel, the St. James restaurant, and the British Turf Club. At this last place, nine British civilians were killed in gruesome fashion, four of them disemboweled and another trampled to death. Additional troops were sent into Cairo from the Suez garrison and succeeded in bringing the rioting to an end on what became known as "Black Saturday," January 26, 1952. The British felt they had made their point, but Truman and his advisers rejected London's appeal for American forces to present a united front. Churchill, now back in Number 10 Downing Street, pleaded with his American ally that such a demonstration would "divide the difficulties by ten." In Washington, however, the administration feared that Black Saturday was only the beginning of real difficulties unless a new approach was adopted. "It did not impress him," Acheson told the British ambassador, "that the operation of Ismailia had been carried out with 'unusual skill'"—as Eden had put it in a telegram to Washington. "The 'splutter of musketry' apparently does not stop things as we had been told from time to time that it would."[8]

British foreign secretary Anthony Eden—in a foretaste of later assertions at the time of the 1956 Suez Crisis—rejected American criticism. Less than a month before the coup that toppled Farouk, Eden received a warning from Acheson that the use of British force in Egypt to hold on to Suez would be a terrible mistake fraught with "consequences in the rest of the Middle East which would be incalculable." Whitehall dismissed the warning, asserting "that January 26th had taught the Egyptians a lesson."[9]

It did teach the Free Officers Movement a lesson: Farouk must go. Led by Nasser they carried off a coup on July 23, 1952. There is some evidence that the movement had CIA involvement—or at least a friendly nod—but Washington was not sorry to see Farouk go in any event. Washington did apparently urge the junta to allow the king to leave peacefully and without a fuss. The movement had originally intended to hand over power to a civilian government but decided there really was no one to carry out such a responsibility right away. Nasser stood back for the time being to allow an older colleague, General Muhammad Naguib, to be the face of the revolution. A few hours after the takeover, one of the plotters met with a U.S. military attaché to assure him of the revolutionary council's pro-Western sentiments and to ask for his help in persuading the British not to intervene.[10]

Ambassador Caffery accepted an invitation to dinner with Naguib and several of his fellow officers. Asked about the agrarian reforms that had been at the top of the list of promised changes, Naguib backed off somewhat. Yes, they must do something about that problem in the immediate future, but they had gone a bit too far in making hasty promises about giving seventeen or eighteen million fellaheen peasants plots of land. "They are somewhat embarrassed at having spoken too much on the subject publicly," Caffery reported. In addition, the officers also now realized they had been too quick in releasing too many Communists and had now "re-arrested [a] lot of them."[11]

It was pleasing to receive such reassurances. In Egypt, as in other places, the military was destined to play a leading role. To do so required a guaranteed source of weapons. As that source, the United States could exert considerable leverage—even more so, it would later become clear, as the final authority on weapons transfers from NATO alliance members. The expected appeals from the Egyptian military were not long in coming. Caffery cabled Washington he had received word from General Naguib that the Egyptians would be willing to give secret assurances to the United States about the long-term objectives of the new regime, including a Middle Eastern Defense Organization (MEDO) and/or partnership with the United States. But before Naguib could do more in the way of public statements, his first job was to sell the Egyptian public on the United States. And to accomplish that would require military supplies and financial assistance.[12]

Yes, Acheson responded, the United States would accept secret assurances—but with the understanding they were only preliminary to open commitments. The United States would carefully monitor Egypt's performance. Commitment to MEDO, however, was only one of three issues of interest. There was the question of a long-term arrangement over Suez guaranteeing ready access to the base. And there was the pressing matter of peace with Israel. In the meantime, the new regime could signal its intentions with "certain gestures," such as a public vow of support for the United Nations' actions in Korea—Egypt had not voted for the original UN resolution authorizing the use of force there—and an offer of compensation to victims of the rioting on Black Saturday. These should not be too difficult for Cairo and would offer evidence of the Egyptian officers' orientation in the Cold War.[13]

Mohamed Heikal, the newspaper editor and Nasser confidant, arrived in Washington in the fall of 1952 ostensibly to cover the presidential election. His real mission was to provide Nasser—the man who would soon assume power—with information about likely attitudes of the new administration, Democrat or Republican. Heikal received a warm welcome in the Pentagon; his host was a general who entertained him with a special map show. The general pushed a button, and behind him descended a huge map of the world covered with buttons and flags, each representing an American garrison or base. The Middle East was largely bare, he said, pointing to the display. "Don't you think we could do with some buttons and flags in your part of the world?" Heikal protested that the real issue was the hopes and aspirations of the people. The general seemed surprised, and not quite aware of Heikal's point. An alternative, the general suggested, was an Islamic pact. Because of its heavy religious content, such a pact would provide a natural bulwark against Communism. Turkey, he went on, was the strongest military power, Pakistan the most populous, Saudi Arabia the custodian of the holy places, and Egypt could supply the cultural focus. Such a pact might even cause uprisings in the Muslim populations of the Soviet Union and China, and have a chastening effect in India. Heikal learned later that the idea did not have State Department backing, but thought it revealed a troubling lack of comprehension about Middle Eastern politics in the postcolonial era.[14]

Heikal's visit to the Pentagon and the general's presentation was only one example of the "friendly persuasion" American officials attempted in an ultimately unsuccessful effort to convince the Egyptians that their future would be best served inside some sort of overarching treaty that would allow Washington to meet at least some of the demands for military aid. Nothing could be done, the Egyptians insisted, until the British agreed to a complete evacuation of Suez. Naguib did go so far as to tell Caffery on one occasion that only if Cairo had promises of serious military aid could it counter the "lies" that were being circulated in the Egyptian press that the Americans were little better than the British. "I may be dreaming but if you could find a way to let us have 100 tanks various doors would be opened including one leading to Middle Eastern Defense."[15]

In early 1953, after the Republicans swept to power on Eisenhower's World War II reputation and his pledge to go to Korea and find a way to end the bloodshed that resembled in many ways the misery of World War I trench warfare, Secretary of State John Foster Dulles promised a "New Look" not only at what the GOP said had gone wrong with the Truman/Acheson containment policy in Eastern Europe and Asia but at the Middle East—especially the Middle East. American policy there had been less than evenhanded, he contended—a transparent reference to the support Washington had given Israel from the time of Truman's quick recognition of the new nation. The challenge was to divert Middle Eastern attention from the Arab-Israeli conflict and channel the emotions into a worldwide anticommunist crusade. Then, it was hoped, it would be easier to persuade the Arabs to make peace with Israel, and, with the security threat removed, easier to persuade Israel to offer permanent borders. Egypt was the key, he thought, to solving the puzzle.

Dulles flew off to the Middle East in May 1953, on his first extended tour as custodian of U.S. foreign policy. Eisenhower and Dulles had chosen an odd gift to present to General Naguib—a .38 caliber pistol with a silver plate on the butt inscribed: "To General Mohammed Naguib from his friend Dwight D. Eisenhower." It was supposed to be presented in private, but one photographer caught the scene. His picture triggered an uproar in the British press. Churchill appealed to his old friend and wartime colleague for an explanation. It had no larger significance, Eisenhower reassured the prime minister. One pistol did not "presage a flow of planes, tanks, and guns."[16]

London was not reassured. In itself the gift might mean nothing, but the least pinprick unnerved British policymakers in the atmosphere of the Iranian oil crisis and anxiety surrounding the stalled Suez Canal negotiations. What were the Americans about? Had they known more about Dulles's objectives than the pistol picture, "pinprick" would not have been the right word to describe the reaction. When Dulles met with General Naguib for the first time, he practically promised to deliver arms to Egypt. If such aid could be *justified*, he said, "the US would be prepared to consider making the Egyptian Army a real force in the world." While it was not possible to aid everybody, "Egypt has great possibilities for the future not only for itself but as an example for others to follow." An example for others to follow—that was the main condition to justify such aid, as it had been when Acheson first addressed the new regime. Egypt must settle the Suez controversy by allowing British forces to return under certain specified conditions; *and* it had to agree to take the lead in bringing the Arab world into a peace agreement with Israel; *and* it had to join in some regional defense pact. The new administration's policies, Dulles said, would be first and foremost directed at the Communist threat.

Look at the globe, he urged Naguib—the Communists already ruled one-third of the world. Stalin's death a few weeks earlier had changed nothing. "Like a religious creed," Dulles described the red menace, Communist pressure "keeps on and on." It had come near Egypt already. Washington had neglected the Middle East for too long. It was the area that gave birth to the great religions and boasted many cultural roots of Western civilization. By meeting American requirements, Egypt would find its reward to be more than just military aid. "In the past the US has perhaps centered too much of its interest on Israel as a result of pressure groups in the US. The new Administration is seeking a balanced view of the Middle East directed against neither the Arabs nor the Jews."[17]

Naguib seemed responsive to these hints, but Dulles pressed for specifics. Would Naguib promise that the British could leave managers on the base to oversee its maintenance? He tried to make a comparison with a Ford plant overseas where there were foreign managers in charge of production. Egypt would win a great political victory when British troops evacuated Suez. "Could it be that the great vision of a new Egypt could collapse over the problems of a few inventory-keepers?"[18]

Why should Egyptians believe the British now, Naguib protested? They had never kept any promises; hence his colleagues' refusal to sanction a demand that uniformed military could stay behind in any capacity. Egyptians could learn all that was necessary to run the base complex. It was precisely because the British negotiators kept expanding the number of causes for reactivation of the base—including supposed threats within the Arab world, as he would tell the American ambassador later—that Naguib and his colleagues could not agree on these points. As for joining a defense pact with Great Britain and the United States, the bad experience over seven decades meant that "everybody is *afraid of pacts and agreements.* There is a feeling that no agreements can be 'respectable' unless they are made between equals. Agreements made on the basis of a master-slave relationship are of no use."[19]

The dialogue continued when Dulles met Colonel Nasser, the key man in the revolutionary council. Left out of the American minutes of their discussion, however, was the opening exchange over Dulles's comments on arrival at Cairo airport. The secretary thought he had been very complimentary about Egypt's great contributions to civilization, hailing General Naguib as "one of the outstanding free world leaders of the postwar world." What right-thinking man could object to praising a defender of the free world? But Nasser astonished Dulles, saying, "I did not like your statement today." For Egyptians, he explained, the phrase "free world" had unfortunate connotations: "We have been occupied by the British to secure the communications of 'the Free World,' and so for us 'the Free World' has come to mean imperialism and domination, and when you used that phrase this morning it created a bad effect."[20]

Recovering from his shock, Dulles initiated a discussion about why the United States had not sent arms to Egypt. He blamed the British. Prime Minister Churchill had called Eisenhower very soon after he began his term in the White House to urge him not to start his presidency by providing weapons that might be used to kill British Tommies who had served under him during the war. Blaming the British only went so far, however, because the United States had no intention of supplying arms to Cairo until all its conditions had been met. Dulles argued that the British who remained behind to run the base would not be allowed to raise the Union Jack. "They would be under the flag of the pact." That was naïve thinking, Nasser countered; no one in Egypt would believe a different flag flying over Suez would make any difference. He had to win the confidence of his people. "If I stop leading my people as a nationalist, then the Communists are going to lead them."[21]

The Egyptian leader had neatly turned the Communist argument for Truman Doctrine–style defense pacts—to protect subversion-endangered countries—inside out. Here was a leader who argued that joining a pact would further supposed Communist aims! As for the argument that there was a Soviet military threat, Nasser had another answer: "How can I go to my people and tell them that I am disregarding a killer with a pistol sixty miles from me at the Suez Canal to worry about somebody who is holding a knife a thousand miles away?"[22]

A real solution to the Suez base problem and the general defense issue could arise naturally as British troops left the area, insisted the American secretary of state. "The US hopes Egypt will lead the Arab States into a new area defense system . . . which, when it is achieved, will find the material in the depots available to it." Nasser responded that Egypt by itself would maintain the base depots and determine access. What Dulles proposed was a lightly disguised ploy to sustain British influence in a new multination alliance. Well, the situation was dangerous, said Dulles, and the base must remain a living organism. "How can we get the [Anglo-Egyptian] talks going again?" Simple, Nasser replied, "By getting the British to agree to the Egyptian point of view."[23]

Reassessments and New Plans

Dulles returned from his first encounter with Nasser and Naguib filled with foreboding and ambiguous about what the next steps should be. He was loath to abandon the idea of well-guided Egyptian leadership in the Arab world, but he believed he must consider alternatives. Eisenhower had told congressional leaders the big problem was how to organize the Middle East into some kind of NATO defense system, including an arrangement that guaranteed the Suez base would always be available. But Israel complicated the problem. On his return, Dulles painted a much darker picture. The Middle East was in the grip of a "fanatical revolutionary spirit." It was not just a temporary problem. "The Israeli factor, and the association of the U.S. in the minds of the people of the area with French and British colonial and imperialistic policies, are millstones around our neck."[24]

As matters stood, Middle Eastern nations were too distracted to appreciate the Soviet threat. The question, Dulles wrote in a memo to himself, was how to increase American influence in the region "at the earliest possible moment." The area had long suffered economic deprivation. No government could gain its people's confidence without holding out the promise of economic improvement. And that meant America had no choice but to extend aid where it could do the most good. Hence the need to send arms to Cairo, to make Egypt stronger. "Such military assistance would be utilized for purposes of internal security, of strengthening defense of the area and obtaining political advantage."[25]

Even so, the State Department remained reluctant to go ahead with arms shipments that would upset the British and the Israelis without guarantees the arms would be used for "internal security" and offer "political advantage." As the intra-government debate developed, CIA representatives in Egypt and Ambassador Caffery favored taking the gamble. There remains considerable mystery about what, if any, role the CIA played in Farouk's overthrow. Because Kermit "Kim" Roosevelt Jr., a grandson of Teddy Roosevelt, who had played a key role in returning the shah of Iran to his throne, had been assigned to arrange a liaison with the Egyptian colonels, there were stories about the "company's" role even at the beginning. And there were many boasts about "my boys," as Caffery supposedly referred to the new regime.[26]

Roosevelt's assignment was to shape Nasser into a positive influence on wayward postcolonial leaders in Africa and Asia. At first,

Nasser seemed a good pupil. Policy statements prepared by Roosevelt for Nasser to deliver were often reprinted on Egyptian presidential letterhead with scarcely any changes. Surely this Egyptian was destined for big things. But little progress was being made on the conditions Washington had set down for welcoming Egypt into full membership in the "free world." For more than two years after the revolution Cairo pressed for arms aid. Nasser asked for $40 million, then $20 million, and finally just $2 million or $3 million for parade items—helmets, pistol holsters, and various kinds of shiny equipment that would look good when the army was parading through the streets of Cairo. There was no question about using this equipment in a war with Israel, wrote one of Roosevelt's CIA operatives in Cairo, Miles Copeland, who agreed with Ambassador Caffery that Nasser was right: a "shabby army [w]as a potentially disloyal army."[27]

In a television report to the nation after his trip, Dulles had said the United States must pursue an impartial approach to Israeli-Arab disputes, so as to win the support of both sides against the common threat of Communism. At present the Arabs were "more fearful of Zionism than of Communism," he lamented, while the Israelis feared the ultimate aim of the Arabs was to push them into the sea. Then he went out on a very narrow limb. "The leaders of Israel themselves agreed with us that United States policies should be impartial so as to win not only the respect and regard of the Israeli, but also of the Arab peoples." He juxtaposed that comment with praise for Naguib as a popular hero, who deserved the praise because he was determined to provide Egypt with a government that will "truly serve the people." Israel, on the other hand, needed to "cease to look upon itself or be looked upon by others, as alien to this [Middle Eastern] community."[28]

Egyptian reactions were muted. "The speech is friendly," said one high official, "but we should not be too optimistic." Meeting with reporters after seeing Assistant Secretary Henry Byroade, Israeli ambassador Abba Eban said he had sought clarifications of some points. Asked which points, he replied, "Well, if you read the speech[,] practically every point." A few weeks later, *New York Times* reporter Dana Adams Schmidt reported from Tel Aviv that the Israelis had sensed in Dulles's remarks an ominous shift in American opinion. They were extremely sensitive to such shifts. "For there is no country in the world so completely dependent on outside—especially United States—economic support."[29] Israelis feared they were beginning to lose the "pathos" argument, Schmidt added, and that the world's sympathies were being transferred to the estimated eight hundred thousand Arab refugees from the former Palestine.

In early June 1953, Dulles went to Capitol Hill to meet with the Senate Foreign Relations Committee in "executive" (or secret) hearings. He was less than optimistic. "We came back with less hope . . . that quite a little could be built around the foundation of Egypt." The basic reason was the intensity of the dispute with the British over Suez. The principal issue, he said, was who was going to manage the military base, who can handle and route the equipment to where it was needed. The Egyptians were not competent to complete those tasks. "They think they are, but they are not, and I think everybody will agree to that."[30]

He had flown over the Suez base area for the first time and realized just how important it was to the West. It extended all the way along the Suez Canal area to a considerable width. "There are a series of air strips, big depots of ammunition, vehicles of one kind and another and there are supposed to be about a billion dollars of military equipment there in one or another of these depots, and from them they route that equipment from those bases, the British fly them to their positions in Jordan where they have an Arab League army, and their position in Cyprus, and from which, if there was a general war, in the advanced position along the frontier with Soviet Russia they would be supplied from there."[31]

Dulles's report on his trip to the Middle East actually made Nasser's point about the purposes of the Suez base being to maintain a Western colonial stronghold in the Middle East. Nevertheless, Washington continued to push London toward a settlement that would provide some sort of transitional assurances the base would be available. Eventually Churchill yielded. He said he did so because of financial pressures, and, he said in a letter to Eisenhower on June 21, 1954, because the American hydrogen bomb tests had lessened the need for keeping up the Suez base. Along with the solid adherence of Greece and Turkey to NATO, and the development of a new front in a Pakistan-Turkey treaty—which might later include Iraq—his mind was relieved.[32]

A new treaty was signed in October providing for a two-year transition to full Egyptian control, and it also ended the standoff over Sudan, with the British agreeing to evacuate and the Egyptians agreeing to give up claims to suzerainty. But it was a tenuous "peace" between the two countries. Nasser came under criticism for agreeing even to a two-year period, and he was the target of an assassination attempt after the agreement was announced. The British were not happy, either, and very wary of what next steps Nasser might take to appease extreme nationalists.

For example, the treaties Churchill spoke of in his letter to Eisenhower were the genesis of the "Northern Tier," or as it was sometimes called, the "Baghdad Pact." These were pokes in the eye, so far as Nasser was concerned, as he sought to make himself the central figure in an Arab awakening. Dulles was increasingly sympathetic with such efforts to "contain" Nasser's ambitions, but he wanted to keep the door open to Cairo's redemption as an American cohort, should Cairo finally recognize where its best interests lay.

With the question of Britain's presence at Suez seemingly resolved—at least for the near future—focus returned to Arab-Israeli issues and Egypt's role in that bedeviling tangle of issues. Israel was anxious to head off any move in the West to give Egypt significant arms under any conditions. Actually, there was little chance of that happening, no matter how many hoops Nasser jumped through, because in addition to all the other conditions, American military aid was given to friendly powers only under conditions that the recipient country accept a Military Assistance Advisory Group (MAAG) along with the hardware. These "minders" were sent along to make sure that the weaponry was used properly, and not for purposes that defeated the American interest in defense pacts. Even if the colonels cleared this hurdle, there remained the other requirements, above all a peace treaty between Egypt and Israel. Congress would never allow the executive branch to forget that. At one point the State

Department considered a onetime $10 million packet funneled through the economic aid programs so as to avoid complaints that Egypt was receiving special treatment. Nothing came of it.[33]

On February 28, 1955, a supposedly retaliatory Israeli raid into the Gaza Strip pushed the arms question to the forefront in new ways. David Ben-Gurion, now defense minister, launched the fateful attack on an Egyptian military post for a variety of reasons. The ostensible cause was retaliation for raids from Gaza carried out by displaced Palestinians, but Ben-Gurion's larger objective was to demonstrate that Israel could not be strangled by Arab economic or military policies. Since the 1948 war, Egypt had kept the Suez Canal closed to Israeli shipping, under a disputed interpretation of the original protocol governing international shipping through the canal. The original protocol governing passage through the canal stipulated it was to be kept open in time of war and peace. Only if Egypt's security was endangered could ships be denied passage. Since there was no peace treaty, Egypt asserted the right to bar Israeli shipping from passing through the canal. In a 1951 conversation with Dean Acheson, Ben-Gurion, then prime minister, had stressed the urgency of demonstrating that Israel could not be destroyed by war or a drawn-out strangulation process. American economic and military aid to Israel, he had said, would prove to the Arab nations that "Israel could not be destroyed."

In recent months, there had been a perceptible decline in cross-border incidents and bellicose talk, along with rumors of secret contacts between Israeli and Egyptian agents, something worrisome to hard-liners on both sides. The February 28 raid left thirty-seven dead and another thirty wounded. While Ben-Gurion hoped a dramatic move like the Gaza raid would force Egypt to reconsider its policies, American officials feared, on the other hand, that the raid would provide an impetus to an all-Arab army—a dangerous prospect increasing the likelihood of a new Arab-Israeli war. Nothing could be worse in terms of exercising control over a Middle East arms race, and, indeed, over Middle Eastern politics. Dulles had long been concerned about a pan-Arab military alliance. He was strongly inclined, he had advised the National Security Council on his return from his original *tour d'horizon*, "to believe we must abandon our preconceived ideas of making Egypt the key country in building the foundations for a military defense of the Middle East."[34]

He had been most favorably impressed with Pakistan's potential, on the other hand, particularly if that country was allied with Iraq as anchors of a "Northern Tier" pact. Add Syria and Turkey, and the Northern Tier would be too high for the Soviets to climb, and too much for Egypt to overcome in a quest to unite Arabs. "As for the countries further south, they were too lacking in realization of the international situation to offer any prospect of becoming dependable allies." There was one problem, however, that would have to be finessed: Dulles did not want to appear to be too close to an Iraqi regime suspect in some quarters as too pro-British. Consequently, while he encouraged the British to take the lead in organizing the pact, he declined full membership.

On the other hand, the Gaza raid made it easy for Nasser to promote himself as the one Arab leader most deserving of support and military aid, and to denounce his competitors as not true nationalists. Nasser's successor, Anwar Sadat, would write later about the Gaza raid that it "marked a turning point in the history of Egypt, the Revolution, and the Middle East." Nasser was under intense pressure from his military to end the long dialogue with Washington; after all, Farouk's fate had been determined largely by the woeful military defeat in the 1948 Arab-Israeli War.[35]

Decision Time

America's new ambassador to Egypt, Henry Byroade, arrived in Cairo just before the Gaza raid. Known as a champion of "even-handedness," Byroade had given speeches urging Israel to behave as a "normal" state, which brought angry retorts from American Jewish groups. Byroade did not define "normal," but his antagonists believed they knew only too well what he meant. At the June 1954 convention of the Zionist Organization of America, Emmanuel Neumann denounced "Byroadeism" as an effort to separate world Jewry from Israel. "Byroadeism would isolate Israel, sever her vital

connection with the Jewish people, block out her cultural hinter-
land, foreshorten her world horizons and reduce her in the end to
an enclave buried away in a corner of the Arab world."[36]

With the British departing, and Byroade coming to Cairo, American rhetorical evenhandedness may well have been one of the trig-
gers of Ben-Gurion's decision to launch the Gaza raid, just as Dulles
had predicted. Nasser summoned Byroade to a private meeting the
very evening of the raid. Gaza was on the agenda, but the Egyptian
leader spent most of the interview denouncing the new Baghdad
Pact, a Turkish-Pakistani-Iraqi security treaty with an open admis-
sions policy. It was clear, Nasser exploded, that the United States
had cast him aside for Iraqi strongman Nuri as-Said. Nasser disliked
Nuri intensely, seeing in him the very model of the comprador
mentality with his disregard for the Iraqi masses and his Savile Row
suits—but that was only part of the problem. Nuri had accused him
of being naïve in not understanding that the Arab countries could
not get along outside the protective shelter of a Western defense
pact. Byroade reported Nasser's anger: "The injection of an actual
new treaty arrangement of one Arab State with Turkey (i.e. West)
he interprets as a great setback to his own plans of bringing into
being a genuine pro-Western sentiment among the people." The
ambassador told Nasser in return that he should be "under no illu-
sions that we can support a unified Arab Army under present circumstances in the Middle East."[37]

Back in Washington no one was thinking anymore about making the Egyptian army into a real force. Instead, Dulles liked the
Northern Tier plan precisely because it put limits on Nasser's aspirations. He was ready, he confided to Anthony Eden, to help Nuri
obtain tanks for an armored division and to supply weapons to
other parties to such a treaty. It was not possible for Washington to
be a formal member of the pact, he said, because Israel's supporters
would object. Eden suspected the real reason was Dulles wished to
take credit in Cairo for standing apart from "colonialist" attitudes.

Nasser lectured the Iraqi leader meanwhile on the real purpose of
British strategy, which was, he said, to drive a wedge in Arab nationalism. Nuri waved off Nasser's warning and accepted American

conditions on military aid, and thereby cleared the way for the Baghdad Pact. The whole diplomatic game depended on each party pretending that containing Russia was the object, when everyone, giver and recipients alike, understood it was about regional politics and keeping internal order. After all was said and done, Nasser concluded, the United States had inherited and made its own the old colonial style of divide and conquer, covering it with a glaze of Cold War rhetoric.

In April 1955, Nasser changed tactics. He would damp down his criticism of both Nuri and the Baghdad Pact, he said, if London ceased trolling for additional members, especially Jordan. British influence had been paramount in Amman since the end of World War I, but Nasser eyed Jordan as a country that could help with the formation of an Arab alliance, and a counterweight to Iraq. When Eden succeeded Churchill as prime minister, Nasser told an American journalist, he promised him "that they will freeze the Baghdad Pact." Besides soliciting promises from the British, Nasser negotiated a military pact with Saudi Arabia and Syria, thereby creating the possibility of a united front of Israel's closest neighbors if Jordan signed on for the alliance.[38]

A month earlier Nasser had submitted yet another request to Washington for arms aid, a list of items so modest that Eisenhower called it "peanuts." The purpose, administration officials reckoned, was simply to embarrass the United States about its sincerity. Very well, said the State Department, behave like Iraq and be willing to accept an American advisory and training group. Besides meeting that condition, payment for the arms would have to be in cash. Nasser had not really expected a positive response, and the American reply gave him a chance to portray Egypt as forging its own path. In a radio speech broadcast from the Cairo Officers' Club, he vowed to organize the defense of the Middle East "without any link or partnership with the West." And he added for good measure, "I think it would be a miracle if we ever obtained any arms from [that] direction."[39]

It was still assumed in the United States that he had little option, in the end, but to capitulate to Washington's demands, even as all the signs pointed in a different direction. British and American diplomats labored over the terms of a response to Nasser's challenge and emerged with something they called Project Alpha. They should give Nasser the impression, said the authors, that he was being singled out as the key leader to bring peace to the Middle East. "We shall therefore need to offer inducements to Egypt." But there could be no yielding to his views on the Baghdad Pact, not even as an inducement "to move towards a Palestine settlement." Military aid would still depend upon a prior resolution of the Arab-Israeli conflict. On the toughest question, the Palestinian refugee problem, the proposed solution was out of Lewis Carroll. Israel was expected to agree to accept 75,000, over several years, while the rest—800,000— would have to be absorbed into other Arab countries. The United States and Great Britain would put up much of the money for resettlement of the 75,000 in the form of long-term loans, but 30 percent of the estimated $300 million would have to come from Israel and "world Jewry."

Indeed, there was actually little new in the Alpha Project except the promise of specific offers of economic aid, for example, on the Aswan High Dam. During Dulles's 1953 visit, Naguib had pressed for American aid to build a new dam on the Nile. The dam was crucial, he said, to bringing additional lands under cultivation to meet the needs of a rapidly growing population. Over the long term, said Naguib, Egypt would need $100 million to start the new Aswan Dam and related projects.[40]

As matters progressed with Alpha, it was hoped Egypt would be drawn into programs to start international water projects on the major rivers that flowed from Syria and Jordan into Israel. Israel would be warned, meanwhile, that refusal to cooperate could prevent the United States from offering a long-sought security guarantee, "and that she would have to bear the onus for failure of our efforts to progress toward peace."[41]

There was little reason to believe that Project Alpha would succeed in persuading Israel to take such steps. In the fall of 1953, when the Eisenhower administration enjoyed almost complete public support after a Korean truce, Dulles found himself fending off a storm of criticism from Jewish groups when he suspended economic aid to Israel to force a halt in efforts to divert water from the Jordan River. In a confrontation with Dulles, the leader of one group, New York congressman Jacob Javits, warned he planned to release to the press a statement decrying the decision as unfair and harmful to Israel's economic development. The statement was full of inaccuracies, Dulles retorted, and suggested "the group might spend some time working with representatives of the Israeli Government to try to change their policy of presenting the world with *faits accompli*. Cooperation seemed to be a one-way street as far as Israel is concerned." A final peace settlement, he insisted, depended very much upon increased American influence in the Arab world, with its "petroleum reserves upon which our military planning depends." On this occasion, the threat worked. Israel agreed to cooperate with the United Nations on an international plan for the Jordan River. But nothing was really resolved.[42]

Ambassador Byroade doubted Alpha had much of a chance; it could do little to relieve Egypt's fears that it was being isolated between Israel and the Northern Tier: "These feelings of frustration could . . . lead [Nasser] to seek neutrality and general non-cooperation with the West." Nasser was now insisting on a land connection with other Arab countries through the Negev Desert—more than a corridor as imagined in various schemes of Project Alpha, but "the whole of [the] Negev south of Beersheba." The Israelis were not likely to go along with that concession, given their own plans for the Negev. And therein was the central problem. There were very few "apparent advantages for Arabs in Alpha proposals themselves."[43]

Byroade's pessimism was well warranted. At the April 1955 Conference of Asian and African Nations in Bandung, Indonesia, Nasser found an opportunity to bring pressure on Washington, by moving in a different direction. Byroade and Kim Roosevelt had attempted to dissuade him from attending a conference where he would be up against the cleverest Communist of all, Chinese foreign minister Chou En-lai. American policymakers had belittled the conference, and Secretary Dulles declared with patronizing contempt that neutralism was "an immoral and shortsighted conception."[44]

Representatives of more than twenty-five nations with a combined population of over 650 million people met at the conference and began their deliberations by declaring "colonialism in all its manifestations is an evil which should speedily be brought to an end." It galled American observers that the Chinese claimed to represent a "neutral" nation in the Cold War, and that Chou En-lai had once again stolen the limelight. What they had not anticipated, however, was that Nasser would broach the question of Soviet arms for Egypt. The Egyptian leader had met Chou at Rangoon on the way to the meeting and asked if the foreign minister thought the Russians might be prepared to sell arms to Egypt. Chou said they might. "Do you want me to explore?"[45]

Nasser came home from Bandung a hero and a major player. He now had good reason to believe the Soviet Union would entertain a bid for arms and provide him with a way around American hurdles. Egypt's cotton exports had fallen by 26 percent in little over a year, the result, in part, of U.S. agricultural subsidies that permitted American farmers to dump cotton on the world market. China and Russia offered an alternative outlet for the cotton—and a barter deal for arms that would not require cash payments in scarce dollars or pounds. Journalist Kennett Love wrote that Nasser's return from Bandung marked the time when his three-year endeavor to base Egyptian policy on friendship with America "began to fade into history's limbo of lost opportunities. . . . It became Egypt's door out of the parochialism of the Arab world into the new horizons of awakening Africa and Asia."[46]

Love's belief that there was ever really a possibility of close U.S.-Egyptian friendship in the Nasser era—given all the obstacles and different objectives of both nations—is more than problematic, as was his conclusion that Bandung provided an escape hatch from neocolonialism. But the conference shook the branches. Out of it emerged a self-named neutralist bloc with its own "Big Three": Yugoslavia's Marshal Tito, India's Jawaharlal Nehru, and Nasser. Nehru had been the one to impress on the Egyptian leader the latent power a neutralist bloc would leverage with the great powers.

Raising the Ante

Rumors that Nasser was interested in making a deal with Moscow, cotton for arms, began to cause some concern in Washington, but they were still not taken all that seriously. Presumably they constituted little more than a bluff to test Nehru's theory. American policymakers kept on refining the Alpha plan as if it really had a chance to resolve the Egyptian-Israeli imbroglio before it produced another war. All the maneuvering about the Baghdad Pact had only made matters worse. Dulles understood the danger. A "pall of fear that hangs over the Arab and Israel people alike," he said in a speech to the Council of Foreign Relations on August 26, 1955, is the central issue. The United States was ready to support an international loan to aid in resettlement of the Palestinian refugees, he said, and was willing to "join in formal treaty engagements to prevent or thwart any effort by either side to alter by force the boundaries between Israel and her Arab neighbors." But exactly what were those boundaries? There had been no final settlement after the 1948 war. The Alpha plan now envisioned a road from Egypt to Jordan under Arab sovereignty that would pass over an Israeli road from Beersheba to Eilat, the direct connection Nasser had said he wanted. But there was no reason why Israel should want to give its likely enemies such a highway for transporting troops and arms.

While American policymakers continued drawing lines across the Negev for a road that would never be built, Nasser continued negotiating with Russia, now nearing a final agreement. Historian Steven Freiberger noted that Dulles tried to persuade himself that Egypt and the Arabs would eventually come to their senses and compare what the Soviet Union and the United States had to offer. "Moscow could provide weapons for war, but only Washington could offer the possibility of redressing Arab grievances."[47]

Nasser encouraged American listeners to believe that he would rather purchase arms from the United States even as the negotiations with Russia reached their final stage. Ambassador Byroade was informed by one of Nasser's aides on September 21, 1955, that the deal was now an accomplished fact. He wanted Byroade to know, said

Ahmed Hussein, that Nasser appreciated all his efforts to convince him the deal was bad for Egypt, but things had reached a point "where he could not hold off revolution in the Army if he did not accept." Others would have replaced Nasser, he went on, an even worse prospect from the American point of view. "There was one point however on which he thought we honestly disagreed, and that was Egypt's desire to negotiate on or deal with, if this should become necessary, the Israeli problem from a position of strength instead of weakness. He had read enough about our philosophy in the East-West situation to hope that would be understandable to [the] United States."[48]

A week later, on September 27, 1955, Nassser announced the deal at the opening of an exhibition of military pictures. When the details came out, the magnitude of the agreement, with Czechoslovakia serving as a thinly disguised middleman, startled observers around the world. It totaled more than $200 million and included 200 MiG-15 fighter planes, 50 Ilyushin bombers, 60 half-tracks equipped with 122-millimeter cannons, and 275 T-34 tanks. Nasser's clever comment about the East-West "situation" and American insistence on negotiations from strength—a phrase Dean Acheson had made famous—hit a soft spot in American prescriptions for ending Middle Eastern tensions. The Egyptians had for some time complained that the United States took the position that Israel was entitled to have weapons equal to, or better than, the entire Arab world.

The Russian agreement to sell weapons meant, first of all, that the United States could no longer control the distribution of arms in the area. The French, for example, were quick to transfer advanced Mystère IV fighters from NATO to Israel. While American policymakers were not happy with this development, they did nothing to block the transfer on grounds that, as Dulles put it at a news conference in October, it was difficult to be "critical of countries which, feeling themselves endangered, seek arms which they sincerely believe they need for their defense."[49]

But that was only the first issue posed by the Soviet move. Where would Russian arms go next? It was possible that the Russians could make similar deals with Saudi Arabia, even threaten the American position at Dhahran air base, which had been the original entry point for the U.S. military into the Middle East negotiated by Roosevelt and Truman. The last thing Dulles wanted to do was push the Baghdad Pact like a stick into Nasser's eye. It was a tough situation. "If Nasser rejects the [Russian] offer," Dulles admitted, "he may well be overthrown and we could get something worse." He worried as well that the deal would be looked on in the United States as "a major defeat." What alternatives were there? A major disaster was in the making. "If Egypt lines up with the USSR, I doubt that U.S. public opinion would permit us to use coercive restraints in the event of an Israel attack."[50]

Fears of an Israeli attack on Egypt were reason enough to up the ante. A greater effort would have to be made to convince the Israelis to be more yielding and to persuade Nasser to agree to make the Russian arms deal a onetime operation. Perhaps, Dulles mused, it was not a completely negative development. Israel would feel new pressure, as well as the Americans. "She might give up a bigger slice of the Negev."[51]

Reports that the Russians were now ready to consider extending aid to build the Aswan Dam added to the pressure to find a way to redirect the Egyptian revolution into safe channels. During one conversation with Byroade, Nasser pointed out the window to the Nile and said, "Mr. Ambassador, we're worrying about all these details while all that water is flowing into the Mediterranean. That's more important." Besides the obvious problems of fending off congressional criticism that U.S. loans for the Aswan Dam rewarded Nasser for playing the Russian card, there were other objections to going ahead with the project. When Anthony Eden wrote Eisenhower to impress upon him the danger that the Russians would act while the West dithered, the president said he had had no appreciation of the magnitude of the Aswan proposal before. Eisenhower added that the complications of the Aswan deal could be resolved in a short time, nevertheless, "we were hopeful that we would be able to make a commitment to go ahead on a general basis within the next week or 10 days."[52]

On November 17, 1955, Mahmoud Fawzi, the Egyptian foreign minister, met with Ambassador Byroade and his British counterpart and informed them that his government was ready to move toward a settlement with Israel at the earliest practical date. Egypt believed there was a "51 percent chance" of success. If Egyptian-Israeli issues could be resolved, Cairo would take the lead with other Arab countries, even in the face of severe opposition. Hence Fawzi was willing to put forward, in general terms, Egypt's position on all outstanding questions. He even agreed that repatriation of a large number of Palestinian refugees was not possible and would, in fact, be "quite restricted." For most, resettlement and compensation was the only answer. A settlement would also include Egyptian agreement to end the economic blockade, and freedom of transit on the canal. As for the Egyptian territorial demands, all Cairo wanted at this stage was an agreement in principle that there would be "continuity of Arab sovereign territory," and not merely a corridor. The only hitch at this stage appeared to be Egypt's unwillingness to meet with Israeli leaders to work out any of the outstanding issues.[53]

The hitch became a major obstacle, nevertheless, when Eisenhower sent his special envoy, Robert Anderson, to talk with Nasser and Ben-Gurion about a way of getting around that obstacle. Meanwhile, the World Bank's Eugene Black, the negotiator who was handling the bulk of the details for an international loan to start work on the Aswan Dam, found the going rough in reaching agreement with Cairo on terms of the contract. As the negotiations dragged on, Dulles intervened with Black to prevent any "take it or leave it" ultimatum. Vitally important considerations were at stake for the entire Western world, cabled Undersecretary Herbert Hoover Jr., and these took precedence over normal business considerations.[54]

Dulles also faced a big problem with Congress, however, and had no idea, really, how he was going to get around objections from diverse pressure groups that included not just pro-Israeli legislators who objected to funding anything that would strengthen Nasser, but also cotton-growing states fearing Egyptian competition in world markets. When Nasser extended diplomatic recognition to the People's Republic of China, he brought into the picture another highly emotional factor working against Dulles's ability to promote a solution to the Middle East imbroglio.

Robert Anderson's meetings with Nasser convinced the Egyptian leader the Americans had no understanding of what they asked of him and what the consequences were likely to be. Anderson was in Cairo for three days, Nasser complained to Kermit Roosevelt, and in that time expected him to agree to and arrange a meeting with Ben-Gurion. Eisenhower and Dulles had impressed on Anderson the need to move quickly, before the 1956 election campaign made it impossible to avoid a partisan shouting match that, while it would not lead to a Democratic victory, would cause more problems in carrying out any Middle East initiative. Roosevelt warned Nasser that his reluctance to move forward totally ignored America's problems. "Specifically it does not recognize the dilemma we will all be in should Israel launch a preventive war."[55]

Israel continued to put pressure on the State Department for arms sales, warning that Egypt was preparing for war, while Dulles watched the progress of Soviet-Egyptian negotiations on a Russian loan for the Aswan Dam. He was more than pleased that a visit to Cairo by a high-ranking Moscow emissary had led nowhere. "The Egyptians were now back," he assured Eisenhower on July 13, 1956, "saying they would take our proposal on the original terms and withdraw their own counter proposals." There were still questions about congressional approval, Dulles said, and "our views on the merits of the matter had somewhat altered." He would "consult" with the president next week.[56]

State Department aides thought Nasser was left in an exposed position as a result of the apparent breakdown in Cairo negotiations with Russian deputy foreign minister Dmitri Shepilov. Nasser was scheduled to go to Moscow, wrote Assistant Secretary of State for Near Eastern Affairs George Allen, and "unless he obtains a commitment from the West before his trip . . . his bargaining position will be severely deflated and he may end up with no dam at all." Allen recommended that when the Egyptian ambassador called, the American offer should be withdrawn—whether or not Nasser proposed to accept the original conditions imposed by the World Bank—and he should be told that future aid for other projects would depend upon "whether Egypt ceases to engage in acts inimical to interests of the West."[57]

Depressed as he watched these events unfold, Henry Byroade warned Washington about the consequences of pushing the Egyptians into the arms of the Soviet Union. "Neutralism exists over a large portion of this part of the world," he wrote. Washington's policy seemed totally wrapped up in the dangerous illusion that the Arab nations must and will support American policy on all Cold War issues. If the United States continued to view them "as either in enemy camp or as 'fellow travelers' I fear that before too long we will begin to appear in [the] eyes [of] these people as being the unreasonable member of East-West struggle."[58]

Dulles met with Eisenhower on July 19, 1956, in the morning and told him the Aswan aid offer should be withdrawn, adding new reasons why—which seemed designed to make a record for future historians—such as whoever undertook the project would be blamed for the "austerity" that the Egyptians would suffer to pay for it. Besides, the Soviets would have a hard time explaining to their own people and to the satellite nations why they were undertaking such a project to benefit Egyptians when living standards remained low at home. After this strangely incongruent argument, the president said he concurred with "the Secretary's view," but which of the two he did not say.[59]

Later that day Ambassador Ahmed Hussein called on Dulles to receive the bad news that, in fact, Nasser had predicted would be the case before he left Egypt. The secretary got right to the point without the usual exchange of pleasantries and began listing the reasons why the United States had decided not to undertake the Aswan project. He began with the claim that the decision was based on a concern for long-term Egyptian-American relations in that the costs would "superimpose" a heavy burden on the Egyptian economy. The immediate impact of an announcement that the United States was undertaking the project might be good but would not likely last long. He had also to consider, Dulles went on, the impact on the American people, who were, frankly, not happy about Egyptian actions over the past several months. He hoped that in the future "tranquility" would return to Egyptian-American relations, so that the kind of cooperation Americans desired could be resumed.

The Soviets would find it hard to undertake such a project in light of the low living standards of their people, Dulles said. Whereas the United States could easily handle the costs "because of the tremendous magnitude of its national production," the Russians would be forced to scrape up the money from an already pressed economy. Dulles's argument sounded no less curious in this second go-around than it did when he first used it that morning in the White House. But he added a new twist: the only way the Russians could justify such expenditure was if they expected great political advantages—so many, in fact, that it would endanger Egyptian independence. "We could not undertake to try to match the Russians in any offers which might be made to Egypt or to other countries." He ended with yet another odd twist. "We did not wish to give the impression that the decision . . . was in any way unfriendly or represented a retaliation for actions of the Egyptian Government." Dulles added that "he still saw a bright future in Egyptian-American relations."[60]

No one doubted the rebuff signaled a turning point in U.S.-Egyptian relations. Catching on to the signal, diplomatic correspondent Dana Adams Schmidt wrote in the *New York Times* that a new tough line might include joining the Baghdad Pact. "It will probably be some time before Mr. Eisenhower sends another pistol to an Egyptian leader."

The Imminent Crisis

The Dulles bombshell landed on Cairo just as Nasser was returning from a "Big Three" conference of neutrals held on Brioni in the Adriatic. On July 24, 1956, Nasser delivered a scathing attack on Washington, with a smiling Russian ambassador sitting close by. The United States, Nasser asserted, had given out false and misleading statements, making it seem that the "Egyptian economy is unsound and throwing shadows of doubt on the Egyptian economy." This was contrary to the principles of international relations. "I look at Americans and say: May you choke to death on your fury!" Interviewed after the speech, the Russian ambassador, Yevgeni Kiselev, confirmed that "we are ready to finance the Aswan High Dam if Egypt asks for it."

Two days later Nasser reverted to the arms deal as necessary to "defend ourselves so that we would not become refugees like the Palestinians" and then turned to the history of the Suez Canal as an imperialist project that had compromised Egyptian sovereignty. The crowd clapped and roared as he related the canal's history, and how "Egypt became the property of the canal. . . . It is no shame for one to be poor and to borrow in order to build up one's country; what is a shame is to suck the blood of a people and usurp their rights." No one expected what came next. Nasser ended by reading out a decree nationalizing the canal company. "Today, O citizens," he shouted over the tumult, "with the annual income of the Suez Company amounting to . . . $100 million a year, $500 million in five years, we shall not look for the $70 million of American aid. . . . Now, while I am talking to you, brothers of yours, sons of Egypt are rising up to direct the canal company and undertake its operation. Now, at this moment, they are taking over the canal company—the Egyptian canal company! Not the foreign canal company!"[61]

Some of Nasser's less-confident aides had reminded him before the speech of what had happened to Iran's deposed prime minister, Mossadegh, who had sought to nationalize his country's oil wells. An Anglo-American-managed coup had stopped the Iranian's plans and put him under arrest, while the shah was returned to his throne. Nasser retorted that once everyone saw that Egypt could actually run the canal, the threat of military intervention would disappear. That was a pretty bold prediction.

In London, Prime Minister Eden had already thought about using force to remove Nasser. It wasn't just the canal at stake, but "losing" the whole Arab world to someone that he called a new Mussolini—a man who would play the role the Italian dictator had as Hitler's ally before World War II. To Eden it did not matter that Nasser had no truck with local Communists; he could still be Khrushchev's man in Cairo. The French, stung by Nasser's support for Algerian rebels, did not have a name to call the Egyptian leader, except enemy. Nationalization of the canal did, indeed, have the appearance of a power move that would put Nasser in a position to dictate political and economic futures not only for the Middle East but, with his hands on a key choke point, Western Europe as well. Sixty-seven million tons of oil had passed through the canal the previous year, vital to European economies.

Nasser's action was not illegal so long as compensation was paid to the company owners. The Egyptian leader promised he would do so, and that the canal would be open to all former users. But that left out Israel. Egypt had now signed, moreover, an anti-Israel military alliance with Saudi Arabia, Syria, and Yemen. Dulles was in a quandary. He had precipitated the crisis by the way he withdrew the offer to build the Aswan Dam, having been assured by colleagues who had negotiated the best possible terms for the loan that Egypt was in a tough spot and could not afford to purchase the East-bloc arms and build the dam. But now he faced the possibility that everything he had tried to build in the Middle East would come undone.

The only thing left to do, he concluded, was to temporize—a very un-Dulles type of approach. He summoned a meeting in London in mid-August to talk about a "Users Association" to ensure international supervision of tolls and canal employees, but all the various schemes he advanced in these sessions assumed Egyptian ownership of the canal, and whatever supervision there would be depended on Nasser's experience. In presenting his proposal he said that the purpose of the meeting was to restore "confidence" to those who normally used the canal after Egypt had "grievously assaulted" the principles of the 1888 convention, yet he ended by saying, "There are some things that this conference is not[;] it is not a conference to make decisions binding on those who do not agree." He would not agree, for example, that the United States pay tolls into a blocked account, thus diminishing any hope of bringing into play economic pressure on Egypt. He also confided to British leaders that the United States could not justify resorting to military measures, because it had sufficient oil. If his way of handling the Aswan loan had been brutal, his treatment of America's Cold War allies was hardly less so. "It might even be necessary to minimize the role of Britain and France," he suggested to Eisenhower. A big problem—one that went to the heart of Dulles's dilemma—was the attitude of Asian countries, he told the president, as they were apt to be swayed by political slogans, "such as 'colonialism,' 'imperialism,' 'Asia for the Asians,' etc." The political consequences of a direct assault on Egypt to restore the company to its old owners could prove disastrous.[62]

Yet he feared, as he told UN secretary-general Dag Hammar-skjöld, that the British and French might try to invoke Article 51 of the charter to justify military action—the clause that the United States had insisted upon at the founding of the United Nations to ensure the possibility of regional defense associations. If they did, he said, they would make a mockery of Western positions everywhere. Force might have been understood at the outset as acting in hot blood, but not now after delay and deliberation. Delay and delibera-tion were, indeed, the purpose of his international conferences—to stall for time. The problem was that Nasser retained the initiative.[63]

During one of the conferences that went on and on that summer, British foreign secretary Selwyn Lloyd cornered Dulles for a moment. London was planning military action, he confided. "There would be a button pushed early in September and after that everything would happen automatically and be irrevocable." Dulles was the only one who could stop this march to war. Recording the encounter in a memorandum, the secretary of state wrote, "During this conversation Mr. Lloyd showed obvious emotional strain." Perhaps that gave him a wrong impression that the British were pulling a bluff, knowing as they must from everything that had been said publicly and privately that Washington would not support the use of force. In the end, they would not push the button—or so Dulles thought.[64]

For Eden, however, the date certainly had been set. If a favorable settlement was not reached by September 10, the military option would be set in motion. Harold Macmillan, chancellor of the ex-chequer, was perhaps the most hawkish of all, arguing that if Nasser got away with it, other Middle Eastern countries, beginning with Iraq, would nationalize their oil, and Europe "would be lost." On September 11, 1956, Eisenhower, at a press conference, gave the British a public response to all their hints. "This country will not go to war while I am occupying my present post . . . unless Congress declares such war. . . . We established the United Nations to abol-ish aggression and I am not going to be a party to aggression."[65]

With Eden becoming more and more obsessed with the Mussolini analogy, his handling of the crisis suffered from emotional swings as he appealed to Eisenhower. In Washington, in early October, the National Security Council discussed covert ways of getting rid of Nasser. Eisenhower had declared himself against a frontal attack, but he mused about various alternative methods for ridding himself of this troublesome priest of Arab nationalism. Meanwhile, the French began planning with Israel for joint military action, plans that were later merged into a tripartite agreement with Britain on how to proceed. Such a plan, with Israel taking the first lead, was agreed upon at a series of conferences in late October at Sèvres just outside Paris. For Eden it was a perfect way around the charge of colonialism: the British and French would ostensibly be acting to restore the peace in an Israeli-Egyptian confrontation—by occupying the Suez! In the ensuing fallout, Nasser would be "fatally undermined."[66]

Much, however, had been risked on the belief that Nasser would be forced out by defeat, and follow Farouk into exile perhaps, or suffer some other fate. It all began to unravel after Israel dropped paratroops into the Sinai on October 29, 1956, and battle was joined in the desert. As decided at Sèvres, London then reminded Cairo that according to the terms of the 1954 treaty covering the removal of British forces, it had retained the right to intervene if Egypt was attacked. Then came an Anglo-French ultimatum on October 30 that fighting must cease or there would be an intervention to protect the canal and base. Israel agreed, but Nasser refused, appealing to the United Nations. So far events were unfolding as anticipated; but now Eisenhower made good on his warnings.

On the eve of the war, Dulles had admitted to Eisenhower that he was "really baffled" about the actual purposes of the British and French. "Perhaps they did not know themselves." Maybe they believed American policy was just for the election period, and after that "we might back them in a policy involving the use of force." Eisenhower was furious that they had acted before the November 3 election, but his response would not have been much different in any case. He was determined that military action would not succeed.[67]

While his advisers were not unanimous, the president instructed them in unequivocal language that the United States would "redeem our word about supporting any victim of aggression." At least two aides, Joint Chiefs chairman Admiral Arthur Radford and CIA director Allen Dulles, suggested waiting to see how things went as British bombers appeared over Cairo. The president wanted none of that. "If we do not now fulfill our word Russia is likely to enter the situation in the Middle East." A British diplomat present at one of these conversations wondered if the United States would not first go to the United Nations before intervening, perhaps hoping for a fait accompli. Ike said that was his plan—but not in order to cause a delay. "We plan to get there first thing in the morning—when the doors open—before the USSR gets there."[68]

It had finally come down to a decision that Washington had hoped all along to avoid: taking sides with its old allies, or striking out on a different path. "When you get into [a] case like this," Eisenhower told an aide, "you just gotta go your own way. . . . What you gonna do—fight the whole Moslem world?" Over the next few days the Suez Crisis grew into a perfect storm of bad news. Soviet premier Nikita Khrushchev threatened to launch ICBMs at the British and French, even as Moscow sent tanks into Budapest to suppress the Hungarian freedom fighters, who, it was claimed, had responded to encouraging broadcasts from Radio Free Europe by taking up arms against the Communist regime. It was doubly infuriating, therefore, that the Soviets could pose as defenders of the Egyptian revolution while smashing down buildings in Hungary to crush the uprising. Eisenhower believed there was a good chance, on the other hand, that the Soviets feared losing Eastern Europe and would flail out in the Middle East in a spasm of desperation. "The British and French took the worst possible case they could to fight on—and proceeded to get all of us in a hole." In an effort to cheer him up, apparently, some aides told him there were CIA reports that Nasser was fretting he might have to go. Eisenhower quipped, "Tell Nasser we'll put him on St. Helena and give him a million dollars." But he was deeply worried. "There has to be some way out of this impasse."[69]

UN resolutions demanding a cease-fire and immediate with-drawal were sponsored by both Moscow and Washington, but the British and French stood fast, not landing additional forces but also not leaving. Matters had reached a point, noted one State Depart-ment aide, where either Nasser or Eden must fall. It was to be Eden. The British were more vulnerable to American pressure than either the French or the Israelis, and Eisenhower was determined to use that pressure in two ways—by not helping London obtain Western Hemisphere oil when Nasser sank ships in the canal to blockade oil tankers, and by denying financial aid to the pound sterling when it came under intense pressure and reserves dwindled quickly to dan-gerous lows. Chancellor of the Exchequer Macmillan saw the hand-writing on the walls of Number 11 Downing Street and became the first to turn in his hawk's feathers for a dove's softer wings. "I'm inclined to think that those who began this operation," Eisenhower told his aides, "should be left to work out their own oil problems—to boil in their own oil, so to speak."[70]

Angry as he was, Eisenhower hated cutting off his "right hand," as he called the British even at the height of the crisis. But there was some good news from the Middle East. Ambassador Raymond Hare in Cairo reported that the American stand turned things around in terms of Arab attitudes toward Washington. Suddenly the United States appeared to the Arabs as a champion of the right. It was pos-sible that vistas were opening in a manner inconceivable a few weeks earlier. This stiffened Eisenhower's stand against doing anything about the British predicament, worsening by the day, almost by the hour. Treasury Secretary George Humphrey told "Rab" Butler, a candidate to succeed the ailing Eden, whose personal health had declined alongside British financial health, that his country was in defiance of the United Nations by not withdrawing its forces, and that American help would not come until a general settlement had been reached.[71]

Far from achieving its objective of toppling Nasser, the Suez op-eration made him stronger. The Egyptian leader loved to ruminate how the crisis had brought the United States into the Middle East as a defender of the new regime, while it finished off the Baghdad Pact as a serious rival. "It might even be said," recalled Nasser's confidant Mohamed Heikal, "that Eden was responsible for Nuri Said's death, for no Arab leader could be Britain's friend and Nasser's enemy after Suez. Suez cost Britain the Arab world." Eden left office ill, his career destroyed. "It was," quipped Nasser, "the Curse of the Pharoahs."[72]

Confronted by dwindling reserves in the Bank of England, and American refusal to help in any way until the fighting stopped, on November 8 the British Cabinet agreed to open negotiations for a transfer of occupied land to a UN emergency force. Eisenhower believed that what the crisis had revealed was a need for the United States to strengthen its relations with other Arab countries as well as Egypt. A new Middle East policy would have to be formulated.

The Nasser gamble had failed. Secretary Dulles's great plan to ease Egypt into the Western Cold War lineup and thereby resolve the danger that Arab nationalism would split into rival camps—some supported by the old colonial powers and others reaching outside for aid to the Soviet Union and China—had been a wager of long odds from the outset. Why it failed was easy to explain, if difficult to do anything about. At each step of the way, from Dulles's initial meeting with Nasser, the secretary left the room disappointed that nothing seemed to work in persuading the Egyptian leader to see why he should cooperate. The very names of the last-ditch efforts, Alpha and Omega, indicated the sense of frustration policymakers felt. At the time of the Suez Crisis, Dulles lamented to a congressional committee that while most Arab nations actually feared Nasser, they feared more his great popularity with the peoples of their own countries. How to contain such leaders and guide the new nations into independence in an orderly way remained the issue. "We must have evolution, not revolution."[73]

When the crisis came, the United States broke with what a later secretary of defense would call "old Europe" to save its reputation as an anticolonial alternative for new nations. It was a leap forward into a Middle Eastern labyrinth centuries in the making. For a time Eisenhower was a hero in Egypt, having forced the invaders to stop fighting and—with considerable arm-twisting—to withdraw from

Egyptian territory. The Suez Canal and base were firmly in Nasser's hands, and he emerged a bolder champion of Arab nationalism—and still a perceived threat to Israel. For a decade the tenuous Suez outcome prevailed, until a new war changed the positions of the actors, but not their objectives.

3

EISENHOWER DOCTRINE
TO SIX DAYS OF WAR

*I hope that our NATO friends will understand clearly that we have
no intention of standing idly by to see the southern flank of NATO
completely collapse through Communist penetration and success in
the Middle East while we do nothing about it. I am sure that they
know that we regard Nasser as an evil influence.*
>—President Dwight D. Eisenhower to John Foster Dulles,
>December 5, 1956

*Right now, of course, your task and mine is not to look back, but to
rescue the Middle East—and the whole human community—from a
war I believe no one wants. . . . I do urge you to set as your first
duty to your own people, to your region, and to the world community
this transcendent objective: the avoidance of hostilities.*
>—President Lyndon B. Johnson to Gamal Abdel Nasser,
>May 22, 1967

Suez marked the beginning of Ike's troubles in foreign policy. He
swamped Adlai Stevenson in a rerun of the 1952 election, but that
was the only good news for quite a while. Indeed, the fallout continued to the end of his second term, with its fiasco-like U-2 affair that
aborted a Paris summit conference with Soviet premier Nikita
Khrushchev when the president refused to disavow spy planes. During the 1956 crisis Khrushchev had wagged a menacing finger at
Egypt's invaders, Britain, France, and Israel, declaring that the Soviet Union possessed large numbers of ICBMs and would use them
if they did not cease and desist.

It was Washington's economic clampdown on Great Britain that really forced the issue, but that did not detract from the impression that the Soviet Union's bullying was a foretaste of what was in store for U.S. foreign policy unless drastic changes were made. Sputnik in 1957 put an exclamation point on the Kremlin's boast and gave the Republican administration fits as Democrats seized on a supposed "missile gap" to propel them into the 1960 presidential campaign. Hidden from the public was the big secret the successful U-2 flights over the Soviet Union had uncovered before the one Russia shot down on the eve of a summit conference: there was no missile gap. Khrushchev's pumping up of the Soviet missile armory was, to say the least, premature.

But clustered around the events of the Suez Crisis were numerous questions and doubts either directly or indirectly related to the immediate events of those days at the end of October 1956. George F. Kennan, the supposed "author" of containment, now retired from the Foreign Service and resident scholar at the Institute for Advanced Study in Princeton, wrote a letter to Washington newspapers in which he declared "the previous foundations of American policy [are] being swept away." Going to the United Nations, as Eisenhower had done, would "destroy what remains of [our allies'] positions in the Middle East and North Africa." In addition, he said, it would "deny the state of Israel—at the establishment of which we so eagerly assisted—the privilege of defending its existence in the face of a mortally dangerous encirclement."[1]

What was remarkable about this last comment, of course, was that Kennan had urged in 1948 that the United States not become embroiled in the aftermath of the creation of the new state. And the best way to do that was not to midwife the Jewish state in the first place. His attitude toward Britain and France was consistent with his earlier beliefs and his long-term concerns about what would befall the West should the United States become the champion of all the new nations clamoring for attention in the UN General Assembly. Kennan feared that the disappearance of Britain and France from the scene would open up the area to Communist penetration and inevitably draw the United States into what was now being called a "vacuum of power."

Suez had yet another consequence—a new arms race that threatened to go nuclear. The Soviet Union quickly replenished the airplanes and other weapons the Israelis and their allies had destroyed, and would thereby, it was supposed, increase its overall influence in Nasser's Egypt. The outcome of the crisis had given the Egyptian leader new stature in the Arab world, which, it appeared, he wished to use to bring the whole area under his thrall. After Suez, Israel would argue, the only way left to stop an Egyptian military move would be to develop an atomic bomb. Washington began to feel that it would have to end its restrictions on arms supplies to Israel, if only to exercise some restraint on Tel Aviv's nuclear ambitions.

The Eisenhower Doctrine

There was a feeling in some Washington circles that the United States should have joined the Baghdad Pact, and that maybe if it had there would not have been a Suez Crisis. However that might be, Kennan's letter did contend that Dulles had caused the crisis by his "fateful inability to maintain intimate communication with our friends, and . . . a style of diplomatic action directed to the grandstand rather than to the realities of our situation." Eisenhower didn't much agree with Kennan about these points, but he did feel that the United States had no choice but to take unilateral action to fill the vacuum of power. On January 5, 1957, even before his inauguration for a second term, Eisenhower sent to Congress a message asking for authority to act to combat the challenge of "International Communism" in the Middle East. "International Communism, of course, seeks to mask its purposes of domination by expressions of good will and by superficially attractive offers of political, economic and military aid," he said. "But any free nation, which is the subject of Soviet enticement, ought, in elementary wisdom, to look behind the mask." The biggest offers of aid, of course, had gone to Egypt, and the point here was to make Nasser look naïve or simply ignorant of Moscow's purposes. Either way he had become a danger to American interests.

A new responsibility fell to the United States, the president's message went on, to assist any nation or group of nations in resisting a takeover by "International Communism." He wanted approval beforehand, therefore, in the form of a congressional resolution to allow the use of military force if it ever became needed to save any of these countries from such a dire fate. "It would . . . authorize such assistance and cooperation to include the employment of the armed forces of the United States to secure and protect the territorial integrity and political independence of such nations, requesting such aid, against overt armed aggression from any nation controlled by International Communism."

It was hardly a surprise that when the president's proposal reached Congress, legislators substituted the name of a country, Egypt, for "International Communism." Among them was Senator John F. Kennedy, who took a different tack. He feared that an extension of umbrella guarantees to Middle Eastern countries could alienate Egypt and other countries such as Syria, and drive them closer to the Soviet Union. The chairman of the Joint Chiefs of Staff, Admiral Radford, had predicted in his secret testimony that if this "Eisenhower Doctrine," really an extension of the Truman Doctrine, was approved, it would halt the flow of arms to Egypt, "in the light of the fact that they will be opposed by the United States if and when they build up these forces." The object of the Kremlin's policy was to turn Egypt into a satellite that in addition to having Russian arms, would by virtue of the military connection host Soviet ideological aims as well. Kennedy was skeptical. He thought it might work the other way around and could even trap the United States in a local war if Egypt and Syria carried out a military invasion into Iraq, and Washington determined they would "qualify as being under the domination of international communism." Radford hastened to say he did not mean to give that impression, although he professed to see long-standing Marxist leanings in Nasser's record.[2]

After Suez, Washington took a number of steps that it hoped would hold matters in check until something happened to change Nasser's attitude. It kept Egyptian funds blocked, supposedly pending a settlement for the nationalized canal company. Other forms of aid were also shut off. Wheat shipments were curtailed, and American technical advisers were recalled from development projects. In addition, the United Nations stationed an international force in the Sinai desert, to ease Israeli fears about any Egyptian retaliation for Suez. When State Department officials were asked whether any aid for Egypt would be forthcoming in 1958, the official response was that economic aid might be resumed after "a decent interval."[3]

In early 1957 Miles Copeland, the man the CIA originally sent to tutor Nasser, was recalled to Washington to provide his estimate of where he thought the Egyptian leader planned to move next. He was told to role play so as to give the home office a picture of the international situation as seen from the Nile. Apparently he did it too well to suit some of those he briefed; one complained that he sounded more like Nasser than Nasser himself. But the real shocker was CIA director Allen Dulles's response. He turned to Copeland with real anger in his voice and said, "If that colonel of yours pushes us too far we will break him in half!"[4]

The keys to turning the situation around, Radford and Dulles agreed in their congressional testimony on the Eisenhower Doctrine, was to counter Egyptian influence with a program to tamp down the rivalries between Egypt and Iraq—each of which threatened to outbid the other in terms of anti-Israel rhetoric—and to create a new "third force" in the Middle East: Saudi Arabia. Saudi Arabia was the country of choice for several reasons, but mostly because, as Secretary Dulles put it, the king "is in a sense the titular head of their religion; their Mecca, their holy places, are in his territory, and he has a very great potential influence in the area. And we have got, in our opinion, to be able to build him up and build around him."[5]

For many who witnessed the collapse of the Nasser gamble, there was a "Here we go again" feeling about the Saudi gambit. Dulles had once praised Egypt as the real seat of Muslim culture and learning, and the least resistant, presumably, to influences from the West—if resentful of British imperial behavior. But Saudi Arabia? Well, if the Eisenhower Doctrine were to succeed, it needed some trusted cohort.

On a cold day, January 30, 1957, Eisenhower stood waiting for King Saud to land in the president's personal plane, the *Columbine*, which had been put at the king's disposal for the flight to the United States. Nasser had never been offered such an invitation even to come on his own airplane. The president was a bit dubious, however, about going out to meet Saud at the airport; but a call from the Saudi ambassador to the State Department had informed Secretary Dulles that the king "would cancel his visit to U.S. if he [was] not repeat not met at airport by the president." This was the first time Eisenhower had done anything like that, and it marked the next step in the relationship Roosevelt had initiated in 1945—but this time with a much higher price tag of $100 million.[6]

King Saud spent a week in Washington, another sign of great favoritism over Nasser's Egypt, but his answers were not always what his listeners wanted to hear. The final communiqué began with a firm statement of Saudi Arabia's "vital importance" to the Middle East and how the interests of world peace required that it be strengthened "for the maintenance of its own stability and the safeguarding and progressive development of its institutions." The communiqué also committed the Saudis to settle "justly" problems of the Middle East area by peaceful means, an oblique reference to the Arab-Israeli imbroglio, and the sort of commitment long desired from Egypt. Saud also agreed that he would work to improve relations between the United States and other Arab countries. In exchange, the United States would provide money to enhance the capabilities of the Dhahran air base, and provide assistance for strengthening the Saudi military.[7]

Dulles confirmed to British ambassador Harold Caccia the details of the military aid program, including plans for the air base and the agreement to sell $100 million in arms over a five-year period, ten times more than Egypt had once been offered as a one-shot deal—and even that had fallen through. Caccia raised his eyebrows about the magnitude of the program, but Dulles appeared unconcerned: "I said that we doubted it would have any serious impact on the area." Another sort of criticism came from Congressman George McGovern of South Dakota: "Do we build strength against communism by contributing American tax dollars to perpetuate this kind of feudal despotism?"[8]

The real, if unspoken, answer to McGovern's question, of course, was that the Eisenhower Doctrine was about containing—and eliminating—Nasserism as a force in the Middle East. "If we could build [Saud] up as the individual to capture the imagination of the Arab world," the president wrote his secretary of state on the eve of the king's visit, "Nasser would not last long." The real problem was there was no other likely candidate for this assignment. Iraq's Nuri as-Said was too polarizing and had disqualified himself by falling in with British plans for the Baghdad Pact; Lebanon's Camille Chamoun was the Christian president of a small, divided country; Jordan's King Hussein could not by any stretch of the imagination be seen as an international figure, being barely able to keep the lid on in his own country.[9]

While the final communiqué contained some ambiguous phrases and did not specifically mention the threat of "International Communism," it could still be read as an endorsement of American policy objectives, including an affirmation that all questions should be settled justly, without war. That was enough to allow Eisenhower to take a strong line with Israel over its continuing occupation of Egyptian territory. He did so in a public address to the nation on February 20, 1957. Although the United Nations Emergency Force was in position on the armistice lines and at the Gulf of Aqaba, he said, the Israelis were still refusing to withdraw. "This raises a basic question of principle. Should a nation which attacks and occupies foreign territory in the face of United Nations disapproval be allowed to impose conditions on its own withdrawal?"

Eisenhower held a powerful hand for the moment, having been reelected with a huge margin, and having obtained from Egypt concessions on international traffic in the Suez Canal and the Gulf of Aqaba. It was hard, even for many pro-Israel senators and representatives, to see why that should not be enough. Ike's promise that the Egyptians would be held accountable satisfied, at least for the time being, nervous Israelis and their American supporters. The emerging American relationship with Saudi Arabia might cause concern in some quarters, but there, again, it looked as if the United States had succeeded in finding a counterforce to Nasser, one whose conservatism contrasted with the supposed incendiary objectives of the Egyptian leadership.

Meanwhile, the administration had succeeded in another objective, making peace with its closest ally, Great Britain. Harold

Macmillan, the sometime Suez hawk who had split with the ailing Anthony Eden, had become prime minister, a development much encouraged by Eisenhower. Macmillan was welcomed in Washington as one who understood the shift in the Anglo-American balance of power in the Middle East, and who could be counted on to play his part with loyalty and enthusiasm. At a dinner meeting in Bermuda's Mid-Ocean Club in late March, the new prime minister raised what he called the sixty-four dollar question: what was the United States going to do about this completely unreliable man, Nasser? Did Washington intend to proceed with a series of inducements to win his favor and in that way solve long-term problems relating to the canal and Israel? Ike replied somewhat ambiguously that one could not at the same time seek his cooperation and combat him. Macmillan persisted. He assumed, he said, that did not mean we were wedded to him and would not be unhappy if indigenous forces in Egypt brought about his downfall. Secretary Dulles intervened to say that the United States was not required to support him internally, "as against internal forces and indeed we would welcome certain types of change in Egypt." But that was different from an international campaign. Macmillan nodded that he was satisfied with this answer to the sixty-four dollar question.[10]

Syria and a Quarter-Turn Back to Nasser

A few months later Macmillan and Eisenhower authorized a top-secret effort to topple a left-leaning Syrian government that had reached several economic agreements with the Soviet Union. The CIA-MI6 (the British foreign intelligence service) plan to stage fake border incidents as an excuse for an invasion by Syria's neighbors and to depose the government by "internal" action failed, in large part because the man the administration had been hoping to build up as the spiritual leader of the Arabs—and successful rival to Nasser— refused to play along. Even while he had been in Washington, King Saud warned Dulles that the United States was exaggerating Communist control in Damascus; and when the Syrians made their overtures to Russia, Saud blamed the United States. Like Egypt, the king wrote, the Syrians had turned to Russia because they could not get arms from the United States, "while at the same time economic and military assistance to Israel is plentiful. . . . If those requests had been heeded, the situation would not have reached the present point."[11]

"The retreat from the initial embrace of the Eisenhower Doctrine looked to be turning into a rout," wrote Robert Vitalis, as the king found himself the target of Arab nationalists like Nasser's confidant Mohamed Heikal, who mocked Saud as nothing but a stooge for the Americans. Secretary Dulles admitted to Senator Mike Mansfield that Arab countries were turning away from any military action against Syria: "The Secretary said that public opinion in the Arab world was such that the Arab leaders felt they had no other choice." Dulles lamented that Soviet propaganda had great influence with the "mobs in the Arab world," a result of U.S. association with Israel. He had been reading over position papers from a decade earlier, just before the emergence of the state of Israel. "It was amazing to what extent and with what accuracy these papers had predicted the troubles which would follow the emergence of a State of Israel."[12]

The troubles had only begun for American policy. In early 1958 Syria and Egypt merged into the United Arab Republic (UAR), a union that lasted only a few years, but looked for a time to be the predecessor of a general movement for unity under Nasser's leadership. As it happened, Nasser had not sought a full union with Syria, and it was a somewhat awkward situation. A big factor, ironically, was that military supporters of Nasser in Syria saw the Egyptian leader as an effective counter to Communist inroads in their country. Nasser had also shown himself to be an opponent of radical religious movements like the Muslim Brotherhood, especially after a failed assassination attempt on his life. These developments brought about another twist in American policy, especially when a crude Saudi Arabian scheme to save Syria from "Nasserism" flopped.

King Saud's first run at being the man of the hour for American efforts to block Nasser's influence was an abysmal failure. A Saudi secret agent had approached a Syrian general with a check for $2 million, an advance payment for having Nasser's airplane shot down as he returned to Cairo after having attended celebrations of

the new union in Damascus. Besides money, the persuasive argument was to have been that Nasser's anti-Muslim feelings ensured
that Russia would gain a back door into Syria. Unfortunately, the
Syrian general who was selected to manage the local end of the affair was in fact an ardent Nasser supporter, who believed Nasser was
the best man to halt the spread of Communism in Syria.[13]

The general promptly turned the check over to Nasser, who scored
yet another public-relations triumph standing on the balcony of the
Diafa Palace in Damascus, waving it in the air before thousands of
chanting Syrians below. Nasser spurred them on, denouncing the
agents of imperialism and their "syndicate of monarchs." In Washington, Secretary Dulles advised the president that a plebiscite had been
planned for February 21, 1958, to vote on the union of the two countries. He had been in touch with several Middle Eastern countries—
Iraq, Jordan, and Lebanon, by now the usual suspects where opposition
might be found to Nasser—concerning the implications of the proposed union. "We have advised those governments that we should be
glad to give active consideration to supporting any feasible common
plan they might be able to devise to thwart or otherwise oppose the
union of Egypt and Syria." So far, he confessed, there was no evidence
"that our Arab friends are able or willing to formulate common action." That being so, there was no option except to recognize the new
government.[14]

There was a silver lining in the UAR cloud, however. Albeit it in
backhanded fashion, it raised the potential for an anticommunist
bloc of Arab states. Nasser might make anticommunism his basic
appeal. "We could not justifiably withhold our recognition of the
United Arab Republic," Dulles admitted to Eisenhower, "without
renouncing our traditional policy on Arab unity and without giving
offense to the popular appeal of Arab nationalism." The UAR demonstrated that Saud could not be the man of the hour under any
circumstances, so why keep hoping for a prophet in Riyadh to replace Nasser? The administration turned back to Cairo, however
tentatively, with offers to resume wheat sales on favorable terms
under a congressional program, PL 480, that allowed poor countries
to use local currency to buy American surpluses. Designed to prop

up domestic prices, PL 480 had some utility as a foreign policy tool. It might even leverage Egypt into more cooperation because of its need to import foodstuffs for a rapidly growing population.

In late April 1958, the new American ambassador to the UAR, Raymond Hare, had an interesting two-hour conversation with Nasser to go over where matters stood between the two nations. "What is your objective?" asked Nasser. In the recent past, he explained, he had been convinced the American objective was to remove him from power. To survive, therefore, he had turned to Russia for military and economic aid. But suppose, now, that relations were to sour with the Soviets. Would the United States hope to take advantage of Egypt's adversity to attempt to dispose of his regime?[15]

It was an interesting way to put the question, because it suggested that Egyptian reliance on the Soviet Union might not be the new reality conditioning relations with the West after all. Lest Ambassador Hare miss the hint here, Nasser went on to say that Cairo had not condemned Moscow's suppression of the Hungarian revolt, had remained "aloof" as Soviet tanks knocked down buildings in Budapest, because his country felt too vulnerable and needy to risk offending the Soviet Union with Anglo-French-Israeli forces at the doorstep of the Suez Canal. It had been a question of survival, not principle. Nasser brought the matter up a second time during their conversation, again lest Hare miss what was being laid out, telling the diplomat that he had been well aware of the facts of the Hungarian tragedy and it "had been preying on his mind."[16]

Hare understood that Nasser was soon to travel to Moscow. What did the Egyptian expect would be the outcome of this meeting? He had a whole sheaf of documents on his desk to take with him, Nasser replied. The top item on the agenda would be to lower the costs of arms already ordered for Syria. But, he emphasized, there would be no more aid requested, and "no specific political commitments will be sought"—or presumably given. The final communiqué, he added, would reflect the spirit of neutrality as voiced originally in the declarations of the Bandung Conference. He even said that neutrality was something of a misnomer; the UAR's position was really nonalignment. Hare's final comment to Washington about the conversation was a plea that an answer be given about America's "objective" as soon as possible, before Nasser left for Moscow.[17]

The idea of a bidding war for Cairo's favor was not very appealing, and there were definite limits on how far Washington would go to "appease" Nasser, as critics, especially pro-Israel critics, complained about the policy steps taken already. Bidding had in fact been going on in Lebanon, where American money was being handed out to anti-Nasser candidates for elections in the fall of 1957, while Cairo aimed its big megaphone, its radio Voice of the Arabs, at Beirut's Christian president Camille Chamoun—second only to Iraq's Nuri as-Said on Nasser's hit list.

Lebanon was close to a full civil war when Chamoun called upon his American allies to secure for him a continuation of his presidency by fair means or foul. He planned to force an amendment to the constitution that would allow him to remain in power. Ambassador Robert McClintlock urged the administration to support him, lest his succumbing to internal pressures demoralize pro-Western elements all through the Middle East. "We must see that he wins and wins handsomely." It was true that Voice of the Arabs spared no epithet to denounce Chamoun, but it was harder to say that Egypt was behind the rebellion. Dulles, nevertheless, told Afghan prime minister Sardar Mohammad Daud that Nasser was a highly volatile personality. "At times he seemed calm and reasonable; at other times he was highly emotional, and whipped up Pan-Arabism, much as Hitler had whipped up Pan-Germanism, as a means of promoting an extension of his power." Pro-Nasser forces were at work in Lebanon; whether the Egyptian leader egged them on or not did not matter to Washington. "This would add to Nasser's prestige," Dulles said, "and seriously discourage Iraq and other pro-Western elements in the area."[18]

Despite being unable to find that "International Communism" had taken over Lebanon, the United States landed nearly ten thousand troops there on July 15, 1958, a demonstration Washington believed would prove it would not desert its friends. Congressional leaders were called to the White House in a repetition of the scene in 1947 when Dean Acheson stepped in to elevate Secretary Marshall's calm briefing about the situation in Greece and Turkey to world-changing proportions. Secretary Dulles duly warned the legislators that sending a military force to Lebanon might start something that could not easily be finished, and thus increase "the anti-Western feeling of the Arab masses." But not to go in would make it appear the United States was weak. "The first consequence of not going in," he said, "would certainly be that the non-Nasser governments in the Middle East and adjoining areas would be quickly overthrown." And if that were not enough, "The impact of our not going in, from Morocco to Indochina, would be very harmful to us. Turkey, Iran and Pakistan would feel, if we do not act, that our action is because we are afraid of the Soviet Union. They will therefore lose confidence and tend toward neutralism."[19]

The marines stayed three months, but the result of the intervention actually increased Nasser's influence. The most miraculous thing about the intervention was that the American soldiers did not fire a shot, while the government that emerged had many pro-Nasser figures leading it. "The Eisenhower Doctrine," wrote Copeland, "was dead."[20]

With a revolution in Iraq that overthrew Nuri as-Said, Nasser's prestige hit its high point in late 1958 and 1959—even as his growing set of disagreements with the Soviet Union made him more anxious to hit the reset button with Washington. On January 19, 1959, Dulles had a conversation with Israeli ambassador Abba Eban. The subject turned to Iraq and the revolution in that country that had brought down Nuri as-Said. Eban hoped that the United States would not throw support to Nasser in an effort to counter supposed Communist inroads in Iraq: "I said if one has to make a choice between the Communists and Nasser, I suppose Nasser is a lesser evil."[21]

Second Thoughts in Cairo and Washington

Nuri as-Said had been one of the original signers of the Baghdad Pact and a redoubt for Western influence in the Middle East, or, in Cairo's view, a lackey of imperialism. As a member of the "syndicate of monarchs," as Nasser called him, he was more than a thorn in

Nasser's side. Cairo had tried cajolery with the Iraqi prime minister, and when that failed used stronger methods in the campaigns fought out on Baghdad streets. After Nuri's demise, Nasser openly sought to shape the government of his successor, Abdul Karim Kassem.

He was spectacularly unsuccessful in trying to do so, just as the United States was in its efforts to tame the new Iraqi leader. Almost as soon as Kassem came to power he began changing the "internal" situation in much more dangerous ways so far as Washington was concerned. He left the Baghdad Pact, with scarcely a nod in the direction of his Western benefactors, then undertook to challenge the Iraq Petroleum Company (IPC), an enterprise with major British, American, and Dutch components, and threatened Kuwait's existence as an independent sheikdom. Nine months after he had overturned the monarchy and killed strongman Nuri al-Said, said *Time* magazine, "the land that some say was the Garden of Eden is a place of terror, plot and counterplot."[22]

Some of those plots were hatched in the CIA. Kassem had welcomed support from the Iraqi Communist Party. "Above all," said *Time*, "Iraq today is a land where cautious men do not openly criticize the Communist Party." Communists dominated the mobs, the magazine claimed, the press, and parts of the government. "Such is the nightmarish atmosphere that in at least one Iraqi city (Basra) the populace is firmly convinced that Communist-led unions have prepared a list of local employers, merchants and professional men to be liquidated as soon as opportunity offers." According to his son, Sergei, Soviet premier Khrushchev was delighted with Kassem's quick decision to disassociate himself from the Baghdad Pact: "According to the standards of the time, that meant Iraq became automatically 'ours,' 'like us.'" Nikita Khrushchev issued a blustery public statement that the Soviet Union would support the anticolonial revolution not simply with words, "but by armed force if necessary."[23]

Khrushchev had blustered during the Suez Crisis that he had ICBMs ready to defend Egypt if the invaders dared to keep up their attacks, but of course the real force that got the British, French, and Israelis to back off came when the United States put pressure on the pound sterling and warned Israel about economic aid. Nevertheless, Stalin's successor believed he had called the tune in both instances, and he was emboldened to seek new ways to agitate nationalist sentiments in the Middle East. At the time of the 1958 revolution Nasser was a guest of Khrushchev. "I liked him very much," Khrushchev wrote in his memoirs.[24]

Nasser wished to return to Egypt immediately because he believed that with Nuri gone, Iraq might well become the third state in the UAR. "This was a completely understandable desire," wrote Khrushchev, "but as it turned out, neither Nasser's hopes nor our own information about Kassem were borne out. Kassem turned out to be highly unstable politically." Actually, the Soviet leader's hopes for Nasser were not turning out well, either. Their Moscow confab proved to be the start of a cooling down of relations between the two. Nasser's efforts to cultivate pan-Arabism in Iraq were getting nowhere, and the divisions it engendered in that country made existing conflicts over religion, ethnicity, and class conflict more serious. Kassem was having a hard time trying to bring all these forces under control, and both Nasser and Washington policymakers feared the Communists would emerge the strongest surviving contender for power out of the free-for-all.

Kassem attempted to counter domestic opposition by encouraging Iraqi nationalism through the creation of a three-man council that would include an Arab Sunni, an Arab Shiite, and a Kurd—an effort to overcome ethnic and sectarian divisions. He closed British military bases, purged the government of Western advisers and contractors, and promised the Kurds in the north greater autonomy. "If you tour any part of this country," he said to rally support for his policies, "you will see how extensive misery, poverty, and deprivation are in the life of the people. You will see the cottages [of the villages] . . . moving skeletons. . . . The wealth of this country was robbed and wasted in the interest of imperialism and the foreigner."[25]

Kassem's rhetoric might not be any worse than Nasser's tirades when he nationalized the Suez Canal, but the canal's fate was not the same as a threat to Western dominance in oil fields that spread across the whole region. And Kassem soon mounted real threats to important American interests, the IPC and Kuwait. These were interlinked questions that would continue to dominate policy debates for a long time to come, no matter who was in charge in Iraq. As far as IPC was concerned, Iraqi attitudes had much to do with the way in which its member companies divvied up oil production among the various Middle Eastern countries. IPC had held a vast concession over much of Iraq since the nation's formation in the post–World War I era, but kept development down to a tiny fraction of the territory, saving areas with oil potential for future use. The oil companies called the tune about current production as well; they decided which fields to pump in which countries.

Immediately after the July 1958 revolution, Kassem, with a look back at Mossadegh's fate, had assured London and Washington that he did not intend to nationalize the oil fields. But he was also aware that even post-Mossadegh Iran, as well as Saudi Arabia, was able to open negotiations on new concessions for land not covered in the original concessions—an option not open to Baghdad, given the size of IPC's concession.[26] Not surprisingly, Kassem then sought to rectify that situation by pressing for negotiations with the IPC for a new agreement. His objective was to persuade the company to relinquish 60 percent of its total concession area to permit new oil exploration arrangements. He also demanded a doubling of output on already developed fields and the construction of refineries in Iraq. The companies made a vague counteroffer to double output "depending on market conditions." But nothing else. A glut in crude supplies gave them an advantage in the prolonged discussions that followed. It was clear that IPC intended to retain full control over every aspect of the industry. "One is forced to conclude that company behavior," wrote a keen observer, "indicated a decision to make an example of Iraq and that there was a strong political flavor to this decision."[27]

The Iraqi leader was not yet convinced, however, that he would be denied his main objectives, despite the companies' many advantages, and despite the divisions opening up beneath him, especially between pro- and anti-Nasser factions. Trying to see a way to promote its interests, Washington quietly supported Nasser's continuing efforts to unseat Kassem with his pan-Arab, anticommunist campaigns. That was far from risk-free, for even if such support was handled with the utmost delicacy, policymakers still could not see what the Egyptian leader's activities and ambitions might produce. It could all boomerang against Cairo in a fashion that would bring something worse into being. Too-open support for Nasser, moreover, might give his Communist enemies in Iraq and other Arab countries the opportunity to call him an "imperialist stooge," noted a State Department paper on the Iraq situation. Yet there were also dangers in discouraging Nasser's efforts. It was a very tricky business all round. "Nasser's current conflict with the Communists, while opening up new opportunities for the West, has not altered his basic pan-Arab goals which include the elimination of the remaining positions of Western, and particularly British, influence in the area," the department noted.[28]

Nasser was a man of many moods and great ambitions, as well as a skilled opportunist who played his cards so as to stir up Americans in a fashion that might provide him with the most options. At one point he dispatched Mohamed Heikal to the American embassy to explain that he had been forced to cancel a plan to crack down on Syrian Communists because of an American diplomat's press leak in an article, which had compromised his position. At the same time he very much resented what the reporter, Dana Adams Schmidt, had indicated in the article were his ambitions to foment a pro-Egypt revolution in Jordan, and an Iraqi-Kuwaiti-Egyptian scheme for oil development. The article ended with a description of the Egyptian leader's predicament: "Soviet help is President Nasser's worst problem. He cherishes the belief that he can drink the wine of Soviet aid without getting drunk, if he can just determine precisely when he has had enough. He would like to get more American aid to offset the Soviet brand."[29]

The tenor of these recent contacts, and Schmidt's leak-inspired assessment of Nasser's predicament, led Eisenhower to take a second look at American-Egyptian relations. At the end of the year, Eisenhower and his top advisers discussed where matters stood with Nasser. From recent conversations at the embassy, they concluded,

"Nasser desires to work with us on Iraq. He is much concerned over Communist influence with Qasim [Kassem] and stated that Qasim refuses to talk with him." The president commented in an almost wistful way that "were it not for the existence of Israel we might be able to do some business with Nasser in that Nasser could oppose Communists better than can the U.S. in the three-cornered struggle of the Middle East." Secretary of State Christian Herter, Dulles's successor, added that Nasser had been much more moderate of late about Israel. Maybe his influence on pan-Arab thinking was not all bad, as "there is a healthy element in the fact of an Arab strong man of such stature that he does not need to compete with other Arab countries in baiting the Israelis." After this discussion, Eisenhower closed the meeting by admitting that "Nasser has grown up a little."[30]

The American effort to get rid of Kassem started in the spring of 1959 when his negotiating demands on the IPC were accompanied by increased influence of the Communist Party and a series of gestures toward the Soviet Union. As events unfolded, Nasser would prove useful in more than one way to the ultimate success of American plans. Inside the Eisenhower administration's deliberations on Iraq, meanwhile, Allen Dulles continued to explain why Kassem was so dangerous. At a National Security Council meeting on April 2, 1959, the president wondered about ways and means of supporting Nasser's efforts to resist Communism. "It seemed to the President," recorded the note taker, "that if we were really going to undertake to save Iraq, we should have to begin to do so now." The situation "was very complicated," cautioned Allen Dulles. Not all of America's friends had the same view of the situation as American policymakers did. But Eisenhower kept coming back to Nasser as a possible ally and instrumentality for getting rid of Kassem. "He still did not understand why Nasser could not make common cause with Qasim against Communism." It just wouldn't work out, explained Dulles; there was far too much bitterness between them to hope for such a solution.[31]

If it became known that the United States was "plotting with the UAR against Iraq," interjected Under Secretary of State Douglas

Dillon, it would drive Baghdad "further and more rapidly into Communism." Two weeks later, at the next National Security Council meeting, CIA director Dulles reported that he was "extremely pessimistic" about the Iraqi situation, although the British and Turkish governments now seemed to agree with Washington about the nature of the threat. The "so-called repatriation of a number of Kurds from the Soviet Union," he said, hid "a number of Soviet agents" destined to carry out the Kremlin's wishes by subverting the Iraqi government.[32]

Dulles had framed the question perfectly in terms of the Truman Doctrine rationale. Throughout the Cold War, from Latin America to Southeast Asia, the Truman Doctrine rationale fit closely with American notions about the "agent" theory of revolution, specifically that since the United States was a trustworthy anti-imperialist nation dedicated to self-determination, those revolutions that mixed nationalism with Marxism were fomented by agents and could not be considered genuine expressions of self-determination.

As the discussion went on, Vice President Richard Nixon commented that "it seemed unlikely that we could find any middle ground between Communistic control of Iraq and control by Nasser." In other words, though Nixon did not say it, Nasser was "our agent" in this particular situation. Nixon had difficulty, he said, in seeing how any of the alternatives they had discussed did not have serious liabilities in terms of American relations with the Arab countries. But in the end, "we simply could not tolerate a Communist take-over in Iraq and . . . we were therefore engaged in building a case to prevent this from happening or for overthrowing a Communist regime in case one became established in Iraq."

Would it be worse than supporting Nasser, however, to use military force? General Nathan Twining, chairman of the Joint Chiefs, picked up on Nixon's point and took it to a logical conclusion: "We could easily take over Iraq by military force if the appropriate preparations were made in advance." But if they went that route, he said, it would be necessary to prepare public opinion. Treasury Secretary Robert B. Anderson warned against repeating the error of talking while the Communists took over half of Indochina. He believed that the domino theory was far more applicable in the Middle East than in Southeast Asia. How long could Washington wait to take action? The people of the United States would understand—after all there had been no fuss when American forces landed in Lebanon the previous summer. The administration should set up a group whose sole duty would be to develop plans to prevent a Communist takeover. "We do not want another [Dien Bien Phu]," Anderson said.[33]

Actually such a group had already been assigned to that task, chaired by Assistant Secretary of State William Rountree. He opened its first full meeting on April 27, 1959, with a statement that there was "a certain amount of confusion regarding our objectives concerning a post-Kassem regime in Iraq." The meetings of this special group continued over the months and ranged across the possibilities, from encouraging Nasser to intervene—an action sure to be vehemently opposed by Israel as well as other American friends in the area—to organizing something of an exile government made up of refugees from the pre-revolution era, to warning Kassem that if he did not want Washington's aid in defeating the Communists, there would be intervention anyway. In October the group reviewed all the alternatives and heard from one member that the most likely path was assassination accomplished by a military coup. "The army could possibly seize control with less chance of chaos in this contingency."[34]

After a failed assassination attempt on Kassem in 1959, one of the conspirators, Saddam Hussein, escaped to Cairo, where, under the watchful eyes of his CIA contacts, he bided his time. A process had been set in motion that eventually led to an army coup and Kassem's removal, but it took nearly four years to come to fruition. Although he was tipped off by a variety of sympathetic leaders, such as Yugoslavia's Marshal Tito, when the plots materialized into a coordinated action, Kassem had convinced himself he could deal with any conspiracy. Inside Iraq the CIA contact man (nominally an assistant military attaché) with dissident members of the armed forces was William Lakeland, an old Egyptian hand from the early days of Nasser. Even before the success of the coup, the embassy contacted the rebels and promised them early diplomatic recognition. Ali Saleh Sa'adi, minister of the interior in the first post-Kassem government, quipped, "We came to power on a CIA train." In the immediate aftermath, hundreds were arrested and tortured before being killed. The point man in this operation was Saddam Hussein.[35]

Best-Laid Plans

How deeply Nasser was involved with Saddam Hussein is not known, but biographer Said Aburish comments that it mattered very little. Nasser was now working with the CIA on the Iraq problem. He had come to hate Kassem, as he had hated Kassem's predecessor, Nuri, and he was willing to work with the Americans to do him in. "He had reached an agreement with the CIA whereby the Agency would rid Iraq of Kassem, and in return, Nasser promised to cede control of Iraq to the CIA."[36]

This alliance of convenience yielded a brutal dictatorship in Iraq and, eventually, two wars, in 1990 and 2003, at the end of which the United States and Egypt, now under Hosni Mubarak, traded compliments for loyal service in managing the affairs of the Middle East. There is a strong historical thread stretching from the arrangements reached between the CIA and Nasser on Iraq in 1963 to the final days of Mubarak's regime in early 2011, after a few weeks of protest in Tahrir Square. The thread broke only once—during the 1967 Six Days' War—and was put back together by Anwar Sadat, who also proved clever in playing the diplomatic game, and two American presidents, Richard Nixon and Jimmy Carter.

Eisenhower met once with Nasser, at the opening of a UN General Assembly meeting in September 1960, little more than three years after Ike stood on the tarmac waiting to welcome King Saud of Saudi Arabia to America—an experimental courtship that never got off the ground in the Middle East. The conversation between Nasser and Eisenhower took place in a suite in the Waldorf Towers Hotel, a place where many talks around UN meetings often were held. The meeting was remarkable for several reasons. At times it almost seemed that the American president and the Egyptian leader had traded

places, with Ike lamenting accusations that the United States engaged in "economic imperialism" when it attempted to give bilateral
aid to foreign countries, and Nasser sounding warnings about Soviet
intentions in Africa and inside the UAR manipulating Syrian Communists. Quite soon, however, the talk turned to the airing of old
grievances. Nasser began by saying that the people of the Middle East
had placed great responsibility on U.S. shoulders after World War II.
And what was the result? Instead of upholding Woodrow Wilson's
principle of self-determination and the ideals of the 1941 Atlantic
Charter, the United States had supported the creation of Israel.

His own efforts since 1952 to establish friendly relations with the
United States had always been thwarted by the Israeli barrier. He had
tried to buy arms from the United States, but could not—so he had
turned to the East. Israel could buy arms, but not Egypt. Moving on,
he discussed American complaints in Congress that the Suez Canal
had not been opened as envisioned after the recent war ended. "If the
U.S. wishes to say that the Suez Canal must be opened to Israeli shipping, the U.S. must try just as hard to get the UN to get Israel to implement the resolutions to which Israel stands in default." Nasser
meant the resettlement of refugees expelled in the first Arab-Israeli
war, in 1948. Eisenhower said that, of course, he would like to see
that worked out. Eisenhower also "agreed that Israel constitutes a terrible problem. However," he added, "Israel is." Perhaps the answer lay
in compensation, rather than resettlement, because the question was
how could the problem be solved without starting a war.

Nasser was only warming up, however. Since its creation, he said,
Israel had received over a billion dollars in American aid, approxi-
mately one million dollars a day. As for the president's thought that
"Israel is," he rejected the premise. "To accept Israel as a fact would
be to permit a thief to keep what he has stolen." Eisenhower brought
the conversation to a close by suggesting that if Nasser thought of
any way to solve the refugee problem, he hoped he would tell him—
but make sure he told him privately, because if a senator caught
wind of the proposal, it would turn into a speech in Congress. With
this "clue" to what he was up against, Eisenhower added a final
note, lest Nasser think he was enthralled by the Egyptian's recital of

the facts of Middle Eastern life. The United States looked forward
to better relations with Cairo, he said, but it was always suspicious
"when the Soviets touch a country.[37]

When it was learned that Nasser was coming to New York for
the UN meeting, the State Department had played around with the
idea of arranging a tour for the Egyptian leader. The idea was
quickly dropped, however, out of fear there would be demonstrations organized at every stop along the way.

When John F. Kennedy entered the White House a few months
later, he hoped to start a new friendly correspondence with Nasser, in
an effort to demonstrate that Democrats were not one-sided in the
Arab-Israeli dispute. In a conversation with Israeli representatives
who were seeking a more-binding security arrangement and more
arms to protect their country against Egypt, one of Kennedy's chief
advisers on the Middle East, Robert Komer, went so far as to say that
the real problem began with the Soviet-bloc arms deal. That was a
common enough statement, but Komer then added that this "military threat to Israel" was brought on in large measure by American
and British mistakes in dealing with Nasser! "We ourselves had con-
tributed to this situation by our policy in the mid-fifties vis-à-vis
Nasser. It was in reacting to US/UK policy that he turned to Moscow,
and we didn't want to make this mistake again."[38]

Komer and others were not always so blunt about supposed past
errors, but they hoped to reinvigorate the lapsed dialogue with
Cairo—or at least not lose touch with Nasser. A few days before a
meeting with Israeli foreign minister Golda Meir in late December
1962, Kennedy addressed the Egyptian leader in very cordial terms
about policies toward Yemen—where Nasser supported a new republican government and Saudi Arabia the old regime—and a variety of other questions. Kennedy said he was pleased to learn that
Egypt was interested in restoring tranquility in Algeria and helping
its economy. "As you know," he wrote, "I have long taken a special
interest in Algeria and I share your judgment that the success of the
Algerian Government in its efforts to bring stability to this key
country is very much in the interest of both our nations." He intended to provide "several tens of millions of dollars in hard relief

aid to Algeria," Kennedy went on, and he hoped Nasser would en-courage that country to pursue such policies as would "enhance our ability to be of such help."[39]

There was much between the lines here, for while Nasser certainly knew that Kennedy's "special interest in Algeria" went back to the 1950s when he had criticized the French efforts to suppress the na-tionalist uprising, he could also take note that JFK seemed now to be repudiating the French for their role in the Suez Crisis. Paris had justified its joining in the Anglo-French-Israeli invasion on the basis not only of the canal nationalization, but also Nasser's support for Algerian rebels. And there was more in Kennedy's message: "We stand with you on the position of principle that the UAR has taken at the Colombo Conference in opposition to the acquisition of terri-tory by armed force. I believe that a similarity of outlook on this and many other issues has created a community of interests which argues well for the success of our cooperative endeavors."[40] Those sentences could be read as both an implied warning to Israel not to start a new war, and some indication of support for the return of Palestinian refu-gees. Nevertheless, however one looks at the message, Kennedy pro-tected himself by sending it to his ambassador in Cairo to be conveyed "orally," not as a formal signed letter. Three days later the president met with Golda Meir at his vacation "White House" in Palm Beach, Florida.

Kennedy's objective in 1962 was to head off a new conflict between Egypt and Israel that threatened war. Foreign Minister Meir began their exchange by putting on the table Israel's belief that Egypt was preparing for war, including recent information Tel Aviv had received that Cairo was "making preparations for radiological warfare." It was believed that the Egyptians were working on some form of dirty nu-clear bomb to contaminate vast areas of Israeli territory. "It seems that if the refugees can't come back, the Egyptians think that at least the land should not be available to Israelis." Her country had information, she said, that Nasser had established a secret budget of $220 million to $250 million per year for developing these weapons.[41]

As for the refugees, what was really behind the Arab demands that they be allowed to return? Already, she said, Arabs living in Israel

constituted 11 percent of the population. Given Arab pronounce-
ments in the United Nations "for hours and hours" that Israel has no
right to exist, the real motive becomes clear. "This is the situation.
Israel knows about Arab plans to bring Arabs back to Israel and then
to make an Algeria out of Israel." The returning Arabs would stir up
trouble, and the Israeli Government would do what any government
would do to protect itself, and the Arab countries would rush in to
help these "refugees." Meir's description fit, of course, the Truman
Doctrine's description of the way subversion worked, and she was at
pains to point out Israel's allegiance to the free world.

After this long presentation, the foreign minister offered Kennedy
some kind words. She said she understood that the president's position "causes all sorts of people to put their problems on his shoulder.
Israel does this too. The United States has taken on the responsibility for the free world. Israel is part of the free world." Kennedy picked
up on her final point. She was right, he said; America's interest in
maintaining the balance of power worldwide had led it into "disputes which are not part of what we see as the central struggle, i.e.,
the struggle of free peoples against the Communist Bloc." He moved
on quickly, however, to say that the United States' relationship with
Israel was comparable only to its relationship with Great Britain.
But if that was so, it was also true that Israel's security would not be
enhanced if the United States abandoned its efforts with the Arab
Middle East and "maintained our ties only with Israel."[42]

From that point, Kennedy discussed various ways that Israel could
help the United States help Israel by not taking unilateral actions on
questions like the diversion of water from the Jordan River, and especially by cooperating with Washington's efforts to monitor its atomic
energy project. Meir was conciliatory but noncommittal, and this issue would continue to disturb policymakers up until Kennedy's death.
Lyndon Johnson was less persistent and, as the Vietnam War ex-
panded, more concerned about not challenging a valued ally. Kennedy had deliberated long and hard, moreover, before agreeing to
supply Israel with Hawk antiaircraft missiles, fearing it would become
a slippery slope to a renewed arms race. He finally concluded that
providing the missiles Israel wanted might offer him some leverage in

arguing with Israeli leaders over the dangers of nuclear weapons, and the willingness of the Soviet Union to match whatever Israel accomplished in that regard. With the 1962 congressional elections impending, JFK finally agreed to the sale. By doing that, he believed he could give bona fides to the Israelis of American intentions to defend their country and there would, therefore, be no need for Israel to develop nuclear weapons.[43]

Israel always had one key trump card to play in negotiations over its arms requests, which was the unwillingness of the United States under either Kennedy or Johnson to countenance a bilateral security treaty. The possibility of alienating the Arab countries—and the fear that the United States could become involved in a nuclear war over boundary lines not settled by the 1948 Arab-Israeli War or the Suez Crisis—were simply risks too great even for the pro-Israel contingent in Congress to overcome. Foreign Minister Meir had played a related card in her December 1962 conversation with Kennedy, suggesting that the next conversation over refugees should be in Jerusalem, with Israeli and Arab diplomats negotiating directly. It was obvious that neither Nasser nor anyone else would accept such a bid, thereby allowing Meir to leave the conversation with a warning: if Egypt would not deal directly, it was because it was planning to carry out Arab threats to Israel's existence.

The Kennedy administration made several complicated moves to try to placate Nasser over the Hawk missile sales, including an aid program that would supply Egypt with essentially free wheat, a deal worth several million dollars. Nevertheless, when the missile sales were announced, the Egyptian press erupted in fury. Every weapon given to Israel, thundered a paper with close attachments to Nasser, "has been used to shed Arab blood." Outside of Nasser's circle, the reaction was more muted in other Arab countries, including Iraq and, especially, Saudi Arabia.[44] By the time Kennedy's administration was cut short by his assassination in November 1963, his efforts to kindle warmer relations between Cairo and Washington had largely failed.

A memorandum to President Johnson on April 14, 1964, authored by the State Department Policy Planning Council's Middle East expert, William R. Polk, neatly summarized U.S. policy toward

Egypt. Egypt's prospects, and therefore its usefulness to the United States, depended upon economic growth, for with its population increasing at the rate of 3 percent a year, and doubling each twenty-five years, demands for a better life, if not met, would force its leaders to turn to more-radical politics internally and closer relations with the Soviet bloc.[45] Why did this matter to the United States? Egypt was a leader of the Arab states and a major force in the Afro-Asian and nonaligned groups, and "occasionally opposes our interests." Polk then listed them. "These include investments in oil, which earn roughly $1 billion yearly, Wheelus Field [an airbase in nearby Libya] in which U.S. pilots assigned to NATO are exercised [sic], the Suez Canal, the use of Arab airspace and landing facilities . . . and security of Israel." On all these, Egypt was in a position to help or oppose the United States. Or simply to keep silent. "In general, our interests are served by Egyptian inactivity."[46]

What about Nasser, then? "Since we cannot, apparently, destroy Nasser or replace him with a viable and more moderate government and since we do not want him to rely completely upon the USSR or to be replaced by a more radical government," the only alternative was to assist Egyptian development. "The U.S. contribution, mostly PL 480 wheat, just about equals the difference between the population growth (3%) and the rise in GNP (5–6%)." This delicate balance, as Johnson's special assistant for national security affairs, Walt Rostow, called it, would have to be maintained as well in terms of other actions. And Polk repeated, "If we cannot destroy Nasser, what we should do is to moderate his positions so that they remain below the threshold of real danger to our interests." There were various ways to accomplish this objective: by direct threats of force, actions in the UN Security Council, supply of defensive arms to Israel, cooperation with friendly intelligence services such as those in Jordan (and outright aid to that country), and diplomatic exchanges.

Quite simply, however, the memorandum concluded, "Nasser will never become our creature." No, and beyond that fact, he would never trust the United States to be evenhanded in regard to Israel. Washington would have to put up with a lot from him, but at the same time make sure that he knew where the lines were drawn, that

Washington had the strength and will to protect its own interests. The key was to prevent a Middle East arms race from reaching a point where Cairo, concerned about an Israeli atomic bomb, called upon the Soviets in a way that could lead to a Cuban-style show-down, "where we would not have all the cards as we did in the Cuba crisis."

Almost all Polk's recommendations were acted upon over the next several years, as Washington sought to keep Nasser hemmed in so that he could not endanger American interests in the Middle East. LBJ also tried to use methods similar to those he employed with Con-gress in fashioning the Great Society, encouraging Nasser to write to him. The "next few years will be a strain on both of us," he wrote early in 1964, but the two nations had so much to gain that "we must both strive to maintain and expand [our relations] rather than letting our two nations drift apart." But a series of events in quick succession spoiled that attempt at a new beginning and sent relations into a downward spiral. On Thanksgiving Day 1964, African students in Cairo burned down the American library next to the embassy. A few days later the Egyptian Air Force accidentally shot down an airplane owned by a friend of LBJ's. These events happened just as the wheat deal was up for renewal; and when the Egyptian minister of supply asked Ambassador Lucius Battle about progress on a new pact, he was told it was a bad time to press President Johnson about a supply of wheat. Somehow this message got garbled into a threat not to supply any more wheat. "By God," Battle was supposed to have said, and what was repeated to Nasser, "I cannot discuss this at all because we do not like your behavior."[47]

Nasser had been on his way to Port Said to deliver a speech on the anniversary of Egypt's "victory" in the 1956 Suez Crisis, and he used the wheat incident as a takeoff point in a bombastic speech attacking Johnson personally. "The American Ambassador says that our behavior is not acceptable. Well, let us tell them that those who do not accept our behavior can go and drink"—he paused and asked the audience, "from where?" The shout came back, "From the sea!" "What I want to say to President Johnson is that I am not prepared to sell Egyptian independence for thirty million pounds or forty million pounds or fifty million pounds. We are not ready to discuss our behavior with anybody. We will cut the tongues of anybody who talks badly about us. This is clear and this is frank."[48]

Nasser soon regretted those words, and there was an apology forthcoming from Cairo that it had all been a misunderstanding. The wheat deal was renegotiated, but on a short-term basis. Johnson returned to personal diplomacy, nevertheless, inviting Anwar al-Sadat, the president of the National Assembly, to visit the United States in early 1966 when Nasser said he could not come because of the tense state of relations and the likelihood he would be subject to protests. "It will do more harm than good," he told Johnson. "I will be picketed and the Zionist groups will demonstrate against me and it will only make matters worse."[49]

Johnson gave Sadat the full treatment, receiving him in the Oval Office and pointing to the walls covered with signed photographs of heads of state. "I like you. I admire your country. . . . I like President Nasser. . . . Now look, I have a space here waiting for a picture of President Nasser. Why doesn't he send me one? Why do we make enemies of each other? We should be friends."[50]

Sadat had brought with him a letter for Johnson expressing satisfaction at the recently improved relations between the two countries. The president seized the opportunity to point out that the United States had given Egypt more than $1 billion in aid in recent years, adding that Cairo's frequent denunciations of American policy had not helped things along. He operated in a goldfish bowl, the president said, never out of sight of the press. They should try to discuss whatever problems they had "quietly among ourselves and not announced to the public over loudspeakers." He knew from his aides, Johnson went on, that the prospect of an Israeli atomic bomb worried Arab nations. "We were watching the situation closely," he assured Sadat, therefore the United States was not as "alarmist" as Egypt was on that subject. But Cairo should know the United States opposed such a development, "because of our firm policy against the proliferation of nuclear weapons."[51] JFK had pressed the Israelis about the purpose of their nuclear reactor at Dimona in the Negev Desert, stressing the importance of international inspections

over and over again, particularly in the summer of 1963. The Israelis evaded Kennedy's questions as best they could and made sure
the inspectors, when they came, were kept away from sensitive areas that indicated work on weapons. Their mantra was that Israel
would not be the first to introduce nuclear weapons into the area,
but it would never be the last. When Johnson took over after Kennedy's death, however, the pressure on Israel was considerably eased.

Despite his assurances to Sadat about the need for cooperation
on big issues, LBJ was anxious not to alienate Israel, as the Vietnam
War threatened to wreck all his hopes for the Great Society—and
Israel, moreover, was an ally he believed could influence Jewish liberals in the United States. On the other hand, and despite Nasser's
letter, Cairo's actions continued to upset Washington. Nasser had
intervened in a Yemeni civil war on the side of a republican movement that also had support from the Soviet Union, setting off alarm
bells in Saudi Arabia. The short-lived UAR had dissolved in 1961,
and Nasser was seeking other ways to burnish his pan-Arab creden-
tials. At meetings of the Arab League he began pushing the idea of
a separate Palestinian political entity. His main objective was to
control the Palestinian movement, particularly the more militant
splinter groups in the Gaza Strip. His sponsorship of the Palestinian
Liberation Organization (PLO), therefore, was an effort to extend
his control over the growth of Palestinian groups advocating armed
struggle, but the PLO's charter called for armed action and the right
of return of all refugees of the 1948 war to the territories of the old
British mandate.

As tensions rose on the Egyptian-Israeli border, the Johnson administration watched the scene with mixed emotions. None of the
measures advocated by policymakers since 1953 had had much
effect in curbing Nasser's ambitions. Even though Egypt and the
United States had shared some objectives in combating a supposed
Communist threat in Iraq, the general trajectory of relations with
Cairo was downward. Nasser's actions in closing the Straits of Tiran,
a narrow passageway that provided Israel access to the Red Sea and
beyond, and demanding the withdrawal of UN peacekeeping troops
in 1967, set the stage for a new war. While no one in the administra-

tion thought a war would really settle matters, or provide a permanent solution to the Egyptian conundrum, the situation was unlike
what Eisenhower faced in 1956, when the United States believed it
could not stand aside and watch events unfold. This time Johnson
determined that while he would not encourage the Israelis to take
the initiative, he would tell them he had no alternative to suggest—
because that was the truth; he had none. And, as the Six Days' War
began, few in the administration would regret seeing Nasser "cut
down to size."

On a mission to probe American intentions if Israel attacked Egypt,
the Israeli chief of intelligence, General Meir Amit, provided a briefing for Defense Secretary Robert McNamara on June 1, 1967, that
sounded like Dean Acheson's famous declamation to congressional
leaders in February 1947 when the British had signaled they could no
longer hold the fort in Greece and Turkey. Acheson had drawn a truly
scary picture that day of the Russians moving all the way to North
Africa and beyond, a rolling Red Tide of subversion and conquest.
McNamara now asked Amit if he thought the Russians knew in advance of the Tiran blockade. He was interested, obviously, in discov-
ering whether this had been a coordinated plan between Cairo and
Moscow. Probably not, said Amit, but they were not reluctant to take
advantage of it. Then Amit held forth on the true meaning of the
blockade. The blockade of Tiran, he began, was merely window dress-
ing. A "grand design" was now evident, which he termed the "Domino
Effect," a loaded phrase sure to bring attention to his next words.

Egypt, with Russian backing, "hopes to roll up the whole of the
Middle East all the way to the borders of Russia, to include Iran,
under Arab domination." While this would affect Israel right away,
"the long range effect would be deeply inimical to U.S. interests."
Amit would not go so far as to say that the "design" was behind
Cairo's "original move" in blockading the straits, but it had offered
Russia an opportunity to implement long-term plans, "whatever the
origins of the present confrontation." The only option for America
was to back Israel with weapons and economic support. Whatever
it did, Amit concluded, "the U.S. is already damned in the eyes of
the Arabs no matter what we do."[52]

Amit's presentation presumed several things about the relationship between Russia and Egypt in a manner certain to stimulate Cold War fears, while suggesting there did not have to be a Russian-American confrontation if the United States aided Israel in eliminating the threat from Nasser. There was the invocation of the "domino effect" and, by implication, wars of national liberation everywhere as a given of Soviet imperial behavior. After the meeting, however, Amit wondered if he had been convincing. McNamara had not really responded to his suggestions for all-out aid to Israel, and Amit asked one of his hosts who drove him away from the meeting if he should try to see President Johnson. No, responded Admiral Rufus Taylor, he could be sure McNamara would convey his position to the White House. "I urged him to get a night's sleep," noted Taylor, "and go back to Israel as soon as possible because he would be needed more there than here."[53]

American leaders had understood the Israeli position on all these issues for a long time and were leery of giving Israel's emissaries, such as Amit and Foreign Minister Abba Eban, any absolute guarantees about borders. The White House did not agree, moreover, that Washington was damned in the eyes of Arab leaders no matter what course it chose. Most of all it did not want to be in a position where a border dispute could drag the United States into military action against an Arab country. Where the White House agreed with Israel was in seeing Nasser as an obstacle—if not quite the threat to the nation's very existence as the Israelis viewed him, or claimed they did.

Though the Yemen crisis had died down, the United States had other complaints against Cairo, and felt it no longer needed any assistance in places like Iraq. Saudi Arabia and Jordan were considered stable—and possible counters to Nasser's ambitions. Best of all, LBJ had good information that Israel would not need help to defeat Egypt in any armed conflict. The administration believed that the Egyptian leader really did not understand the implications of what he had done in demanding the removal of UN peacekeeping forces. As soon as they were gone he sent his own troops into the Sinai and closed the Gulf of Aqaba to Israeli shipping. It had been opened as a result of the compromises made after Suez. Nasser now declared that he was determined to correct that mistake. Recent weeks had seen an Israeli-Syrian confrontation, and Nasser's reputation was at stake. CIA director Richard Helms told Johnson, however, that Nasser did not desire war. He had sent his troops into Sinai in large part out of guilt feelings about not helping out Syria when the Israelis took over borderlands. They made "a big show of marching into Sinai, partly to show good faith, partly in hopes of deterring the Israelis" from more retaliatory attacks. Nasser knew that his army was not ready for war.[54]

That might be so, but he had overplayed his hand with bellicose speeches to the Egyptian National Assembly and Egyptian trade unions. On May 29, 1967, he told the National Assembly that the blockade at Aqaba had been established to take a stand for "the rights of the Palestinian people," as if that would really help the million or more refugees. And to the trade unions, he boasted, "We are now face to face with Israel and if they want to try their luck without Britain and France, we await them. . . . The Israel flag will not pass through Aqaba Gulf and our sovereignty over the Gulf entrance is not negotiable. If Israel wants to threaten us with war they are welcome."

Israel sent its most skillful negotiator, Foreign Minister Eban, to Washington to learn if the United States had any plan for international action to force open the narrow waterway. If there was no plan, that left the way open for Israel to take unilateral action. But was there any chance the Johnson administration would repeat the American performance in 1956 and force Israel to give up its gains? President Johnson made a statement in one of their discussions that is sometimes interpreted as his giving Israel an amber light. "With emphasis and solemnity," read notes of this meeting, "the President repeated twice that Israel would not be alone unless it decides to go it alone."[55]

One way of interpreting that statement was that while it meant the United States would not approve of military action, it would not condemn it. Just before the often-quoted statement, Johnson had told Eban, "Israel must not make itself responsible for initiating hostilities." Such a statement covered many vague possibilities, including not simply manufacturing an incident, but also using the previous Egyptian actions to make out a legal case for war under international law, which clearly applied to Aqaba. Eban countered this ploy with one of his own. Would the president consider a formal Israeli-American security pact modeled on NATO? Johnson replied coolly, as if what Eban proposed was simply superfluous now and in the future: "You will whip hell out of them."[56]

LBJ could look back and say he and Kennedy had tried to give Nasser a "break," but that from the beginning the Egyptian had brought all these woes on himself by not paying attention to what the Americans were trying to tell him, how they were trying to guide him. His was not a reasonable position for the leader of a nation that desperately needed what America had to offer. On the eve of the Israeli attack, National Security Adviser Walt Rostow wrote Johnson a memo that summed up where matters stood and how the United States could now achieve its main objective because of Israeli determination. Whatever they said about the plight of the Palestinian refugees, Rostow told LBJ, moderate Arab elements—and that meant "virtually all Arabs who fear the rise of Nasser"—"would prefer to have him cut down by the Israelis rather than by external forces." Beyond the immediate crisis, Rostow continued, the "radical nationalism represented by Nasser" was waning. "Arab socialism and other such doctrines have not proved successful." Then this: "Just beneath the surface is the potentiality for a new phase in the Middle East of moderation; a focusing on economic development; regional collaboration; and an acceptance of Israel as part of the Middle East if a solution to the refugee problem can be found. But all this depends upon Nasser's being cut down to size."[57]

At the outset of the Russo-Japanese War in February 1904, when the Japanese fleet attacked Russian ships at Port Arthur, President Theodore Roosevelt was relieved that the burden of opposing the czar's ambitions had been taken off his shoulders. Japan was "playing our game," he wrote in a private letter. LBJ's attitude to the Six Days' War was virtually the same, with the added factor that Johnson also saw the war as a way to get the American Jewish community to give him more support in Vietnam. Ultimately, of course, Japan posed a much bigger problem for American interests in Asia, culminating at Pearl Harbor. Similarly, events in the Middle East did not work out the way Rostow predicted. Dean Acheson, who was among those "realists" who had criticized Eisenhower and Dulles for stopping the 1956 Anglo-French-Israeli invasion, and who was now summoned to Washington to offer advice, mused on the central dilemma that would now confront policymakers who cheered Israel's prowess. The occupation of new territories, the creation of more refugees, he foresaw as troubles ahead with no apparent solution. "Mr. Acheson," noted Rostow, "looked back on the whole history of Israeli independence and, in effect, said it was a mistake to ever create the State of Israel."[58]

On June 5, 1967, Israel struck at 7:30 in the morning, an attack that had been planned, wrote one of the Israeli strategists, for ten years. It was a walkover. Within hours, more than three hundred out of four hundred Egyptian planes had been destroyed. By evening of that day the Israeli army had reached well into the Sinai. Egyptian army officers ran from the front back to Cairo. It was a worse debacle than what happened in 1948 in the last days of the Farouk regime. Both sides agreed to a truce on June 12, 1967, but by then Israel occupied all the Sinai, the West Bank, and the Golan Heights. During the first days of the war, Arab peoples had no information about how bad things really were. When they learned the truth, the shock wave across the Middle East would not die down. Appearing on television, Nasser announced in a lifeless voice that he was resigning and turning the government over to his vice president, a relative unknown. The resignation did not last long, and he clung to power until his death just a few years later, a disastrous interim that held back any significant changes to improve the economy. During that period, moreover, he assumed even greater dictatorial powers, as the high hopes of the 1952 revolution curdled into bitter clots of anger and frustration. Washington felt great satisfaction, however, about the elimination of the threat of "Nasserism." Prospects for transforming the Middle East, Rostow had insisted before the Six Days' War, were just below the surface.

As the effort began to construct a postwar framework for that transformation, Nasser's voice was muted, and it seemed there was a new tone in the words he used about Egypt's future role. Talking to an American he knew from years past, Robert Anderson, the Egyptian leader said, "Above all else, try to make clear to your government and your people that we are eager for a political settlement, for a political peace." Other Arab leaders had warned him not to recognize any Israeli claims of a right to exist. He had told them, "We are no longer talking about Israel's right to live. We are talking about our own right to live." He believed Israel's new aim was the economic destruction of Egypt. He had no income from the canal and tourism, and his refineries had been destroyed in the war. "Therefore, my task is now to build a strong economy within my own country. This is the best way I can retaliate."[59]

The Nasser years had seen the United States recognize Egypt's potential as a cultural and intellectual leader of the Middle East, as well as military guardian of the canal and Suez base, both of which were considered essential assets if America was to be successful in replacing the old colonial suzerainty. This vision of Egypt's destiny had been on display from the very first meeting of Dulles and Nasser. The purpose of any arms sale to Arab countries, from Washington's perspective, was then clearly spelled out in Admiral Radford's testimony to Congress in the aftermath of the Suez Crisis, when Nasser had fallen out of favor in Washington.

Radford had come under heavy fire during questioning about whether the Eisenhower Doctrine would not lead to an arms race in the Middle East, and he repeatedly stressed in reply that there was no intention to send much heavy equipment into the area. The object was to influence military behavior within the countries, and build up national pride so they would be able to resist the temptations that had seduced Egypt into error. Senator Richard Russell had asked if the military aid under the doctrine would build up a military force "of real value to the free world?" The admiral then laid out the whole purpose of the doctrine: "Well, first the consideration is to generate forces in friendly countries that can maintain internal security." Pride was a big part of it. "They love to have the heavy equipment that they can parade down the main street on independence days and things like that, and show the people that they have what they feel is real armed strength."[60]

After Nasser that purpose would grow into something bigger, as Washington put more responsibility on, and constructed a symbiotic relationship with, an Egyptian military regarded as fully trustworthy on all the big issues.

4

LIFE WITH ANWAR SADAT:
OR A STORY OF EMPIRE BY INVITATION

*The State visit of President Sadat will be the first ever by an Egyptian
Chief of State to the United States. The visit will dramatize the extraordinary change which has occurred since the October 1973 war not
only in U.S.–Egyptian relations, but also in the U.S. position in the
Middle East. . . . Sadat has based his policy on the belief that peace
in the Middle East on terms satisfactory to Egypt and the Arabs can
be achieved in cooperation with us. We have an interest in seeing Sadat's
policy succeed. In the longer term, we hope to develop a relationship
with Egypt that will endure beyond Sadat.*
    —Henry Kissinger to President Gerald Ford, October 27, 1975

Three American presidents attended Anwar el-Sadat's funeral on
October 10, 1981. Richard Nixon, Gerald Ford, and Jimmy Carter
were there to lead the assortment of Western dignitaries who came
to Cairo to honor the assassinated Egyptian president. The occu-
pant of the White House at the time, Ronald Reagan, did not come
because of security concerns. But he sent a message: "America has
lost a great friend, the world has lost a great statesman, and man-
kind has lost a champion of peace." Also lining up in the mourners'
ranks were Henry Kissinger and Israel's Menachem Begin, who, a
Time magazine reporter wrote, "enjoyed an immeasurably complex
relationship and history with the deceased."[1]

In truth, however, everyone who was at the funeral—and all of
Sadat's enemies who stayed away—"enjoyed" such a relationship and
history. Only one representative showed up from a Muslim country,
the president of Sudan. The rest boycotted the ceremony. From

Algeria, the exiled general who had been Sadat's chief of staff, Lieutenant General Saadeddin Shazli, called upon the Egyptian armed forces to follow up the assassination by wresting power from those committed to "Zionism and Imperialism."[2] Sadat's uneasiness about his enemies at home and in the Arab world had led him to mass arrests—between 1,500 and 2,000—in the month before his death. Included in the roundup were former close associates of Nasser, perhaps the most shocking being Mohamed Heikal, the journalist and special adviser who edited the Cairo daily *Al-Ahram* and who, standing in the corridor at the hour of Nasser's death, had praised Vice President Sadat's elevation to the presidency as reassurance to the country that its leadership was in good hands.

The assassination occurred on October 6, 1981, as Sadat reviewed a military parade on the eighth anniversary of what he considered his greatest accomplishment—"the Crossing." The term was Sadat's favored Egyptian usage for what others called the October War, or the Yom Kippur War. On that date in 1973 Egyptian armies had swarmed across the Suez Canal to attack Israeli fortifications and troops and drove them back from the advanced line they had occupied since the Six Days' War in 1967. Since that time, the moment Sadat believed had cleansed the record of the humiliating defeat, "the Crossing" had taken on several new meanings—especially for those who plotted his death.

The assassination occurred despite heavy security surrounding the reviewing stands, designed and paid for by the American CIA, whose relationship to Sadat—as it had been with Nasser—was highly complex. The agency kept tabs on what was going on in Egypt, but Sadat used these contacts as his separate channel to Washington, since, during the years 1967–74, there had been no formal diplomatic relations. "Helping to keep Sadat in power," wrote Washington insider Bob Woodward, "had been a monumental task for the Administration and the CIA, which had provided covert security assistance and intelligence to his government."[3]

Woodward's comment also suggests why we must not forget the complexity of the term "the Crossing," because the attacks on Israeli forces that began on Yom Kippur were designed to force a political opening for diplomacy. Those who professed astonishment that the Egyptians should lash out in a lost cause to satisfy some notion of honor missed the point. "Rare is the statesman," observed Henry Kissinger, Sadat's initial negotiating partner, "who at the beginning of a war has so clear a perception of its political objective; rarer still is a war fought to lay the basis for moderation in its aftermath."[4] Even Kissinger is guilty here of understatement. Sadat's ultimate objective with "the Crossing" went beyond simply laying the basis for negotiations with Israel. It was a symbolic crossing all the way over from Nasser's efforts at neutralism in the Cold War, and his vision of himself as one of the Big Three of the neutral bloc, to reliance on the United States under terms that Presidents Richard Nixon and Jimmy Carter used to describe Iran's designated role—regional stabilizer or rock of stability. Indeed, while he knew that Egypt could not have the same sort of "special" relationship with Washington that Israel enjoyed, Sadat imagined that Cairo could enjoy equal status with Iran in the Middle East—a far better deal than Nasser had managed.

After Nasser

Convinced that Lyndon Johnson had aided Israel by giving a green light to the 1967 invasion, Nasser had broken off diplomatic relations with the United States. They were not restored until 1974, but that did not mean Cairo and Washington lacked contacts. Both sides took soundings of the other's positions from time to time, particularly after Sadat succeeded the charismatic Nasser. The CIA was always there to listen and report, and Sadat determined very quickly after he came into power that he would not pursue the same course as his predecessor. Nasser had made irritating the United States a specialty, of course, from the time he turned down John Foster Dulles's overtures in 1953.

He had recognized Communist China, bought arms from the East bloc, criticized American allies in Asia, and allowed the National Liberation Front to open an office in Cairo at the height of the Vietnam War. He had also gotten deeply involved in the three-way struggle in Yemen with Saudi Arabia and Great Britain. When the Six Days' War ended, Egypt was thrown back to Suez, and Israel held the Sinai as well as newly occupied lands sliced away from Jordan and Syria. Nasser tried to resign at that moment, but returned because of popular outcries. But his image—along with his health—had been shattered. It was a dark time for Egypt.

In the United Nations, meanwhile, the aftermath of the Six Days' War was addressed in Resolution 242, which called for the restoration of lands taken during the war, and steps by both sides to move the Arab-Israeli question off the battlefield. But ever since 242 passed, a debate has raged over the language and meaning of the resolution: did it mean "the lands" or simply "lands," the latter a much vaguer requirement on Israel? Then Secretary of State Dean Rusk tried to have it both ways in his memoirs: "There was much bickering over whether that resolution should say from 'the' territories or from 'all' territories. In the French version, which is equally authentic, it says withdrawal *de* territory, with *de* meaning 'the.' We wanted that to be left a little vague and subject to future negotiation because we thought the Israeli border along the West Bank could be 'rationalized'; certain anomalies could easily be straightened out with some exchanges of territory, making a more sensible border for all parties." But despite these words, he insisted the United States never meant to grant Israel title to lands taken in war.[5]

What Rusk doesn't say, of course, was the difficulty of pressing the Israelis on *any* version of Resolution 242, given domestic political realities. Ironically, when Sadat came to power, Resolution 242 would trap him, albeit in a different fashion, when he tried to negotiate on the Sinai before and after the famous Camp David conference in 1978. Sadat's vision of a peace settlement concentrated on what was called Nile Valley nationalism, and he was loath to give the Palestinian refugees or their cause a veto over Cairo's negotiating positions; but he could hardly throw Resolution 242 overboard publicly. He needed the support of Arab countries to put himself in a position to negotiate.

But of course that was all sometime in the future. Nasser had managed to persuade Moscow to replenish all the arms lost in the war by playing on the idea that leaving Egypt in the lurch would be bad for Soviet foreign policy in general. The Russians, on the other hand, were badly disappointed by the performance of their Egyptian clients in the war, and wary that they might try to seek revenge without thinking through their position. The Americans—absorbed at the end of LBJ's term and well into Richard Nixon's in trying to get out of Vietnam with a "decent interval" before Saigon collapsed— were happy just to let things bump along around an endless circle of incidents called the war of "attrition." Opinions about Sadat's ability to do very much about the standoff did not credit the new leader with much more than braggadocio. Sadat had been one of the younger colonels at the time of the 1952 revolution, and many observers saw him as a lightweight who would not last long, a man who enjoyed playing center stage but lacked the character (or the means) to change the Israeli-imposed new order.

Sadat's Year of Decision

Sadat kept declaring from 1970 on that the next year would be the "Year of Decision," a pattern that only added to the impression he was all talk and no action. Nixon sent an aide to Nasser's funeral, Elliot Richardson, who met with Sadat before returning home. The new Egyptian president had collapsed during the funeral ceremonies and received Richardson at his bedside. Apparently this confirmed other impressions that Sadat would survive as president only a few weeks and that nobody could predict what would happen in that event.[6]

Sadat believed that this report was one reason Washington did not take seriously a message he had sent Nixon via Richardson that he now approved the "Rogers Plan" for overcoming the stalemate in Arab-Israeli negotiations. The first attempt to translate UN Resolution 242 into a lasting peace settlement had failed when its negotiator, Gunnar Jarring, had gotten nowhere with either side. One supposed stumbling block had been Egypt's refusal to negotiate bilaterally with the Israelis. Nasser had feared taking such responsibility for the negotiations' impact on his self-chosen role as leader of the Arabs. He was not opposed, however, to negotiations under UN auspices, or if proposed by Washington. Secretary of State William Rogers then picked up the thread in a December 1969 speech that proposed peace talks on the basis of an Israeli withdrawal from Sinai, security assurances, Israeli-Jordanian negotiations over the West Bank, negotiations over the future of a united Jerusalem, and vague promises of a fair settlement of the refugee problem. The speech caused an uproar in Israel, where only a few were willing to retreat from any land, and certainly not the whole Sinai.[7]

Despite all his previous resistance to American conditions from the time of Dulles's first visit to Egypt in 1953, Nasser had announced in 1970 that he would accept the Rogers Plan. "Listen, Anwar," he told Sadat at the time, "whether we like it or not, all the cards of this game are in America's hands. It's high time we talked and allowed the U.S.A. to take part in this." Until then, Sadat wrote in his memoirs, "we had authorized the Soviet Union to talk on our behalf to the United States." What frustrated Sadat most was that Washington failed to pick up the signals he sent out during the next three years until the October War.[8]

The Rogers Plan would go through several permutations over the next year and a half down to the summer of 1971, when it was finally dumped in a White House wastebasket located in the basement offices occupied by Nixon's national security adviser Henry Kissinger. The "war" between Kissinger and Rogers doomed the plan from the start, but it never had much chance, even had Nixon been willing to confront the Israeli lobby and press image. Kissinger's basic view of the Middle East during this period, moreover, was that the whole area was a Cold War battlefront. When Sadat signed a new treaty with the Soviets in 1971, it confirmed in Kissinger's mind that anything to Egypt's advantage—at least so long as the Soviets were there—was bad for the United States. Israeli defense minister Moshe Dayan recalled that in his White House meetings, the question of Tel Aviv's deep raids into Egypt during the war of attrition came up, but not in a negative way. As for shooting down Soviet-built planes, the attitude he encountered was, "Shoot the hell out of them!"[9]

Kissinger also felt, even after the October War disabused him of many notions he had about the essentially "romantic" character of Arab political decisions, that the Rogers Plan in all its variations lacked logical coherence in that it envisioned an end solution without intermediate steps. When he became involved in the so-called "peace process," he tried to substitute his own formula, "sovereignty and security," for the more limiting phrase "land for peace," which neither side would accept. He could never have gotten far, nevertheless, without Sadat's support and, indeed, determination to take part in a new Middle East *Pax Americana*. That fact is the key to understanding all that followed.

Sadat felt that the original treatment he received from the Nixon administration was scarcely friendly. He had been warned it was futile to expect the White House to put any pressure on Israel to commit itself to a settlement that involved a significant retreat from the truce boundaries after the Six Days' War. If nothing happened to change the situation, these boundaries would become permanent. In February 1971, therefore, Sadat undertook the first of a series of unilateral actions that would ultimately lead to the October War of 1973. He began with a speech to the Egyptian Peoples Assembly that proposed a partial Israeli withdrawal from the Sinai to the strategic passes, reestablishment of diplomatic relations with the United States, and direct negotiations for a peace treaty. The Egyptian people welcomed the speech, he wrote in his memoirs, except for the remaining "political leadership" left him by Nasser—who, he charged, took a pro-Soviet position on all matters. Sadat's purge of these Nasserite elements was also a tip-off—albeit one that went unrecognized—that he had no intention of sacrificing any Egyptian lives for the Palestinian cause. He might talk the talk, as the current saying goes, but he would not walk the walk. That stance would get him far with the United States, but it also led to his assassination.

Not only had Sadat proposed something in the speech no other Arab leader had dared to do, but he hoped the signal would be understood in Washington. Certainly it would, he thought, when he later dumped the Nasser carryovers: "If the United States or Israel had shown enough interest in that Initiative, the October War would not have taken place and the process of peace would have started in February or March 1971."[10] But nothing at all happened until May 1971, when Secretary Rogers made a trip to Cairo and congratulated him on his speech. "Do you know," Sadat recalled Rogers saying, "you have found a solution to the problem." "How?" asked Sadat. Israeli prime minister Golda Meir had said that if any Arab leader declared a willingness to negotiate with her country, she would be prepared "to put all her cards on the table." Rogers had come to Cairo to put the negotiations on track. What was he expected to do? asked Sadat. "Nothing at all," Rogers said—he had already done what was needed. Rogers would now go to Israel and tell Meir it was time to keep her promise.

Again nothing happened, until July, when another American emissary appeared in Cairo to ask if the Egyptian president still meant to stand by his initiative. Sadat said he did. "Fine. According to my instructions, I would like to tell you that now I have received your reply, the U.S. President, as from midnight [July 6/7, 1971] will personally intervene to start the ball rolling for a peaceful solution to be reached."[11]

Sadat's memoirs are not always perfectly accurate, but in this instance he accurately recorded the jockeying in the American policymaking community as it stumbled around the Rogers Plan. Meanwhile Sadat waited to hear. "He went, and I waited. Midnight—and many other midnights came and went but nothing stirred." Sadat's first signal was too weak to be heard over the din of clashing personalities and ambitions. Henry Kissinger had received reports, however, of Egyptian coolness toward the demands the Soviet president made on a visit to Cairo, and the negative response he got to his insistence that Egypt turn down any U.S. peace initiative and put an end to the American "economic advance" into Egypt. Sadat had agreed that Cairo would consult with Moscow before launching a new war, but that only lessened Washington's sense that it needed to pay much attention to the Egyptian leader's talk about a "Year of Decision."[12]

At about the same time, Sadat gave the head of the American Special Interests Section in Cairo, Donald Bergus, a letter for President

Nixon. In it, he said "that if he could come to an agreement about disengagement and reopening the [Suez] canal, he would remove the Russians from Egypt." Bergus added in an "eyes only" cable of his own to the president that here was a major breakthrough for peace; once Egypt spent millions on clearing and opening the canal, "My thought was—you can write off war as a viable alternative in the Middle East."[13]

Kissinger had actually taken account of Sadat's initiatives, but he also knew Israel would argue that as long as the Soviet bases remained in the Middle East there was little use pursuing efforts to get Tel Aviv to retreat to pre-1967 borders. Politically it would be impossible, even if Sadat wished to move in that direction, which he did not. The State Department's top political adviser, Joseph Sisco, argued, on the other hand, that when—and if—a settlement was reached, the Arabs would handle that problem themselves. "Russian influence will go down." But Kissinger wanted them out first.[14]

Eleven months later, in January 1972, Sadat took that step on his own and started to send the Russian military advisers home, with a final decision to complete the job coming in July. It amazed some policymakers in Washington, who were not quite sure what to make of this seeming reversal of Egyptian policy that went back to the 1955 arms deal with Czechoslovakia. On the other hand, however, Egypt continued to receive military aid from Moscow, including SAM-3 surface-to-air missiles that had proved effective in Vietnam against American planes. Israel had put pressure on the United States for more arms to counteract these Egyptian weapons, and the spiral continued to increase in velocity despite Sadat's efforts to find an alternative to a new war.

Removal of the Soviet advisers, far from encouraging the dramatic response in Washington that Sadat hoped for, gave the White House a sense that the Middle East could wait while other, more pressing, matters were arranged, especially a path out of the Vietnam War. The so-called "Madman Thesis" Nixon had boasted about—threats in the manner of Eisenhower's supposed warning he would use the A-bomb if the Korean War continued—had only proved that he was *not* a madman, and had given way to diplomatic maneuvering to bring China into the big-power equation. In that way, it was hoped, Vietnam could be removed from the Dulles invocation of a crusade against something called "International Communism." For by ending the diplomatic embargo on Beijing, Nixon and Kissinger were essentially removing the rationale for the Vietnam War, even if they remained loath to admitting the final defeat that was surely coming with the predictable failure of Vietnamization.

Sadat and his advisers, meanwhile, watched these developments closely, pondering the implications of "détente," the term used to describe the bundle of agreements Nixon and Kissinger wrapped up at a series of summit conferences beginning with the May 1972 meeting in Moscow. The most well known, of course, were the arms control treaties known as SALT I and SALT II, but what interested Cairo most was the joint statement at this first summit advocating military relaxation in the Middle East with its implication that Egypt's interests mattered little to the United States. "It was a violent shock to us," Sadat wrote in his memoirs, "because . . . we lagged at least twenty steps behind Israel and so 'military relaxation' in this context could mean nothing but giving in to Israel." When he sought clarification from the Soviet ambassador about whether there had been any discussion of the tenuous situation where Egyptian and Israeli armies confronted one another in the Sinai, Sadat was told that while the Russians had pressed Nixon that Security Council Resolution 242 should be implemented, "no progress had been achieved on the Middle East question."[15]

Sadat had reason to doubt his Soviet friends had made much of an effort, and he had already drawn the conclusion from the Rogers Plan fiasco that attempting to work through the State Department was useless, a conclusion more than confirmed by the results of the Moscow summit and the apparent ground rules of détente that assigned no priority to Middle Eastern questions. Worse yet, Sadat was still obliged to seek arms from Moscow, since he still had no other choice. If the atmosphere in Washington had not changed, it had gotten worse in the Soviet capital, where interest in supplying Egyptian requests had lessened since the summit conference. As an explanation for their change of heart, the Russians gave the Egyptian leader a two-page analysis that concluded certain weapons could not be shipped because a new war could not be won.[16]

Reflecting on this period, Sadat blamed the Soviet-American quest for a recalibration of superpower interests in capping nuclear weapons, along with a suspension of Cold War rhetoric to sort out Vietnam and Berlin's future status, for neglect of the Middle East. "The Americans were naturally stunned to hear of my decision on July 16, 1972, to expel the Soviet military experts from Egypt; but they tried their best to play it down in their media in view of the 'Age of Détente' that had been already ushered in with Nixon's visit to the Soviet Union in May 1972, that is, two months before I took my decision. It looked as though it was a conspiracy of silence."[17]

Egypt's fate, it now seemed, was firmly attached to the kite tail of a joint Soviet-American hegemony. That was the meaning of détente. The very worst aspect of the predicament was not the tense situation in the Sinai, therefore, but the long-term problem of Egypt's economy while the "no war, no peace" situation continued. The 1967 defeat had not only left Egypt's military in almost total disarray, but Nasser's concentration on getting new arms—and the problems of paying for them—forced a cruel choice between arms and butter. Military spending consumed about one-third of the Egyptian budget in the immediate post-1967 years. Egypt was seriously short of hard currency. There was no income from canal tolls. Tourist revenue had all but disappeared. (It is significant in this regard that the first new minister named to the post-Mubarak government in February 2011 was the all-important minister of tourism, the department responsible for 18 percent of Egypt's GNP.) Egypt's domestic oil production had been located in the occupied Sinai, but now the oil wells supplied Israel's energy needs. Rapid population growth and urbanization strained food production, creating a greater need for imported foodstuffs of all kinds. Oil-rich Arab countries helped enough to stave off imminent disaster, but "the Egyptian economic outlook was decidedly bleak."[18]

Nasser's legacy was, according to Sadat, largely to blame for Egypt's economic situation as well as its military weakness. "We had, with crass stupidity, copied the Soviet pattern of socialism, although we

lacked the necessary resources, technical capabilities, and capital."
After the 1956 Suez Crisis, budget matters were more than satisfactory, he argued, but instead of a takeoff period, based on both a
healthy public sector and a flourishing private sector, "our socialism
began to be tinged in practice with Marxism. Any free enterprise
system came to be regarded as odious capitalism and the private sector as synonymous with exploitation and robbery. . . . It was that
shrinking back from active individual enterprise that marked the
beginning of our abysmal economic collapse."[19]

"In 1970 I read a report issued in the United States which analyzed
the economic situation in Egypt that said: 'Let Nasser shout as loud
as he likes. He will soon be down on his knees, economically.' At
the time we were relying totally on our own resources; there was no
foreign aid of any kind—Soviet, American, West European, or
Arab. All that we received from the outside world was abuse."
While he believed the "report" was part of a psychological warfare
campaign to force Cairo to accept the status quo with Israel, he had
few doubts that with an increased population to feed and hungry
for consumer goods as well, "within two years at most from 1970,
the Egyptian economy would be reduced to zero."[20]

American experts had predicted this situation (as noted in the
previous chapter) as early as 1964, when Walt Rostow, then chairman of the State Department's Policy Planning Council, forwarded
a memorandum to President Johnson on April 14 of that year, authored by Middle East expert William R. Polk, proposing an answer
to the key questions about how the United States could go about
getting what it wanted from Egypt. It was the best statement of the
problem he had seen, said Rostow, laying out why it was necessary
"to maintain the delicate stick and carrot balance with Cairo."
Egypt's prospects, and therefore its usefulness to the United States,
insisted Polk, depended on economic growth.[21]

The problem for Sadat was to force a change in American "inac-
tivity." As his complaints about Nasser's economic policies suggested,
Sadat was disillusioned about the Marxist tinge that had, as he saw
matters, ruined prospects for Egyptian "socialism." On several occasions he would assert that the United States held 99 percent of the

cards. He had visited the United States in 1964 and come away an admirer of the American economic system, and with a conviction that "United States involvement in the pursuit of his internal and external goals was a practical necessity. The trick . . . was to attract American interest in Egypt's predicament and to persuade the U.S. government to play the cards it held."[22]

The Crossing

After several false starts, Sadat managed to get a special emissary admitted to the Oval Office in late February 1973. Before the Egyptian arrived, Nixon had received a letter from the Yugoslav leader, Tito, who told him that he had met with Sadat and agreed with him that the present situation was intolerable. The rights of Arab peoples, including the Palestinians, must be part of a final settlement. He, Tito, wanted the American president to know that nonaligned nations stood behind Egypt's demands, although détente had significantly weakened the neutralist bloc. What followed was more interesting, as Sadat had told Tito that he was ready to take additional steps to secure peace: "Egypt also takes as its point of departure the reality of the existence of the state of Israel." From that "point" onward discussions about formal diplomatic recognition of Israel was really a negotiating point about a final settlement, not a retreat from this assertion.[23]

Henry Kissinger appeared briefly at the outset of the tête-à-tête with Sadat's emissary, explaining that he must not stay because it was important to maintain the impression that the State Department still had charge of Middle Eastern affairs. Kissinger had ceded "control" of that aspect of American policy, in large part, not only because of his Vietnam and China "duties," but also because that area promised little but grief, given all the cross-currents with domestic politics. Nixon was gracious enough, however, remarking that he had greatly enjoyed his 1963 visit to Egypt, felt respect for Nasser, and wished to play a part in building a permanent peace. He then invited his visitor, Hafez Ismail, Sadat's national security adviser, to give a frank expression of Egypt's point of view on all matters.[24]

Ismail took up the challenge and laid out Cairo's case. Egypt had no wish to be part of the sphere of influence of any country, he began, and desired only to play its historic role in the Middle East. With a strong Egypt, the Middle East was strong; with a weak Egypt, the Middle East was weak. In short order, then, Ismail had shoved aside Nasser's ambition to play a leading role as leader of the neutralist bloc, in favor of Nile Valley nationalism. The cause of U.S.-Egyptian frictions—the only cause, he went on—was the total military and political backing Washington gave to Israel. One day, he predicted, Israel would seek to get the United States out of the Middle East, just as it had gotten rid of Great Britain when it stood in the way.[25]

Here was another fascinating shift Nixon could hardly miss, because Egyptian determination to remove the British antedated the struggle that armed Zionist terrorists had undertaken. Now, Ismail seemed to be saying, Egypt would welcome greater influence by Britain's successor in the region. The central issue, he said, was Israel's determination to keep the lands it had acquired by war, and to deny the Palestinians any sort of a decent settlement of the refugee problem. What Israel must do, in other words, was behave as a Middle Eastern state, stop relying on outside aid that gave it a special position over all others, put an end to immigration, and cut its ties with world Zionism. Ismail could not really have expected a favorable response to those demands, but what he was looking for were American counterproposals.

Nixon gave him little in return. "Instant peace is [a] dream," the president told Ismail. "Permanent peace can't be assured, but some movement off dead center is a major goal." Nixon then launched on a discussion of why the peace process had to go along at a slow pace, moving from one interim stopping point to another. He did assure Ismail that the United States would not seek to trap Egypt at some place where Israel would be happy to call it all even. "You have my word. . . . This must be the beginning of a dialogue." He and Kissinger should put their minds together to see what the next steps must be; but it was crucial that everything be kept a secret. Nothing could be achieved without such precautions. The president added that secrecy was needed as much for the Egyptians to protect themselves against radical extremists as it was for the United States. "This is very sensitive—it must be kept quiet and private."[26]

During the conversation, according to Egyptian notes of the meeting, Nixon observed that the Israelis felt they would be giving up very material advantages and Cairo would have to consider what it was prepared to offer to induce them to take part in the process toward a permanent settlement. The concessions expected were territorial and political, even though Egypt was actually the occupied country. It was here that the president introduced the formula "sovereignty and security" as the key phrase for a successful mediation, with the accompanying implication that there could be no blanket settlement of "land for peace"—that is, Israel giving up the occupied areas of the Sinai, the Golan Heights, and the West Bank in exchange for peace. Instead there would have to be a series of bilateral agreements.[27]

As Cairo saw the result of the White House meeting, American insistence on secrecy was determined by a desire to keep the Russians out of the talks, yet not disturb the atmosphere of the "Spirit of Moscow." The desire to work for individual agreements was a natural follow-up to traditional policies of pursuing a "bicycle spoke" bilateral approach that would discourage the reemergence of a Nasser-like Arab "front" against Western interests. (The party most likely to suffer from that approach, of course, were the Palestinians, who lacked a state to negotiate anything by way of a settlement with Israel.) "The end result," concluded Mohamed Heikal, still a Sadat adviser, although an increasingly skeptical one, "should be a *Pax Americana* guaranteeing American interests in the area."[28]

Over the next months there was scarcely anything stirring as Egypt felt its economy sinking, its reputation abroad suffering, and its Arab allies unforgiving of its passivity. A second Russian-American summit occurred, and around the edges of that meeting Kissinger met with Ismail to assure him that the superpowers were working on a framework for negotiations. On one occasion Kissinger told Ismail that very little could be accomplished before Israeli elections in October.[29] During their conversations, Ismail raised the issues of America's increased military and technological aid to Israel, the White House's inability to resist congressional demands for pressure on Russia to increase Jewish emigration to Israel, and its total support for Israel. What options were left to Egypt? Either it would have to accept the current situation as permanent, make enormous concessions for peace, or take military action. Kissinger asked about that last option, and Ismail demurred. It would be too "adventurous" for now; what he meant was in the longer term.[30]

The ambassador had accomplished his purpose, even though he seemed to dismiss a near-future military action. What had been at least a wisp of a changed atmosphere in February, however, had now disappeared in the summer heat. One day Mohamed Heikal said to Sadat, "I'm afraid it looks as though the détente is going to become a reality and impose itself on us before we can impose ourselves on it. The détente will set conditions for the Middle East problem instead of the Middle East problem setting conditions for the détente." "Maybe," Sadat answered, "we will just be able to catch the last part of the tail of the détente."[31]

In the late summer of 1973, Sadat began patching up a détente of his own both at home and among other Arab countries. He forgave critics and reinstated some enemies; he traveled to Libya to calm a fire-eating Gaddafi and to Jordan to meet with King Hussein. He also traveled to Saudi Arabia in search of a new weapon, oil, which could be wielded against Israel's allies. And on the third anniversary of Nasser's death he spoke at a public ceremony: "We know our goal and are determined to reach it. There is no effort, no sacrifice that we shall not accept in order to do so. I won't promise anything or go into details. But I shall simply say that the liberation of our territory is the fundamental task before us. With God's help we shall carry it out, we shall succeed, we shall regain what is ours. That is the will of our people, the will of our nation. It is the will of God."[32]

Given all his previous rhetorical salvos about taking dramatic action, and "Year of Decisions," followed by nothing, it was not surprising that Sadat was not taken seriously this time. The most that was expected was a series of pinprick attacks. Only recently Israel had shot down more than ten Syrian jet fighters with hardly more reaction than a raised voice from Cairo. When Kissinger became secretary of state in September 1973 while still holding the position of national security adviser, he promised Arab ambassadors that they should not pay attention to his Jewish heritage, because he would be an evenhanded protector of American interests, not an Israeli partisan. Yet since 1971, military aid credits to Israeli had increased nearly tenfold from the end of the 1960s: $545 million in 1971, $300 million the next year, and $307 million in the third. And despite what Nixon had told Ismail, noted William B. Quandt, who would himself be part of a later peace process, "Kissinger was not convinced of the need for a major American initiative in the Middle East."[33]

And why should he be? it was argued. Sadat had divorced himself from the Soviets and was stuck with aging military weapons, the Egyptian economy was barely treading water, and Israel had an overwhelming military advantage on the ground and in the air. But those were the very reasons why Egypt would attack. And so it did on Yom Kippur, October 6, 1973, when Egyptian troops carried out a successful crossing of the Suez Canal and began driving back the Israeli troops. Syria also joined in the attacks against Israeli forces on the Golan Heights. What might have appeared as a desperate foray against overwhelming odds surprised the rest of the world, as all across the line the Egyptian army and air force performed much better than in 1967.

Yet despite the initial success of the attack in forcing an Israeli retreat, the *New York Times* sampling of experts concluded that Arabs simply did not calculate their behavior by Western standards. "Winning is less important than recovering a sense of dignity and honor" seemed to sum up the general opinion. The former head of State Department Intelligence, Thomas Hughes, added, "The Arabs do what they think they have to do even if it seems suicidal." And yet there was some feeling as well that perhaps the "Arabs" (a term often used in such articles in place of Egyptian or Syrian) did have in mind Kissinger's newly strengthened position as both secretary of state and national security adviser that would tempt him to impose an American peace plan and stick to it come what may. The Yom Kippur War, in this estimate, was also a preemptive strike against Kissinger—or, on the other hand, to force him to act under circumstances of Cairo's choosing.[34]

For a few days it even appeared that Egypt might win a great military victory over its longtime enemy as its advance in the Sinai sent a wave of panic through the Israeli leadership. A week into the war the Egyptians gambled on a big offensive, sending four hundred tanks into battle against the Israelis under cover of missile attacks. But once Egypt's infantry emerged ahead of the protective cover, the Israelis—using new weapons that had just arrived from the beginning of an airlift that signaled U.S. determination not to allow a defeat—crushed the offensive. The battle began at 6:15 in the morning of October 14; by noon it was all but over. The Egyptians had advanced less than twelve miles, "not far enough to achieve anything but their own destruction." And the Israeli commander telephoned Prime Minister Meir, "It's been a good day. We are back to being ourselves and they [the Egyptians] are back to being themselves."[35]

But it was the beginning of the war that had changed the situation. Egypt had demonstrated that the post-1967 status quo was simply not tenable, and could be shored up only by a constant infusion of more and more military aid, and a permanent war mentality that itself would produce instability. On the Cairo side, Sadat believed that he had restored Egypt's position in the eyes of the world, and could make concessions if he got the Sinai back and the oil wells restored to his control. He also believed that "the Crossing" meant that the United States would, as Nixon had promised, stay with the process to the end.

Sadat had risked a great deal. There were moments, as when part of his army was cut off and surrounded by Israeli forces on the banks of the Suez, that all appeared lost. He now had enough leverage with Washington, however, to have pressure brought on Israel to allow foodstuffs through to the besieged. Egypt's new leverage consisted not of moral suasion, but the oil weapon when Saudi Arabia's Prince Faisal declared an embargo on shipments to the United States and Europe. Other Arab oil producers followed suit. Citing American military support for Israel, the Organization of Arab Petroleum Exporting Countries cut off supplies to Europe, causing near panic in England and on the Continent. Long lines at gas pumps, emergency restrictions on the use of electric power in public buildings, and other restrictions followed. The prospect of long-term higher oil prices presaged a general economic crisis in the Western world. But perhaps more important, the actions of the oil producers signaled a tectonic shift in the relationship between the industrial countries and raw materials producers. For the first time since the beginning of European expansion and the establishment of the colonial world order, the upper hand now belonged to countries outside the industrial world. The greater firepower colonial armies had employed to maintain their rule, from the Gatling gun to modern automatic weapons, was essentially useless against the oil weapon, which exposed the vulnerability of the industrial nations.

Complicating the effort to deal with the immediate need to secure a cease-fire and peace negotiations was the unprecedented Watergate crisis. From a seemingly small-time break-in during the 1972 presidential campaign, carried out at Democratic headquarters in the Washington Watergate apartment complex by former CIA operatives paid by CREEP (Committee to Re-elect the President) funds, Watergate had now put the Oval Office underwater after the discovery that tapes existed that might incriminate Nixon in a possible cover-up engineered from his office. Nixon made matters worse, if that was possible, by firing the Watergate special prosecutor, Archibald Cox, who had subpoenaed the White House tapes. Rather than carry out the order to fire Cox, Attorney General Elliot Richardson and his number-two man, William Rukelshaus, both resigned. Nixon's apparent seclusion during and after the "Saturday Night Massacre," as the firings were called, fed speculation that the president was determined to save his presidential hide by creating an international crisis, no matter the risks involved.

It came about this way: during a dispute over whether Israel had broken a temporary truce by continuing to attack Egyptian positions, Moscow proposed joint military action to bring the situation under control—and suggested it would go in alone if necessary. Kissinger turned down the suggestion and ordered the nation's alert status to be raised, as if a general war was possible—an exclamation point, certainly, on Washington's refusal to consider any suggestion that might indicate willingness to see Russian troops in the area of Suez. The exact purpose of the exercise has always been debated. But here was an opportunity to skewer Soviet pretensions to pose as Arab defenders against Israeli-American imperialism. Ever since the 1956 crisis when Khrushchev brandished ICBMs at Britain, France, and Israel, American leaders had yearned for such an opportunity to call Moscow's bluff, if it was that, or force a humiliating back-down if the Soviets actually meant to intervene.

Washington had not taken time to consult its allies, however, and to its dismay, NATO balked at approving use of European airspace to carry out maneuvers that would inflame the situation. Some European nations and Japan publicly sought to disassociate themselves from the U.S. Middle East policy. Whereas in 1967 opinion in the United Nations had been pro-Israel, except for the Arab countries and their supporters, now world opinion had swung the other way, despite Egypt's role in initiating the conflict.

So Washington did not hold all the winning cards after all. Kissinger complained in his memoirs, "Our allies did not take comfort from the fact—as they might have—that even during the crisis of authority over Watergate, the United States was prepared to run a major risk to defend the global equilibrium. Instead, they concentrated on the indisputable fact that there had been no prior consultation over an alert that involved U.S. troops stationed in Europe." The crisis in "global equilibrium," then, was the issue, an abstraction not everyone agreed was really at stake, nor did Kissinger's plea that there was not time for consultations given the Soviet démarche satisfy his international critics.[36]

If things were not bad enough with the allies—who, Kissinger admitted, did have a case, if not a compelling one to his mind—Kissinger faced questions at home from reporters about the likelihood Nixon had seized on a diplomatic note to divert attention from his Watergate troubles. Kissinger replied—more in sorrow than anger—that such questions were unworthy and a disservice to the American government's integrity. He added, however, that, "One cannot have a crisis of authority in a society for a period of months without paying a price somewhere along the line." Perhaps the Soviets had acted as they had because they believed the government had been weakened by the Watergate furor.[37]

In Cairo, the situation looked a lot better, even though the United States had come to Israel's rescue with large-scale arms shipments. Sadat could claim to potential critics in the Arab world (and outside) that without this aid, his forces would have accomplished their major goal of recapturing the Sinai. By making Israeli dependence on American support even more imperative, on the other hand, he had actually increased his leverage. Nasser had said late in life, and Sadat firmly believed, that the Russians could give Egypt arms, but not peace. Only the United States could do that, but something had needed to be done to force the issue, something that would persuade Washington it had to put pressure on Israel. The Crossing, in this estimation, had made Israel weaker diplomatically, because it was more reliant on Washington's approval.

How quickly Sadat adapted to the situation on the battlefield—and the uses he could make of the successful Israeli counterattacks—demonstrated considerable political skill. Kissinger went overboard later in comparing him to the German unifier, Otto von Bismarck, but nevertheless, Sadat accomplished goals by adroit maneuvering that caught both his supporters and critics by surprise, from the time of the October War through the Camp David meetings five years later. Addressing the People's Assembly soon after the war began, Sadat had boasted that the flood of American weapons to the Israeli side did not frighten Egypt. His audience had gone wild. But two weeks later, with his armed forces in retreat, he told foreign correspondents that the United States had shipped powerful new weapons, previously unused weapons, that Egypt did not have an answer for, weapons that destroyed his tanks and his missile batteries. He compared the American effort to innovations in World War II. "I recalled," he would write in his memoirs, "what the United States had done on the German front during World War II, and then on the Japanese front." He even raised the specter of the A-bombs on Hiroshima and Nagasaki. He told foreign correspondents: "I am not going to fight America—I fought the Israelis for eleven days . . . but I am not ready to fight America." Given these words, what followed amazed his listeners. "I can say that America's stand with regard to the establishment of peace is a constructive one."[38]

With Henry Kissinger's help, it seemed, Egypt had found a way to disentangle itself from its old partner, the Soviet Union. "A mere twenty-four hours after the United States had demonstrated, with its worldwide nuclear alert, to what extraordinary lengths it was ready to go to in support of its Israeli protégé, [Egyptian foreign minister] Ismail Fahmi, in Washington, was posing with Dr. Kissinger's arm round his waist. Two days later, the pictures graced the front pages of Cairo's newspapers; readers were speechless with shock."[39]

Then came the beginning of "shuttle diplomacy." Kissinger sent word that he wanted to come to Cairo. He arrived in the Egyptian capital on November 5, 1973, for his first meeting with Sadat. They appeared together on the balcony of Tahra Palace in suburban Cairo, an incongruous pair, writes Kissinger biographer Walter Isaacson: "Representing America to the Arab world was a plump, German-born Jew wearing an ill-fitting, rumpled blue suit; greeting him as if a long-lost friend was a tall, erect, swarthy former terrorist, peasant born but aristocratic in bearing, wearing a crisply pressed khaki tunic with a Savile Row cashmere coat draped over his shoulders. Each was quickly and lastingly charmed." Kissinger began the talks, "You've created an international crisis, and that's why I've come to see you. What are your requests?"[40]

Henry and Anwar

Sadat lost no time, in November and again at a second meeting in December, in outlining his requests to "my friend Henry." He wanted Israel out of the Sinai, of course, but he was quite willing to accept the American position that a peace settlement had to be a step-by-step process. Where Egypt had held out against that idea for fear it would be interrupted at a favorable point for Israel, Sadat now placed his trust in Kissinger. From the outset, moreover, Sadat agreed, indeed volunteered, that Egypt would not make its policy dependent on an "Arab" consensus of what constituted a satisfactory solution. Since Syrian demands on the Golan Heights were likely to be a major stumbling block, this was very good news to Washington.

Even before the American secretary of state finished getting his papers out of his briefcase, Sadat told him he was far less interested in temporary truce lines than planning out an overall strategy. He talked a bit about what he called the failure of the "socialist experience." He wanted to develop the country along other lines, as he had already discussed with the American banker David Rockefeller. He had one specific request for the immediate future: he wanted the United States to become responsible for his personal safety— because he knew that there were those plotting against him: Russians, Arabs, and even some inside his own country![41]

Sadat's request for the United States to organize his personal bodyguards as he made unpopular decisions was startling in a number of ways. Of course, ever since the 1953 restoration of the shah to the Peacock Throne that ended—for a generation—the threat of an Iranian revolution, the CIA had been deeply involved in a similar exercise to build up the secret police in that country. But the forwardness of Sadat's approach, with its repudiation of Nasser's fundamental desire for nonalignment, went beyond anything Kissinger had expected. It sent a message almost as important as those from Indian princes to British viceroys a century earlier requesting protectorate status. Whatever he felt about the meaning of the request, Kissinger promised it would be answered.

Sadat's special bodyguards were sent to the United States for training. A new police unit trained in counterterrorism was established in Cairo. "A CIA employee called John Fiz, who could read and speak Arabic, was installed in the presidential office and had the task of dealing with all matters regarding security."[42] Even in the absence of a formal treaty, what began in November 1973 was both symbolically and actually a new military alliance—instigated by Sadat, and linking the United States to Egypt and Iran. There was no formal treaty, but there need not be now. In the 1950s Nasser had fought against the Baghdad Pact as essentially a control mechanism Dulles had invented to contain and shape Arab nationalism; now Sadat was embracing the role of regional stabilizer. The final pieces would not be put in place until the Sinai Agreement of September 1975, and Sadat's trips to Tel Aviv and the Camp David peace conference, but the outline was already there.

During his second meeting with Kissinger, in December, Sadat elaborated on his position vis-à-vis the Soviets. He had accompanied Nasser on his last trip to Moscow, he said, and Nasser had returned broken-hearted and ill. Sadat said that he himself always felt humiliated after trips to the Soviet Union. Yet he knew he must rely on Russian arms in the near future. He would rather have American arms but understood how difficult that would be for Washington. Nor was it possible to break completely with the Soviets "before he could point to a concrete achievement." It was just the right mix of arguments to impress Kissinger that he was dealing with a "statesman" of some consequence.[43]

For his part, Kissinger asked for help with Saudi Arabia and the others in getting the oil embargo lifted. Even before the first meeting in Cairo, the secretary of state had said that "our desire [is] to have Sadat, once the ceasefire is consolidated, urge Faisal to relax the oil boycott when negotiations begin." It was important to let Sadat know that American ability to stay close to Egypt in the peace negotiations to follow could not be sustained over the necessary period of time if the oil situation did not improve.[44]

Immediately after the December meeting, Sadat sent word to Kissinger that Israeli tactics in delaying a stable cease-fire were aimed, as always, at disrupting any genuine improvement in Arab-American relations, and the outline he had presented to him to make progress had stalled. "The situation on the ground continues to be very tense," Sadat said. Kissinger admitted to Ambassador Ashraf Ghorbal that Egypt had received "many expressions of intentions by well-meaning U.S. officials previously, but they have generally not produced results." He meant to produce results now; but, inevitably, he needed time to prepare American public opinion. "We have, moreover, worked hard on Israel at the same time." But what about American military supplies to Israel, asked Ghorbal; they are still continuing—what was Cairo to think? "It is our impression," Kissinger replied, that Arab countries were receiving more than Israel. "In any case," he continued, "this is no longer the issue. The Israelis now know how dependent they are on the U.S. and that means they are going to listen to us."[45]

It now looked very much as if Sadat's calculation in launching the Crossing had been on target. In addition, where the United States had once left Egypt to fend for itself with the Soviet Union, an unsatisfactory indirect process for negotiations, it appeared that Washington was operating in certain respects as Egypt's advocate with Tel Aviv. Nixon followed up Kissinger's comments to the ambassador with a letter to Sadat confirming that his administration would present the arguments for its disengagement plan to Israeli defense minister Moshe Dayan when he arrived in Washington. "For my part, I pledge myself to do everything in my power to ensure that my second term as president will be remembered as the period in which the United States developed a new and productive relationship with Egypt and the Arab world."[46]

In the letter, Nixon made another appeal for Egyptian aid in lifting the oil embargo. It was essential that it be ended at once, and not wait to the end of current talks on disengagement. "With the opening of the talks on disengagement, we have now reached the stage where the United States influence could prove decisive." By January 18, 1974, Kissinger had negotiated an Israeli troop withdrawal from parts of the Sinai, and the promise of a negotiated settlement between Israel and Syria was sufficient to convince Arab oil producers to lift the embargo in March 1974.

Prospects for a lasting settlement that would return the Sinai oil fields to Egypt were still uncertain, however. Kissinger and Sadat met again at the end of April 1974. The Egyptian joked that Leonid Brezhnev had sent him a warning not to trust Kissinger. This led into a discussion of the difficulties "Henry" was having with the recalcitrant Syrians, who remained stubborn about reclaiming all the Golan Heights. Unlike Egypt, which had real military leverage in the Sinai, the Syrians were unable to do much about the Israeli salient. If Damascus was unhappy with what Kissinger could get for them, and wanted to go to war, would Egypt support Syria? "No, definitely not," promised Sadat. Exchanges between the two like this one had become almost ritualistic. Kissinger would then in-form Sadat of progress on other fronts outside the area of territorial conflict. He had been active in seeking sources for economic aid to Egypt in European countries—West Germany, for example. Willy Brandt had visited Cairo recently, replied Sadat, where it was agreed that a bilateral committee would be set up to study the matter of how aid could be best accomplished.[47]

Work was going forward, as well, on the clearing of the Suez Ca-nal, with the United States supplying several million dollars to speed up the progress. Referring to American helicopters being used in mine clearance, Sadat "half-jokingly" said he wanted to keep these. "The Secretary suggested at the conclusion of the operation, one might be left behind." This vignette suggested a larger reality behind the Egyptian-American dialogue: Sadat had achieved his goal of get-ting the United States involved, but he was still the supplicant. Everything had *not* changed, obviously. The Egyptians were now trying to nudge the United States to find a way to supply needed arms. Foreign Minister Ismail Fahmi told Kissinger that the Soviet Union was offering more arms than Egypt was asking, but not the replacements Cairo really needed. Kissinger took the hint and sug-gested they get arms from India, "and we could make it up in eco-nomic aid." Fahmi then asked the real question. "When will you deal with us openly?" The end of the year, said Kissinger, but first there had to be a Syrian disengagement. "Then a next step with you. . . . I will talk to Sadat. Then we will start a military program."[48]

As these conversations continued, Kissinger added new countries to the list of those he had encouraged to send economic aid to Egypt: Great Britain and even, remarkably, China. And in regard to arms sales, it was still too soon to talk about very much from the United States, but Kissinger had an idea that arms could be sold to Saudi Arabia or Kuwait and then transferred to Egypt. He warned that Israel had started a campaign in the United States against arms for Egypt. It was essential, therefore, to avoid discussing the subject publicly. They might even try to kill bills for economic aid. The talk went on this way over several meetings. Sadat thought the list of weapons that Kissinger suggested could be included when direct arms sales began was "marvelous." But it was becoming something of a desert mirage, always gleaming out ahead, but fading away the closer one got to where the oasis was supposed to be.[49]

When Sadat raised more questions, Kissinger put him off by saying that it would not be wise to talk about a "final settlement," because Egypt would then be accused of attempting to make a separate peace. Kissinger's concern for Sadat's reputation in the Arab world was no doubt genuine, but he was also able to use that ploy because of the various pledges the Egyptian leader had given him that he would not fight for Syria's goals, or for those of the Palestinians. It had been agreed between them that Washington would overlook Egyptian rhetoric in the United Nations and other places, because it was just that, rhetoric, not to be confused with policy.

Sadat pressed hardest on the question of the Sinai oil wells, complaining "Israel had already taken six million tons of Egyptian oil." He planned to demand compensation for what had been expropriated in this manner. Kissinger responded by asking what would Egypt do, in return, by way of compensation for the territorial compromises Israel was being asked to make? Sadat replied somewhat sharply that the Israelis should by now be convinced of his determination to make peace. That was compromise enough. After all, all the land they were talking about had come to Israel by military conquest.[50]

Behind Kissinger's questions was Washington's concern that Egypt, if no longer allied to the Soviet Union, was still as much a problem as it has always been, especially in Congress, where large-scale aid, especially before a final settlement, would have a rough time getting accepted. The memory of the recent oil embargo made the Arabs seem less like trustworthy friends than schemers ready to take advantage of any opportunity to improve their position, literally, at American expense. Although both Nixon (and then Gerald Ford) were sincere in promising that the United States would be there to the end, the administration was not above volunteering all sorts of suggestions about the transfer of weapons from Arab countries, or sales from Great Britain and other places, that it knew would not be approved, given the tough requirements Congress put on all credits and cash exports.[51]

Kissinger had promised, for example, that the question of arms sales for Egypt could be taken up in the fall of 1974. On another trip to Cairo in November—now for the new president, Gerald Ford—he had to admit that it could not be done. Moreover, he had to report additional sales to Israel, which he sought to convince Egyptian leaders were actually designed to put pressure on Tel Aviv. "As you know," he began, "our strategy is to use arms assistance to get the Israelis to take the kind of decisions which will make practical reconciliation in negotiations possible." As for Egypt, he had to report that the third-country transfers he had talked about could not be done "in the way in which we discussed it together." President Ford would now have to decide what he could do. "It cannot be done in any other way than openly. I suppose this would raise a huge public debate in the United States."[52]

Sadat showed more resistance to his friend's arguments in this conversation than he had before. Kissinger had also asked for help with Faisal to ward off another oil boycott if an early settlement was not reached, and with Syrian opposition to settling without getting everything it wanted. What should he tell Syrian president Hafiz al-Assad about their conversation? Nothing, said Sadat. "Tell him that you have not offered anything concrete. Incidentally, I cannot open the Suez Canal until there is more progress." Kissinger was taken aback. "You will be blamed for breaking the Disengagement Agreement if you do this. I need to tell the Israelis that you are going to go ahead on the opening of the Canal." Sadat did not yield as usual. "This time, Henry, you must put the squeeze on them. The situation needs it. They must feel that you and we are planning together."[53]

"The Arabs must help," Kissinger insisted. Sadat brushed that aside. "I need to get the oil, and I need to have the passes. This is the minimum, Henry."

Another Dramatic New Initiative

The days of "Henry and Anwar" were growing short. Shuttle diplomacy continued, becoming less effective than in the early days after

the October War. In August 1974, the Watergate crisis had finally
ended with Nixon's resignation and Gerald Ford's surprising elevation to the Oval Office as an unelected president. The changeover
illustrated the difficulty with the Nixon-Kissinger "step-by-step" approach. It had been undertaken, purposely so, without a clear picture of what a final peace would look like. Egypt had been the
easiest to deal with, of course, because Cairo had the most to gain,
and the Israelis were not entirely convinced that being in the Sinai
was best in the long run for their security needs. With Syria and the
West Bank, however, there were additional motivations that helped
to freeze matters on those fronts. Syria continued to push, moreover, for a general settlement made by all the parties, not individual
arrangements that would isolate each of the countries in unequal
negotiating positions. The Palestinians had the most to lose by the
"step-by-step" procedure. Keeping Egypt and Syria from joining together was therefore imperative for Washington. Sadat had given
pledges he would not support Syria if it went to war, a war Damascus was sure to lose, but which would raise again Arab determination to use the oil weapon.

Back in early 1973, a special Egyptian emissary had argued with
Nixon that a strong Egypt meant a strong Middle East, and a weak
Egypt would mean a weak Middle East. The argument was also an
appeal for American aid. The same point could be made to Gerald
Ford, for the problem was how to give Egypt enough to keep it in
the "process," without at the same time stirring up a furor in Congress. Negotiations over the Sinai continued to stall, with the Israelis insisting that Egypt make a formal statement of renunciation of
belligerency. Sadat said that was precisely what he had feared would
happen all along. Once Egypt promised not to go to war, nothing
further would happen, and Israel would have no reason to return
the oil fields or allow Egyptian military forces to occupy the vital
passes. There were instances, moreover, where such a promise could
not be reconciled with, say, an outright attack by Israel on Syria.
Sadat had pledged not to support Syria if it opted for war, but he
could never promise not to come to Damascus's aid in the case of
an Israeli invasion. No Egyptian leader could promise such a thing

and survive. Kissinger pleaded that he was trying very hard, and the Israelis were trying very hard. Unfortunately, they had made a public statement that they would not give up the passes and the oil fields without a nonbelligerency pledge. The most Sadat would give up was the right to fortify the eastern end of the passes.

An agreement worked out in March 1975 fell apart over the nonbelligerency pledge, and things plummeted back to step one. Sadat met with Ford and Kissinger in Salzburg, Austria, on June 1. On the eve of this meeting, a letter signed by seventy-six senators had declared that the White House needed to "be responsive to Israel's economic and military needs." Ford had told Sadat that half of those who signed the letter had not even read it, let alone understood what it meant. But the letter also illustrated the limited freedom of action the president had in Middle Eastern affairs. After Vietnam, a general reaction against presidential unilateralism in foreign policy set the tone in Washington, a situation that further hampered efforts to make good on promises of economic aid to Egypt.

Sadat helped move things along by announcing on June 5, 1975, that he would reopen the Suez Canal—yet another concession he had been withholding pending a signed agreement. There also emerged a new willingness on Washington's side to consider Americans as part of a buffer force between the Israelis and Egyptians. Hard negotiations over the summer led to an agreement on September 4, 1975, dubbed Sinai II. It was accompanied by several bilateral secret agreements. In these Israel gained promises of oil supplies to make up for what it lost in giving back the oil fields, as well as assurances the administration would look favorably on its requests for F-16 aircraft and Pershing missiles with conventional warheads. And there was more. The United States agreed that it would not recognize or negotiate with the PLO unless it recognized Israel's right to exist. Ford also sent a letter to Prime Minister Rabin that the United States had not developed a position on the borders between Israel and Syria. In any consideration of this matter, the president said, he would give great weight to Israel's position that it must remain on the Golan Heights. The only bilateral agreement with Egypt, on the other hand, was a promise to try to bring about

Syrian-Israeli negotiations, to provide assistance for its early warning system in the buffer zone, and to "consult" with Cairo on any Israeli violations of the agreement. *Time* magazine's bureau chief in Jerusalem, Donald Neff, summed up the meaning of the agreements and bilateral commitments: "To state it crudely, it appears that since the U.S. cannot negotiate peace in the Middle East, it will buy it."[54]

While Sinai II came as a relief, or, better put, a respite, nothing permanent had been settled. Sadat had long ago conceded that he would not do more than give rhetorical support to the idea of an overall "Arab" settlement, but the bilateral commitments Ford gave to the Israelis made it definite that Egypt had been isolated. Nasser had followed the path of taking arms from Moscow in an attempt to establish a neutral position in the Cold War, not for Egypt alone, but for the Arab countries, with, of course, himself as the leader. Sadat began shedding that legacy as soon as he succeeded Nasser, in favor of Nile Valley nationalism, although he continued to insist that Egypt had to play the leading role as the most important Arab country—at least to the United States.

After Sinai II was signed, it did become easier for Egypt to obtain arms from the West—if on far less favorable terms than those given to Israel. In the previous twenty years, Egypt had purchased a total of $2.2 billion in arms from the East bloc, and repaid some of its debt; in the next seven years, however, Cairo indebted itself for $6.6 billon in arms from the West. "By switching to America as Egypt's source for arms Sadat ensured that there would never be any alternative to negotiating with Israel," according to Mohamed Heikal. It was still going to be hard, however, for Sadat to get Israel to negotiate—until he finally made it clear that not only would he not go to war in support of Egyptian claims, but also not to prevent Israeli ambitions elsewhere. And even with all that, Washington guaranteed that Israel would be guaranteed superiority in arms.[55]

If Russia was a less desirable political partner it was also, in Sadat's view, a poor model for Egypt economically. Disproportionately heavy spending on the military was one reason for Egypt's declining economy, but it was also a result of discouraging the anemic private sector. It was another Nasser legacy, Sadat believed. With those beliefs guiding him, he set out to encourage foreign investment. The new policy he called *Infitah*, or "opening," formally launched in an April 1974 speech. The delays in the peace process held up economic aid to Egypt, but the promises the Ford administration made to supply both food under various government programs and development loans were realized. The lack of economic infrastructure to support higher levels of foreign investment remained a key problem, however. On the eve of Sadat's state visit to the United States after the signing of Sinai II, Henry Kissinger summed up the problem well. Egypt's economy was a mess, he advised President Ford, because of Nasser's policy of nationalization of industry, a labor system based on full employment and featherbedding, and reliance on short-term, high-interest commercial loans. What made the next few years critical to Sadat's success, moreover, was the danger that other Arab countries, angry at his policies, would "seriously cut their payments to Egypt." Sadat will therefore "be looking to us to keep up the momentum of the peace-seeking process and encourage continued Arab assistance as well [and] provide important public and private economic assistance on our own."[56]

Jimmy Carter defeated Ford in the 1976 election and made an early promise to devote himself to finding a political solution that would include a homeland for Palestinian refugees "who had suffered for many, many years."[57] Prospects for a new American policy foundered, however, when Carter provoked a storm of opposition by suggesting the Soviet Union be included in fashioning an overall peace settlement. In May 1977, Menachem Begin's Likud Party came into power, and the new prime minister struck an inflexible note on any advance on the Sinai II agreement, especially any that involved the Soviet Union.

Egypt's economic situation continued to worsen despite Sadat's courting of foreign investment; if anything, it was said, his policies had produced a sorry amalgam of the worst of socialism and the worst of capitalism. In January 1977, acting on recommendations from the International Monetary Fund (IMF) about necessary reforms to encourage investments, Cairo ended government food subsidies and other supports, triggering the most serious protests and riots since Nasser's time. These were put down, but there was a desperate note now in debates over economic policy.[58]

In mid-October 1976, Sadat had had a long conversation with the American ambassador, Hermann Eilts, about Cairo's difficulty in implementing the IMF recommendations. Washington had tried to help with "passing the hat" around to potential lenders to Egypt, and Sadat had been in discussions with Germany, Iran, and Saudi Arabia. Eilts told him that the major problem was the unhappiness of potential donors—Western, Arab, Japanese, and Iranian—because Egypt had not adopted the austerity measures. "I had to tell him in all frankness that, while we recognize the political problems that acceptance might entail, I thought he would have difficulty getting any responsible Western state to assist if these recommendations are not soon accepted."[59] The result had been the riots that threatened his government. Somehow, without American help initially, Sadat would have to find a way to force a new opening in the brick wall that confronted his diplomacy, one that would finally allow Egypt's economy to recover and flourish.

At the same time as he was deciding upon a dramatic step, Sadat received hints from Washington and Tel Aviv that direct talks with Begin were not only possible, but that Israel was ready to do serious business. Sadat's subsequent announcement that he would go to Israel to address the Knesset was something no one expected, and it sent a shock wave through the Arab world. Suddenly, the American media converged on Cairo, lauding Sadat as a true statesman. He would be named *Time* magazine's "Man of the Year." PLO leader Yasser Arafat had been advised by Sadat beforehand that he was going to make a statement he would want to hear. Arafat was furious when he heard what it was. King Khalid of Saudi Arabia offered up a prayer on the day the Egyptian leader left for Israel. "Oh God, grant that the aeroplane taking Sadat to Jerusalem may crash before it gets there, so that there may not be a scandal for all of us."[60]

"It was as if a messenger from Allah had descended to the Promised Land on a magic carpet," began *Time* magazine's account of

Sadat's arrival at Ben Gurion airport in an American-built Boeing
707. His plane had been escorted to its destination by four American-
built Israeli jet fighters. In Jerusalem, ten thousand policemen, two
thousand special security guards, and a special antiterrorist com-
mando unit stood in readiness for his visit to the Knesset. "We cannot guarantee his survival in Egypt," quipped an Israeli security
official, "but here with us he is as safe as if he were at his well-
protected palace." Sadat's speech was the strongest acknowledgment
he had yet made of Israel's right to exist. "You want to live with us in
this part of the world. We welcome you in sincerity. . . . Israel has
become a fait accompli recognized by the whole world."[61]

Sadat then called upon Israel to abandon its territorial conquests
in the 1967 war, and to recognize that the Palestinians deserved the
same opportunity for self-determination that Israel claimed in 1948.
"Even the U.S., your first and foremost ally, chose to face reality."
Begin's response was to remind his visitor of the long history of suffering and exile of the Jewish people, who "never for a day" had forgot-
ten that Eretz Israel was their homeland. And he called on other
Arab states, Syria, Jordan, and Lebanon, to "come and talk to us." He
added that he planned to open Israel to all visitors from Egypt, and
that he hoped to make a return visit to Egypt. "In these matters there
is reciprocity. One day, God willing, I shall visit Cairo, and I shall
also go to see the Pyramids." And he added, with a smile, "After all,
we helped to build them."[62]

The immediate aftermath of "Jerusalem" produced a problem for
both Sadat and Carter. Begin invited himself to Washington, wrote
William Quandt in his insider's account of the peace process, where
he hoped to have the administration endorse his proposals for opening direct negotiations on substantive issues. In response to Sadat's
appeal for an Israeli evacuation of the contested territories, Begin
proposed "home rule" for "Judea, Samaria, and the Gaza District."
Begin would claim after they met in Ismailia on Christmas Day that
Sadat was on the verge of accepting the proposed solution but had
been discouraged by his hard-line advisers. Whether that was so or
not, Sadat insisted that Begin had not grasped the importance of
the Jerusalem visit and wished to "haggle and tread on sovereignty."[63]

There matters stood until President Carter invited the two to come to Camp David in September 1978, to see if there was not some way to get past recrimination and into a serious dialogue. What emerged from Camp David after very long, and very tough, negotiations was an agreement on Sinai, and a general statement of principles about the ultimate future of the Palestinians—nothing more. The process for achieving even that much agreement involved President Carter meeting separately with Begin and Sadat until the final wording was worked out. Carter applied pressure on Begin to agree to a complete withdrawal from Sinai, but the Israeli premier turned down his efforts to get UN Resolution 242 adopted in full; all he would accept was language that made reference to "the legitimate rights of the Palestinian people." As in the past, there would be no real linkage between an Israeli-Egyptian peace treaty and the question of Palestinian authority—beyond the establishment of a committee composed of Egypt, Israel, and Jordan to oversee the transition to some form of autonomy over a five-year period. At the end of that time, supposedly, final decisions would be made on the future of the West Bank and Gaza.[64]

Carter hoped, like his predecessors, that by giving up linkage at Camp David in favor of an Egyptian-Israeli agreement, the participants would thereby engender the trust that would lead to bilateral negotiations between Israel and other Arab countries. And like his predecessor, he put up cash to sweeten the deal. According to Scott Kaufmann, "as part of the Camp David accords, Washington promised Egypt $1.5 billion in military aid, which Cairo used to buy three dozen F-4 fighter jets, hundreds of missiles, and numerous other weapons." For its signature, Israel received an offer of $3 billion in weapons and aid in building two airfields lost once it left the Sinai Peninsula. Begin hoped this would increase his leverage with all the parties.[65]

The End for Sadat

Within weeks of the signing of the Camp David Accords, Prime Minister Begin told the Carter administration that he was ready to sign a peace treaty with Egypt, but not to accept any wording "setting out a timetable or target date of any sort for negotiations or elections or setting up of a West Bank / Gaza interim regime." Sadat had tried to get some sort of an explicit linkage between the treaty coming into effect and West Bank / Gaza elections—but to no avail. As matters went forward in early 1979, moreover, Israel rejected any language that characterized its presence in Gaza as an "occupation."[66]

The treaty signing ceremony went ahead anyway on March 26, 1979, on the White House lawn in Washington. It was broadcast live on television, with special commentary by the BBC: the two leaders sealed the deal with a firm handshake, read its account, watched by a smiling President Jimmy Carter. Sadat then praised President Carter as "the man who performed the miracle." "Without exaggeration," he said, "what he did constitutes one of the greatest achievements of our time." Carter, however, was more cautious, saying the treaty was "a first step on a long and difficult road. . . . We must not minimize the obstacles that lie ahead."

In their speeches following the ceremony, Begin and Sadat re-vealed just how far there still was to go. Begin spoke emotionally of how the city of Jerusalem could never be divided, while Sadat was unreservedly frank about the question of Palestinian autonomy. News of the signing ceremony was greeted by angry demonstrations throughout the Arab world. Crowds stormed the Egyptian embassy in Kuwait. PLO leader Yasser Arafat told a rally in Lebanon that Sadat had betrayed the Egyptian people, and they would eventually eliminate him: "Let them sign what they like. False peace will not last."[67]

To protest the treaty, the Arab League moved out of Cairo and relocated in Tunis, a sign not only of Egypt's emerging isolation in the Arab world, but also of the new insignificance of the League itself. One of the few close friends Sadat had left in the Middle East was the shah of Iran, and when the 1979 Iranian Revolution top-pled him, the shah, fatally ill, and after an unhappy stay in Panama, was welcomed to Cairo with ceremony befitting a sitting monarch. President Carter was worried about what would happen if he went there. "Anwar's got enough problems without having us dump the

Shah in his lap." When he called Sadat to express his misgivings, Sadat reportedly replied, "Jimmy, don't you worry about Egypt. You worry about your hostages."[68]

Carter's difficulty trying to set free the hostages taken from the U.S. Embassy in Tehran the previous fall when Iranian students seized the building in anger over Washington's hosting the shah in his early exile would become a key issue in the 1980 presidential campaign and one of the reasons for Carter's defeat by Ronald Reagan. Hosting the shah in Egypt during his final days was one of the reasons for Sadat's assassination on October 6, 1981. One witness to the assassination was *New York Times* reporter William Farrell, who was in the reviewing stand erected for the anniversary of the beginning of the October War. Of humble origin, Farrell wrote, Anwar el-Sadat assumed power on Nasser's death. Sadat forged his own regime single-handedly. He was bent on moving his country into the late twentieth century by abandoning the alliance with the Soviet Union and embracing the West. His reputation was based "in large part" on the decision to journey to Jerusalem and then to Camp David. "That rule ended abruptly and violently today. As jet fighters roared overhead, the killers sprayed the reviewing stand with bullets while thousands of horrified people—officials, diplomats and journalists, including this correspondent—looked on."[69]

Seven hours after the assassination, Vice President Hosni Mubarak, an air force general who had distinguished himself in the October War, spoke to the nation. "I hereby declare in the name of the great soul passing away and in the name of the people, its constitutional institutions and its armed forces, that we are committed to all charters, treaties, and international obligations that Egypt has concluded."

5

THE $50 BILLION GAMBLE: THIRTY YEARS OF EGYPTIAN-AMERICAN CO-DEPENDENCE

General Petraeus, welcome to Egypt. Your visit will be, I hope, the first in a regular process of dialogue and consultation with Egyptian leaders who view the U.S.-Egyptian security partnership as the cornerstone of the bilateral relationship. This visit provides an opportunity for you to assess the state of our military partnership and to identify new opportunities.

—Ambassador Margaret Scobey, December 21, 2008

Even before the assassination of Anwar Sadat on October 6, 1981, the pressing challenge for Washington policymakers was the need to reward Egypt's leaders for making peace with Israel. Sadat's murder by extremists demonstrated that a serious response could not wait any longer. The most obvious answer, of course, was to provide Cairo with a reliable source of arms now that it had severed its military ties with the Soviet Union. The Carter administration had already begun to lay the foundations for a lasting relationship with Egypt by initiating sales of modern weapons on easy credit terms. Ever since the 1952 revolution, Egyptian-American relations had turned on the vexed question of finding a way to satisfy Cairo's desires without appearing to forsake the commitment to Israel's security. Secretary of State John Foster Dulles's failure to persuade Nasser to accept American conditions on military aid in the 1950s began twenty years of American-Egyptian wrangling that seemingly had no solution.

Sadat pointed the way out by taking on the burden of making peace with Israel. But almost immediately other new factors came into play. The 1979 Iranian Revolution removed the shah from the

Middle East power equation and left the Persian Gulf area without a strong American ally directly across from Saudi Arabia. Then came the hostage crisis for which the Carter administration seemed to have no answer. On top of those woes, the Soviet Union's military intervention in Afghanistan that began on December 25, 1979, led President Carter to declare that Moscow's decision constituted "the most serious threat to the peace since the second World War." His call for increased defense spending and the creation of a rapid deployment force to protect American interests in the area provided more impetus to the need to build up a strong position elsewhere in the Middle East, including—especially including—Egypt. Finally, there was the Iran-Iraq War, which continued through the decade of the 1980s. Before it ended in 1988 when Iran accepted a UN peace proposal, the war had cost $150 billion and perhaps more than a million lives in a conflict that resembled nothing so much as the massed armies fighting across the no-man's-lands of World War I.[1]

Iraq's Saddam Hussein used poison gas in that war, but the Reagan administration viewed the chemical weapons issue as primarily a public relations concern and did not allow it to take priority over the desire that Iraq should provide the force to contain Iran's Islamic revolution before it spread across the Middle East. The White House sent a special emissary to Saddam Hussein to convey this message, restored diplomatic relations with Baghdad (broken off at the time of the 1967 Six Days' War), and gave Iraq large export credits to enable purchases of more goods from the United States. Still, the United States had played both sides in the war. In an almost farcical attempt to reach out to supposed "moderates" inside Iran, a scheme was hatched for transferring antitank missiles to Tehran through Israel. Ostensibly, this aid was intended to help in the release of American hostages held in Lebanon by Muslim extremists with connections to Tehran, and to provide funds for Reagan's favorite anti-Communist guerrillas in Central America, the Contras. An underlying factor, however, was a concern expressed in an American intelligence estimate that Iran's "Khomeini regime is faltering" and that, as matters stood, the United States had no "cards to play" in the event of an upheaval.

The whole episode was fraught with so much intrigue and ill-conceived presumption about the motives and influence of the Iranian "moderates" who took part in the negotiations that, when it was exposed, "Iran-Contra" opened the Reagan administration to questions not merely about the extralegal nature of the dealings, but about its competence in managing anything to do with the Middle East.[2]

By contrast, relations with Egypt under its new leader, Hosni Mubarak, *appeared* to be much easier. In exchange for military aid that would total $1.5 billion yearly over the next three decades, second only to the aid extended to Israel, Mubarak would keep the peace treaty Sadat had signed in 1979, provide the United States with a number of other valuable assets, such as his ability to maintain contacts with the PLO's Yasser Arafat, and, eventually, to offer special services in the Global War on Terror (GWOT) that allowed George W. Bush to avoid some difficult questions about the use of torture in attempting to gain information about the September 11, 2001, attacks and possible future plots against American citizens and their property.

By the end of Mubarak's thirty-year reign, the American and Egyptian militaries were regularly involved in joint training maneuvers known as Bright Star, highlighted by American marines storming ashore near Alexandria to practice desert operations. Egyptian co-production of American Abrams tanks and other military hardware offered other benefits, moreover, to Mubarak's favored local industries. The Washington buzzword about these military connections was "interoperability." It perfectly suited the whole range of Egyptian-American relations while Mubarak reigned. The Egyptian ruler was well aware of his value to Washington, from the time of Ronald Reagan to that of Barack Obama. On several occasions, particularly when challenged by complaints of one sort or another—usually about political repression and civil liberties—Mubarak or his chief aides would remind the American ambassador in Cairo about the services Egypt performed and what Mubarak called the "untouchable compensation" he was owed in return—all those jet fighters and other military hardware that insured the army's health and loyalty.[3]

Mubarak Takes Over

Hosni Mubarak was seated close to President Sadat in the reviewing stand when the assassins turned their military vehicle out of
line and into the stands. Lieutenant Khalid al-Islambouli and three
other conspirators leaped out and tossed grenades into the crowd.
Islambouli then rushed forward, firing his machine gun at Sadat. "I
have killed the Pharaoh!" he cried out. Blood was everywhere. Eleven
others in the stand were killed, and many more wounded. But
somehow Mubarak, though wounded, escaped death. There would
be other attempts on the former air force general who had become
Sadat's favorite from the time of the October War, but none would
succeed. Over the years, a succession of American diplomats would
marvel at his survival skills.

Secretary of State Alexander Haig represented President Reagan
at Sadat's funeral. A few days after the assassination, Haig wrote
that he felt sure of the new Egyptian president's determination to
uphold the peace treaty with Israel and cooperate with the United
States in resisting any "threats from the Soviets and their surrogates"—
meaning he would not backtrack from Sadat's turn to the United
States. The principal worry, however, as the "very limited attendance"
at the funeral made clear, was that Egypt remained "seriously isolated
in the Arab world."[4]

Haig felt that the Arab-Israeli question could be put on hold for a
time as a "local issue," while the administration concentrated on its
tough new Cold War policies. That view prevailed for only a few
months, however, as an Israeli confrontation with PLO encamp-
ments in Lebanon exploded into an exchange of artillery fire and
rockets, and then an Israeli invasion. Before all that happened, Israel
had persuaded some in the Reagan administration that it could
handle the situation in Lebanon, and in doing so would also eliminate Syrian support for the PLO. The idea appealed to Haig and
those who agreed with his view because Damascus was the Soviet
Union's strongest ally in the region. But when Israel invaded Lebanon to eliminate the PLO force and Reagan saw the scenes of violence, he reacted by sending one of the harshest notes to an Israeli

prime minister ever dispatched by the White House, demanding that Menachem Begin agree to a cease-fire.

Already sidelined on a number of issues by other influential voices near the president, Haig was furious that his view that Israel should be permitted to finish the job was ignored. But the president was now listening to those other advisers, especially the man who would replace Haig, George P. Shultz.[5] Where Haig had been convinced Israel could do the United States a big favor by eliminating the PLO as an "irritant," the new secretary feared the Israeli invasion of Lebanon would force Egypt to change its policies and weaken America's position in the long run. Mubarak, meanwhile, had written an op-ed piece in the *Washington Post* about the Lebanon crisis that brought a very sympathetic response from the White House. Reagan wrote in a "Dear Hosny [sic]" letter that he agreed with the Egyptian leader that the questions involved went beyond the immediate location of the fighting. "Rather, that crisis has confronted us squarely with the need to move toward a solution of the Palestinian problem in all its aspects. I was particularly struck by your words that 'from the ashes of devastation and destruction, we must spare no effort to resurrect the spirit of peace and hope.'" The letter went on to praise Mubarak for Egypt's "unambiguous commitment to peace" and for standing by "that commitment despite the stresses of recent weeks." And, it added, "We want to proceed in this endeavor in full partnership with Egypt."[6]

Shultz—who was probably responsible for this letter—had an idea it would be possible to get around previous failures to realize the stalled Camp David promise of negotiations to resolve Palestinian questions by involving Jordan in order to co-opt Arafat's PLO. Israel's current position was that it would not negotiate with the PLO on anything until the PLO publicly recognized the Jewish state's legitimacy—and demonstrated its own right to represent all Palestinians, not just a faction. Shultz's new idea was that Israel should agree to give up much of the territory taken in the Six Days' War as part of a final settlement. He had no love for Arafat or his organization, but he imagined that if Jordan's King Hussein took the lead, the plight of the Palestinians would be put onto a different agenda. Israel showed no interest in the plan, and the vagueness of the final settlement fell short of PLO demands. The Reagan initiative, as it was known, never got off the ground, as it became clear Jordan could not move on its own, despite Washington's promises of military aid if Amman did its part. King Hussein called Reagan to give him the news that there was no prospect of developing a negotiating position the PLO would accept. "We in Jordan, having refused from the beginning to negotiate on behalf of the Palestinians, will neither act separately nor in lieu of anybody in Middle East peace negotiations."[7]

Meanwhile, the events after the Iranian Revolution had caused a reassessment among Arab nations leading to reconciliation between Egypt and the Arab League, which moved its headquarters back to Cairo from Tunis. A tilt toward Jordan as the negotiator of choice, therefore, was not likely to succeed without Cairo's backing. Reagan's reelection in 1984, however, encouraged Arab nations who had hopes for a renewed attempt to resolve the Palestinian question through an international conference at which Palestinians would form part of the Jordanian delegation. It had been previously stipulated by the American administration that the Palestinians involved in any negotiations would have to be acceptable to Israel, thus eliminating Arafat and others from taking part. With all these caveats, the possibility for real negotiations seemed remote. Even so, in early 1985 there was a parade of Arab leaders to Washington to see if some basis existed for hoping the new initiative would have a chance.

On February 11, 1985, Jordan and the PLO had signed a statement in which both parties agreed that their goal was a Jordanian-Palestinian confederation to be established once Israel had withdrawn from the territories taken in 1967. The first step in the negotiating process, proposed the Arab representatives, would be an American-Palestinian dialogue. Mubarak acted as the major spokesman for the Arab plan. The idea behind it was to find some way to involve the United States as Sadat had done with the October War. After a meeting with King Hussein at the Red Sea resort of Hurghada, Mubarak told reporters that he had never said the Palestinian delegates should not be PLO members. The Arab League had said that the PLO was the sole representative of the Palestinian people, he asserted, and "we cannot deviate from this because this is not our sole right."[8]

Hussein then told the reporters he fully agreed with the Egyptian leader and that this might be the last chance for peace. There was a very narrow window for hope. "It is the last chance. . . . It is up to the United States to decide." Mubarak went to Washington to press his idea, and attempted to sound a softer note. As he had said many times, he told reporters in the American capital, the delegation should include representatives from the occupied West Bank of the Jordan River, the Gaza Strip, as well as others mutually agreed to by the parties. "These are wide parameters. They provide ample scope—they should be put to use." Mubarak's proposed solution recalled, in fact, the 1978 Camp David Accords, which provided for a delegation to include elected mayors of West Bank cities as well as other Palestinian leaders to negotiate a final settlement. Israel had taken the position that the PLO was a terrorist organization and that no delegate with ties to Arafat's organization—which refused to recognize Israel's right to exist—could be part of any negotiations.

When reporters turned to administration officials to ask if the United States would indeed participate in preliminary talks with a Jordanian delegation that included Palestinians who were not part of the PLO—a backhanded way of putting the question of whether the United States would accept the Mubarak plan—the response was equally opaque: "The answer is, there is no answer to that." Behind the public scenes it was made clear to Mubarak and King Hussein that their attempt to foster negotiations between the United States and such a delegation was a nonstarter. Hussein was even warned that the arms he had been promised had no chance of congressional approval unless he committed Jordan to direct negotiations with Israel. Hussein gave his answer in a speech to the UN General Assembly. Jordan would negotiate directly with Israel "under suitable, acceptable supervision, directly and as soon as possible, in accordance with Security Council Resolutions 242 and 338." One month later, the U.S. Senate rebuffed Jordan's request for arms, stipulating that no major sales could take place until "direct and meaningful" negotiations had begun. Translating these two statements, Hussein had said that negotiations had to be on UN Resolution 242, which required Israeli withdrawal from the occupied territories, and the Senate Committee had said that Jordan must be prepared to extend full recognition to Israel, thereby bypassing the PLO. The administration finally withdrew the request for a $2 billion arms package for Jordan early in February 1986.[9]

What Mubarak learned from the events of 1985 and the attempt to start the peace process with a PLO-U.S. dialogue was that he could not repeat Sadat's successes, either in the October War or in setting the stage for Camp David. Despite Reagan's "Dear Hosny" letter about the need for a new attempt to find a solution and his promise to "proceed in this endeavor in full partnership with Egypt," there were definite limits on what Washington would entertain as a proposed agenda. Whether Israel would consent to the agenda was always a key factor in obtaining the American government's approval.

Complicating any idea of putting pressure on Israel to agree to an agenda for starting peace talks was the deepening involvement of the administration in what later became known as the Iran-Contra affair. Arab governments knew about the flow of arms to Iran via Israel, wrote William Quandt, and assumed American complicity in the deals at the same time that Washington seemed to be tilting toward Iraq in the Iran-Iraq War. "How could the two strands of policy be reconciled? At a time when American credibility was important for possible success of the peace process, Egypt and Jordan seem to have developed doubts about the reliability of the United States."[10]

At this point, there was very little Mubarak could offer his American benefactors in terms of a new Arab-Israeli peace initiative beyond the proposals he and King Hussein had launched in the past two years. For Mubarak the situation presented two aspects: one bad and the other not so bad. It was bad because his troubles at home were in part a consequence of Sadat's mission to Jerusalem and all that followed in terms of anger and frustration culminating in the assassination, and which now attached to him; it was not so bad because by advancing the failed proposals he had made himself an indispensable link to Yasser Arafat—an uncomfortable position, perhaps, but one that helped preserve his role in future negotiations (if any developed) and solidified his position in Washington.

The Internal Struggle

In the aftermath of Sadat's assassination, Egyptian police had swept up thousands of prospective conspirators. The actual perpetrators of the attack were put on trial, and Lieutenant Islambouli and the three other shooters were executed in April 1982. Twenty-three others were identified as part of the immediate conspiracy. Their trials and those of others arrested went on and on, lasting for nearly two years. One of Islambouli's comrades survived in prison until the Tahrir Square protests in January 2011 led to Mubarak's downfall, and he was released along with other long-held political prisoners. The most revealing aspect of Islambouli's motive was that he had acted after the blind Muslim cleric Omar Abdel-Rahman had issued a fatwa (or ruling on a point of Islamic law) approving the assassination. Abdel-Rahman would later turn up in New York as the mastermind behind the first attempt to blow up the World Trade Center, in 1993.

Also arrested in the sweep was another figure later to become famous in al-Qaeda, Ayman al-Zawahiri, a young physician from a middle-class professional family. A brilliant student, Zawahiri early on exhibited traits that would make him a leader, but one with a good deal of self-righteousness about his possession of the total truth. A major influence in his life was Sayyid Qutb, an intellectual leader of the Egyptian Islamic Jihad movement, who, with several companions, was executed by Nasser in 1966.[11]

Zawahiri was fifteen years old when Qutb went to the gallows, and was already in the process of forming an underground cell dedicated to overthrowing the government and establishing an Islamist state. What Zawahiri and Nasser agreed on was their belief in Egypt's unique destiny as the intellectual center of the Arab world. For Nasser, of course, it was all about escaping the Cold War straitjacket to lead the Arab countries into the modern era on their own terms. For Zawahiri it was also about finding the true meaning of Egypt's destiny, but only through Islam—a quest to reestablish the caliphate, the rule of Islamic clerics, who had not exercised real power since the thirteenth century. He believed that Egypt would become a rallying point for the rest of the Islamic world. "Then history would make a new turn, God willing," he would write later, "in the opposite direction against the empire of the United States and the world's Jewish government." Before dealing with the "distant enemy," however, it was necessary to defeat the "near enemy," for it would not be possible to succeed until Islam had reformed itself. Egypt was where the process had to begin.[12]

Zawahiri had not been part of the assassination conspiracy, but he was certainly a leader of the Egyptian Jihad. After medical school he served in the Egyptian army, then traveled to Afghanistan and became enthralled by the fight of the "Afghan freedom fighters," or mujahideen, against the Soviet Union. He also became excited by Iran's new ruler, the Ayatollah Ruhollah Khomeini, and supported the revolution in Iran with leaflets and cassette tapes urging all Islamic groups in Egypt to follow the Iranian example. His mission was not an easy one, to unite all the groups that professed a desire to overthrow the government in the name of Islam—"until Sadat's peace agreement with Israel united the disparate Islamist factions." There was also the new law sponsored by Sadat's wife that granted women the right to divorce, something not granted in the Quran. Sadat's last speech before his assassination ridiculed pious women who wore Islamic garb, and he banned the veil from universities. The radicals responded by calling Sadat a heretic, which under Islamic law was "an open invitation to assassination."[13]

Zawahiri's odyssey began during the trials, when he was recognized as a leader of the defendants, who, after he spoke, chanted in unison behind him, "The army of Mohammed will return, and we will defeat the Jews!" Zawahiri was ultimately released after three years in prison and resumed his medical practice for a time before going to Afghanistan to join in the fight against the Soviet Union. "It is as if 100 years were added to my life when I came to Afghanistan," he later wrote. After the victory of the Afghan resisters, he dedicated himself to the overthrow of the Egyptian government,

operating from Yemen and then Sudan. In 1993 he became head of
Egyptian Jihad, launching bloody attacks, including a famous one
against tourists in the Valley of the Kings. He was also the primary
figure in a plot to assassinate Mubarak during a meeting of the Organization of African Unity in Ethiopia in 1995, which failed when
a grenade launcher malfunctioned and Mubarak's limousine sped
back to the airport at Addis Ababa.[14] As a result of these activities
both Zawahiri and Osama bin Laden, who had also been involved
in financing the plot, were finally expelled from Sudan and went to
Afghanistan. It was there that bin Laden convinced his colleague
that it was time to think about striking the "far enemy" as the first
priority.

Mubarak's response to the wave of terrorism—the emergency laws
that had been promulgated after Sadat's assassination, the arrests and
secret trials, the widespread use of torture—went hand in hand with
economic policies that only helped to drive more and more Egyptians
into the kind of despair that produced extremists. His rule depended
upon the military's loyalty, which was purchased not simply by the
arms he obtained from the United States, but also by the favoritism
he bestowed on high-ranking officers who became capitalist "entre-
preneurs" owning increasing sections of the Egyptian economy. Retired officers expected, and received, special perks including titles to
lands that could be converted into expensive housing developments
or ownership of tourist hotels (a major contributor to Egypt's GDP),
or they became growers of agricultural products such as olive oil. Although businessmen might sit in Mubarak's Cabinet, the military
exercised a veto on contracts. In Egypt, instead of fostering a rising
middle class, the industrialization that took place was of a semifeudal
nature.

This system could not have been sustained without the military
aid from the United States. It was not that the Americans wanted
to promote uneven development in Egypt, but that they could not
bring together otherwise conflicting goals in any other way.

In a "scene setter" cable to Washington on May 19, 2009, Ambassador Margaret Scobey summed up the nearly three decades
of Mubarak's domestic and foreign policies, beginning with the

prediction that despite his advanced age he would seek office again in the 2011 elections. "The election will not be free or fair, and . . . he will likely stay in office until he dies." Mubarak had no single confidant or adviser who could speak for him. He had prevented any of his main advisers from operating outside their strictly circumscribed spheres of power:

> Defense Minister Tantawi keeps the Armed Forces appearing reasonably sharp and the officers satisfied with their perks and privileges, and Mubarak does not appear concerned that these forces are not well prepared to face 21st century external threats. EGIS [Intelligence] Chief Omar Soliman [sic] and Interior Minister el-Adly keep the domestic beasts at bay, and Mubarak is not one to lose sleep over their tactics. Gamal Mubarak [Hosni's son and reputed heir] and a handful of economic ministers have input on economic and trade matters, but Mubarak will likely resist further economic reform if he views it as potentially harmful to public order and stability.[15]

Later in this message, the Cairo embassy gave the new Obama administration a devastating picture of where Egypt had gone over the years Mubarak ruled. Egypt continued to be a major regional economic power, but "problems" continued to frustrate many Egyptians. This was a classic understatement, as the next sentences revealed: "Egypt's per capita GDP was on par with South Korea's 30 years ago; today it is comparable to Indonesia's. There were bread riots in 2008 for the first time since 1977." Political reforms had stalled, while Cairo continued to use heavy-handed methods against individuals and groups. Economic reform momentum had stalled as well. Even the high GDP growth rates of recent years had failed to lift the lower classes out of poverty. "High inflation, coupled with the impact of the global recession, has resulted in an increase in extreme poverty, job losses, a growing budget deficit and projected 2009 GDP growth of 3.5%—half last year's rate."[16]

This could all be forecast, argued one observer, from day one of Mubarak's presidency. He had no vision of the future comparable to either Nasser's grandeur or Sadat's boldness; there was no "Egyptian project." In the late 1980s and into the 1990s, Egypt began to feel the full effect of the internationally mandated "economic reforms" that made the country a stable place for investments but did little to lessen the people's suffering. The best option Mubarak could think of was the post–Cold War *Pax Americana*, wrote Tarek Osman, "where greater security was founded on American guarantees and regional economic integration. In return, Egypt would be rewarded with increased foreign direct investment, a leading place in an emerging system and continued international support; its success in the effort would be measured by investment dollars, trade surpluses and regime continuity rather than any true internal regeneration, the achievement of long-term strategic objectives or sense of historic fulfillment."[17]

The First Gulf War

On July 25, 1990, Iraqi president Saddam Hussein summoned the American ambassador, April Glaspie, to a late-night meeting. It was to be the last high-level contact between the two nations before the Iraqi invasion of Kuwait eight days later on August 2. The Iraqi dictator had a long list of complaints about American policy over the past decade, beginning with what the Iran-Contra scandal had revealed about Washington's two-faced policy in regard to the Iran-Iraq War. But now there was evidence, he said, that the United Arab Emirates and Kuwait were contriving to drive down the price of oil. Moreover, Kuwait was engaging in slant drilling in areas along the border between the two countries. Such acts were economic warfare against Iraq, he said, as it struggled with a $40 billion war debt. Without Iraq's resistance to Iran, he went on, the Middle East would look very different today. He understood the American interest in keeping prices down and oil flowing, but the United States should not seek to prevent him from righting a very serious wrong. In other words, all those countries that benefited from his willingness to take on the Iranian mullahs now owed it to him to stand aside while he dealt with the problem.[18]

Glaspie responded to these complaints by assuring Saddam that President Bush was a wise man who had no wish to wage an economic war against Iraq. Indeed, she had instructions to seek closer relations with Baghdad. Then came the famous quote that would be pored over and studied for the next three decades in an effort to determine if Glaspie had given Saddam a green light to go into Kuwait. It was even argued at times that she had planted a lure in order that the George H.W. Bush administration could use military force to initiate the post–Cold War "New World Order." "I know you need funds," she began. "We understand that and our opinion is that you should have the opportunity to rebuild your country. But we have no opinion on the Arab-Arab conflicts, like your border disagreement with Kuwait." Despite later efforts to sensationalize this statement, the ambassador had gone on to say that she had been instructed to ask about Saddam's intentions "in the spirit of friendship" and to insist that the United States wanted to see a speedy and peaceful solution to the looming crisis.[19]

Also less well known about this exchange was Glaspie's suggestion that Iraq seek to call upon some Arab leader to mediate the dispute, such as Hosni Mubarak. Saddam said his attempts to involve other Arab nations in the resolution of the dispute had failed. "Now tell us," he finished, "if the American president found himself in this situation, what would he do?" It turned out that President Bush had no desire for Mubarak's mediation efforts, either, although the Egyptian leader had put himself forward as a possible go-between. Bush would say repeatedly over the next several months that his greatest fear was that there might be a move for some sort of an "Arab solution" that would exclude a principal role for the United States as the arbiter of all things to do with an act of aggression—especially, it seemed, when there was the matter of control of oil resources. By adding Kuwait's reserves to his resources, said Bush, Saddam Hussein could become the key decision maker in OPEC and a challenger to American suzerainty.[20]

When the invasion began, Saudi Arabia's King Fahd asked Jordan to urge Saddam to restrict his efforts to the actual disputed boundary areas "until the whole dispute could be resolved peacefully." Jordan's King Hussein felt he should see Saddam personally, but first he wanted to talk with Mubarak to see if the efforts of all three powers could be coordinated. Mubarak was upset that Iraq had resorted to force, as Saddam had promised not to do so before Iraq and Kuwait met face to face at a planned conference. But Mubarak's initial reaction was to seek a way to mediate the dispute—precisely the Arab solution the White House feared. On his way to Alexandria to talk with the Egyptian leader, meanwhile, King Hussein called President Bush. He had been trying to reach them, Bush said. He was quite upset with Saddam's aggression and had already made a public statement to that effect. What Bush had said in comments at the White House was: "This will not stand. This will not stand, this aggression against Kuwait."

"Saddam had challenged the United States," he now warned Hussein, and he was ready to "accept the challenge." Bush wondered why the other Arab countries had not condemned Iraq's actions, or offered their help to Kuwait. "The United States will act independently," Bush added, "regardless whether other countries cooperate or not." Hussein asked him to give the Arab countries at least forty-eight hours. Mubarak suggested that a mini-summit be called to meet in the Saudi Arabian city of Jiddah on the Red Sea. But beforehand, Iraq should withdraw from Kuwait and restore the legitimate government. Hussein insisted that these were questions to be discussed at the proposed conference, not prerequisites.[21]

When he went to Baghdad, the Jordanian king found Saddam open to the idea of a summit conference, provided it met without prior conditions, and provided that the Arab League foreign ministers then meeting in Cairo did not condemn Iraq's action. King Hussein felt comfortable with conveying that message back to Fahd and Mubarak. Before he could return to his capital, however, the Egyptian government had issued a statement that condemned the invasion, and reported that the Arab foreign ministers had also proposed condemnation of Iraq.[22]

What had happened? Mubarak's explanation to Hussein was that he was "under great pressure." He had also spoken with King Fahd, he added, who was very angry. Therefore, he no longer supported the previous agreement he had made about a summit conference, and he now demanded Iraq's immediate withdrawal from Kuwait and restoration of the Kuwaiti ruling family. What Hussein did not know was that Bush and Mubarak had had a long telephone conversation, during which the American president offered to forgive Egypt's debts to the United States. The embargo on Iraq would produce economic hardships in Egypt, Bush wrote in his memoirs. "If they did not find some relief there could be serious political problems in the country." He knew he would have trouble with Congress, wrote Bush, as forgiving foreign debtors never played well in Peoria. But he needed Egypt's support. "Mubarak was crucial to the entire Middle Eastern peace process and the coalition."[23]

Mubarak's withdrawal from any association with the Jordanian initiative gave Bush precious time to send Defense Secretary Dick Cheney to Saudi Arabia to secure Fahd's approval for stationing American troops in his country. The king was persuaded in part by Cheney's presentation of questionable intelligence about the likelihood that Iraq was preparing to move onward after Kuwait into Saudi Arabia. Fahd was assured that the U.S. troops would not remain. At the time of the Cheney mission, Osama bin Laden, who was in the country, protested that he could raise an army to liberate Kuwait without using American forces. When his offer was refused, he stormed out of the royal palace, declaring that he would be heard from again.[24]

What bin Laden was after was not merely to command an Islamic army against the apostate Saddam Hussein, but to sever the ties between Saudi Arabia and the United States that went back to the end of World War II when Franklin D. Roosevelt secured the first foothold by nonbelievers in "the sacred land of the two holy mosques." American policymakers were well aware of the danger of treading too heavily on religious sensibilities, but the Middle East could not be ruled out-of-bounds for expanding American interests, particularly one as important as oil was to the world economy, in order to satisfy the feelings of a bin Laden and his cohorts. Bush subsequently called upon Egypt to send a token force to take part in "Operation Desert Storm" to make sure that the attack on Saddam

Hussein's army in Kuwait had at least a thin coating of military support beyond resolutions by the Arab League.

Ambiguous Outcomes

Getting Congress to agree to forgive Egypt's debt was a straightforward matter compared to all the complexities that arose out of Gulf War I. The war itself was a quick and easy affair. But Bush stopped short of going to Baghdad, leaving Saddam Hussein in power and Bush's own successors with a dilemma about how to unseat the dictator. Fahd and Mubarak had both told Bush before the war that they thought it highly unlikely Saddam would be able to back out of Kuwait and stay in power. Bush hoped that defeat in what Saddam had boasted would be the "mother of all wars" would provide a nudge toward something less disturbing than a revolution, something like a coup d'état, maybe? It didn't. And the next decade saw President Bill Clinton try to force change on Iraq by continuing sanctions, which didn't work, either. The discovery of how far Saddam Hussein had gotten with work on weapons of mass destruction before the first Gulf War added to postwar uneasiness.

Ostensibly aimed at forcing Saddam to agree to unlimited inspections, the larger goal of the sanctions regime begun shortly after the invasion of Kuwait (and continued after the war and throughout the Clinton administration) was to remove Saddam from power. Whatever was hoped, the sanctions backfired. They did not have much of an impact on Saddam's coterie, which continued to enjoy life in the many palaces he built for himself and his sons; but they caused a good deal of suffering for Iraqi citizens, especially children. And, inevitably, they were a source of anti-Americanism across the Arab world. "I think this is a very hard choice," Clinton's secretary of state Madeline Albright told an interviewer in 1996, "but the price—we think the price is worth it." In her memoirs, she said that of course she did not mean to justify the death of innocent children, but Saddam Hussein could have ended the sanctions by cooperating with inspection regimes.[25]

Whatever else they accomplished, the sanctions were a powerful stimulus to Arab terrorists. Both Osama bin Laden and Ayman al-Zawahiri declared the September 11, 2001, attacks—the infamous 9/11 airliner suicide missions against the United States—were a just response to the miseries the West imposed on Iraq. Besides extremist critics of the aftermath of the first Gulf War, there were those in Egypt who spoke out, like Boutros Boutros-Ghali, a former secretary-general of the United Nations who had returned home to run a government human-rights agency in Cairo—an unpromising assignment for someone who had once had real influence on world affairs. "In 1992," he told a visiting American writer, "I had the illusion that the United Nations would manage the post–Cold War world. I was mistaken. The U.S. felt it should manage the post–Cold War world, based on free markets and democracy, with the idea that one democracy will not fight another. But this ideology failed. The new Administration moved from a policy of persuasion to a policy of coercion and preventative war."[26]

Egypt, meanwhile, became in the 1990s a central target of terrorists acting under the guidance of Zawahiri and other jihadist leaders. Not only was there was the attempted assassination of Mubarak in 1995, but in the years before 9/11 more than fifty different attacks were carried out on government officials in Egypt. These were dealt with, wrote Stephen Grey, author of *Ghost Plane: The True Story of the CIA Torture Program*, "with ruthless repression." No one was more ruthless than Mubarak's chief of the intelligence services, Omar Suleiman. Appointed to that position in 1993, Suleiman, an army general who had trained in the Soviet Union, was the CIA's go-to man in Cairo for more than a decade.

Mubarak's resentment toward American insistence that he move forward with reforms and ease up on political opponents appears highly ironic in light of the infamous CIA "rendition" plan devised in the mid-1990s and operated with Egypt's close cooperation over more than a decade. (The now-notorious concept of "extraordinary rendition" involved the extrajudicial transporting of suspected terrorists to other countries, where they could be subjected to harsh interrogation practices not allowed in the United States.) The self-identified author of the 1995 rendition plan was Michael Scheuer, head of the bin Laden unit in the CIA during the late 1990s. In 2007 he testified before Congress that the CIA had warned President Clinton and the National Security Council that the State Department would identify "as human rights abusers" the countries to which the "captured fighters" (another ambivalent phrase) were being delivered. In response Clinton and "his team" asked if the CIA could get each "receiving country" to "guarantee that it would treat a person according to its own laws." For Scheuer that was a perfect solution! "This was no problem and we did so." He had now learned, he testified before Congress, that "Mr. Clinton, Mr. [Sandy] Berger [national security adviser] and Mr. [Richard] Clarke [White House counterterrorism adviser under Clinton and Bush] have said, since 9/11, that they insisted that each receiving country treat the rendered person it received according to U.S. legal standards. To the best of my memory, that is a lie."[27]

Michael Scheuer infuriates people—and he relishes every opportunity to shock anyone who comes within range of his verbal blasts. But in this instance he has well put the question of the policymakers' response to terrorism and what it has accomplished for the nation. Egypt is central to the rendition discussion. "In the world of renditions," writes Stephen Grey, "Egypt has been torture central." And he quotes another CIA official, Robert Baer, who served before and during the period when rendition began: "If you send a prisoner to Jordan, you get a better interrogation. If you send a prisoner, for instance, to Egypt, you will probably never see him again."[28]

Cables sent from Cairo and subsequently disclosed by WikiLeaks make it plain that the United States knew about Suleiman's reputation as Mubarak's "consigliere," if they did not discuss his specific role in the torture of political prisoners as revealed in other sources. Suleiman was not "squeamish" about participating in interrogations, and on one occasion tried to break a prisoner by having him witness a man killed by a vicious karate kick.[29] The "host" countries, *Washington Post* investigative reporter Dana Priest wrote in a famous article that infuriated Scheuer and other rendition operators, had signed the UN Convention Against Torture and Other

Cruel, Inhuman or Degrading Treatment or Punishment," "yet CIA interrogators in the overseas sites are permitted to use the CIA's approved 'Enhanced Interrogation Techniques,' some of which are prohibited by the U.N. convention and by U.S. military law. They include tactics such as 'waterboarding,' in which a prisoner is made to believe he or she is drowning."[30]

Nearly every visiting American policymaker was lined up for an interview with Suleiman to receive his opinions on international affairs such as Iran's baleful influence on Middle Eastern politics or how well Egypt was cooperating with efforts to isolate and weaken Hamas, the dissident Palestinian political movement that won a surprise 2006 electoral victory in Gaza, a test case (which went the wrong way for Washington) of President George W. Bush's effort to spread democracy behind the path of American soldiers in Iraq.

There was no doubt that Suleiman was the key man to see in Egypt after Mubarak, although in later years it appeared that he might be shoved aside as a successor to make way for Gamal Mubarak, the president's son, a situation that prompted much speculation about prospects for Egyptian stability. (What part this "rivalry" played in the endgame at Tahrir Square, especially the military's role in providing the final coup de grâce to the Mubarak regime, remains an intriguing subject.) Either way, however, the prisons that held thousands of Egyptians throughout the 1990s—and possibly more than a hundred rendered by the CIA after 9/11—poisoned the nation's politics. And when the American cables discussed the situation in various shades of diplomatic obliqueness, all they could say was how difficult it was to strike a balance for American policy. A few days after Barack Obama was inaugurated, for example, Ambassador Scobey wrote, "Mubarak now makes scant public pretense of advancing a vision for democratic change. An ongoing challenge remains balancing our security interests with democracy promotion efforts."[31]

Under Suleiman, the Egyptian intelligence services had built up "a trove of information on al-Qaeda and other radical Islamist groups in the Middle East." During the Cold War, wrote one terrorism expert at Georgetown University, Bruce Hoffman, the United

States had a window into the Soviet Union through Iran. "We have the same kind of window into Iran and other countries via the Egyptians," he said after Mubarak's fall. "Whatever happens next, this will never be the same."[32]

The dilemma for policymakers, however, was that rendition and all that flowed around and from that operation endangered the long-term stability of American allies, could not be kept secret, and stimulated more anti-Americanism than it provided vital information. Suleiman's cooperation—and ingenuity at torture—might have won him praise from some as the best "spook" in the Middle East, but it did not work well for American national interests. This sort of cooperation with spy services in Egypt and Libya, asserted Dennis Blair, Obama's first director of national intelligence, had a bad result. "Not only did these intelligence relationships interfere with our ability to understand opposition forces, but in the eyes of the citizens of those countries they often identified the United States with the tools of oppression."[33]

As a key nation for American policymakers trying to resolve the seemingly interminable Arab-Israeli conflict, and as the linchpin of so many other initiatives in the Middle East since 1952, Egypt continued to present a formidable challenge to policymakers hoping to see the political development of the area along liberal, pro-Western lines. At the heart of this problem, to some, was the annual $1.5 billion in military aid to Egypt and its relationship to the possibility of persuading Egypt to adopt political reforms. And that issue, in turn, became involved inside a related debate about whether Egypt was storing up such aid for another war with Israel. These were vexed issues, indeed, and came to the fore in Congress and the media often during the later years of Mubarak's reign. It can even be argued that the neoconservative determination to go to war with Iraq was part of a larger concern that included conclusions about the unreliability of continuing to build up the Egyptian military as a counterforce to Palestinian agitation or Iranian radicalism. After all, during the run-up to the 2003 invasion of Iraq, it was widely assumed that a quick victory would set in progress, if not a cascade of democratic forces, an irreversible trend across the Middle East.

That argument is not necessary, however, to the related question of whether congressional efforts to put a check on arms sales had to do not only with the absence of political reforms in Cairo, but Egypt's calls for serious negotiations on a Palestinian state. Diverging opinions on how far to travel with Egypt sat uneasily alongside the older belief that arms insured a strong government on the Nile, whose military was, as the new buzzword had it, committed to "interoperability" with the Pentagon. Questions about the plans Egypt had for its arms began to be raised in the late 1990s. Hosni Mubarak explained in 1995 that Egypt's large military was necessary to deterring its enemies. His longtime minister of defense, Field Marshal Muhammad Hussein Tantawi, asserted, "Peace does not mean relaxation. . . . Any threat to any Arab or African country is a threat to Egypt's national security." Another Egyptian military figure made the purpose of the nation's arms more specific after a military exercise in 1998: "The exercise affirms to the world the effective role of the Egyptian armed forces, to lighten the path of Egyptian diplomacy to impose the peace of the strong which began on October 6." The reference to the 1973 war, and Sadat's political purposes, could hardly go unnoticed. Almost all the Egyptian forces, wrote an Israeli commentator, Hillel Frisch, who cited these generals in his article, were "concentrated on one front to engage one force only: the Israeli Defense Forces."[34]

Frisch also pointed to the army's success in maintaining its strength not only by reliance on American largesse, but also because of the perks Mubarak bestowed on his loyal friends in the military services. These were characteristics of a premodern army, "a long way from making the transition to the post-modern, globally oriented service state" that American policymakers, from the administration of George H.W. Bush to that of Barack Obama, had envisioned for Egypt. Indeed, from 1991, when the first president Bush asked Egypt to participate in the Gulf War, to Obama's speech in Cairo in June 2009, American presidents have attempted to persuade Egypt to broaden its missions in both politics and the military—yet without sacrificing anything essential from American ability to arbitrate the outcomes in the Middle East.

9/11 and Mission Impossible

Resolving the conflicts in Washington's approach to dealing with Hosni Mubarak's government reminded some of an old adage: "If it ain't broke, don't try to fix it." For the CIA, Egypt was a vital ally. The Pentagon also had good relations with the Egyptian military—as exemplified in Operation Bright Star. Egypt might push for a Palestinian state, but it seemed determined to put a check on radical forces like Hamas. On the other side of the ledger, the Egyptian economy—despite constant reports of outstanding growth in GDP—seemed unable to cut the Gordian knot of poverty tied around one-third of the nation, which, it was argued, owed much to the way favors were doled out to the military. Instead of making progress toward political freedoms, Egypt under Mubarak was a police state, with no incentive for him to change his ways, even as his methods absorbed energies that could be used to move in a positive direction.

In reply to American efforts to prod him toward political reform, Mubarak used to great advantage U.S. fears of Muslim radicalism, pointing to what had happened in Iran, and, after the Second Gulf War, the chaos in Iraq caused, he asserted, by the efforts to install democracy in that country. Saddam Hussein had been a dictator, true, he would say, but he held the line for Arabs against ayatollahs. The outcome of the war had been to increase Iran's influence even in his own country, he charged, where the Muslim Brotherhood already posed a threat to stability. Did Washington really wish to shove him down that dangerous path?

After the shock of the 9/11 attacks on the World Trade Center and the Pentagon, more and more questions arose about putting so much military aid into the hands of Middle Eastern rulers who had no intention of changing their ways. And those who asked such pointed questions began to own more of the debate about strategy. The Cold War was over, after all, and the Soviet Union was no more. So on that level why was it necessary to go on supplying the militaries of those countries? Even during the Cold War, moreover, the real purpose of American weaponry was not to provide a serious front against the Red Army, but to keep order within those states. It was sold to Congress and the public, of course, as a significant part of the Western deterrent against Moscow; but it was a deterrent only in the sense that it built morale and patriotism, bulwarks against internal discontent and radicalism.

It was also the case, of course, that the United States, before and after 1979, had been determined to promote a balance of military power in the region that favored Israel—but not to such a degree as to make another war likely. Maintaining that delicate balance had preoccupied American policymakers, while leaving unattended fields where the real threat to national security was growing far faster than the renditioners could keep up. The United States had invested $50 billion in arms for Egypt—and what had been the result? The result of supporting Middle Eastern dictatorships, it was argued, had been the attacks on 9/11. "The ringleader," wrote one skeptic in the *Christian Science Monitor*, "and four of the 9/11 hijackers were Egyptian." Mubarak's repressive policies had not shut down radical extremism, and his argument that opening up Egyptian society courted danger hardly seemed convincing to Americans on both the right and left.[35]

In some interesting ways the debate growing inside the United States over military aid to Egypt and other countries, such as Saudi Arabia, was, albeit in distorted fashion, mirrored in internal debates among members of al-Qaeda. Zawahiri and several of his Egyptian cohorts formed a kind of brain trust in Osama bin Laden's organization, but Zawahiri's penchant for attacking the "near enemy," the government of Hosni Mubarak, eventually gave way to bin Laden's argument that the only way to bring change to the Middle East was to attack the "head of the serpent," the United States, "the far enemy." When the question arose about attacking apostate Muslim governments, bin Laden retorted, "Leave them alone and do not preoccupy yourselves with them. They are scum. . . . When they witness the defeat of the United States, they will be in their worst situation."[36]

The rough agreement here was that the United States called the shots for the Middle Eastern governments. Change American behavior and you could change the balance of power within the Muslim world. Was that so far distant, after all, from Anwar Sadat's refrain that the United States held 99 percent of the cards? He had invoked American involvement and power, he boasted, in the October War. He got what he wanted—at first—but then it brought him down. But in his place came Hosni Mubarak. The task for jihadists, bin Laden maintained, was to remove American influence, then the natural course of things would produce what he and Zawahiri so ardently desired.

The political attacks on American military aid to Egypt divided the George W. Bush administration. Before 9/11 those who raised such questions were dismissed as naïve, but not so in the wake of the blow that left nearly 3,000 dead in New York and elsewhere, and a shattered sense of security nationwide. Former ambassador to Egypt Edwin Walker said that "aid offers an easy way out for Egypt to avoid reform. They use the money to support antiquated programs and to resist reforms." The first Bush revision of the national security strategy in 2002 articulated a new doctrine: the money should go to "countries whose governments rule justly, invest in their people, and encourage economic freedom."[37]

Among those who generated great interest in neoconservative circles was James Woolsey, a former CIA director at the very time the rendition program got going. He left that post in 1995 but became a very vocal proponent of bringing down Saddam Hussein. He declared himself convinced immediately after 9/11 that Iraq was behind the bombing. In 2004 he told a college audience that the United States was now engaged in World War IV. It would last much longer than World War II, he said, but hopefully not as long as the four decades of World War III, the Cold War. America's enemies in this war were the religious rulers of Iran and the "fascists" of Iraq and Syria, he went on, along with extremists like al-Qaeda. The war had been going on for some time, but the United States had "finally noticed." What would win the war was American backing for democratic movements across the Middle East, something that was already making rulers there uneasy. "We want you nervous," Woolsey declared in a stem-winder of an address during a teach-in at UCLA sponsored by Republican groups under the rubric "Americans for Victory over Terrorism." "We want you nervous. We want you to realize now, for the fourth time in a hundred years, this country and its allies are on the march and that we are on the side of those whom you—the Mubaraks, the Saudi Royal family most fear: We're on the side of your own people."[38]

Strong stuff, indeed. But change a few words and you have one of Osama bin Laden's tirades against the United States. Neoconservatives did not own a monopoly on what would be called by Bush's national security adviser and then secretary of state, Condoleezza Rice, "muscular Wilsonianism." In the House of Representatives, California Democrat Tom Lantos, who received high marks on many "progressive" issues, called for a reassessment of Egypt's military aid program. Cairo, he complained, treated such aid as an "entitlement"—Washington-speak for automatic appropriations like Social Security or Medicaid. Seizing on the first President Bush's rationale for forgiving Egypt's foreign debt before the first Gulf War, Lantos pointed out that Egypt had not sent any military units to join the coalition forces in Afghanistan. "Egyptian military exercises," Lantos said, "are ominously geared toward an Israeli enemy that doesn't obviously exist."[39]

The only Holocaust survivor to serve in Congress, Lantos was a dedicated supporter of Israel, who put challenging military aid to Egypt at the top of his agenda. Like Woolsey, moreover, he believed that the answer was to shift to economic aid and educational support. Cutting military aid, he believed, would "help thaw the peace." Of course, such a shift would entail more interference in Egypt's internal affairs—something the Mubarak government had made plain did not interest it very much. President George W. Bush joined in as well, most famously in a speech in London on November 19, 2003, at Whitehall Palace. He began with a reference to Woodrow Wilson, the last American president to stay in Buckingham Palace; Wilson's idealism, Bush said, was needed to guide both the British and Americans in undertaking the mission the Iraq War had begun. There was an attitude, he claimed, that seemed to suggest that Middle Eastern countries did not desire, and were not capable of, democratic government. "Perhaps the most helpful change we can make is to change our own thinking," he said:

We must shake off decades of failed policy in the Middle East. Your nation and mine, in the past, have been willing to make a bargain, to tolerate oppression for the sake of stability. Longstanding ties often led us to overlook the faults of local elites. Yet this bargain did not bring stability or make us safe. It merely bought time, while problems festered and ideologies of violence took hold.

Now we're pursuing a different course, a forward strategy of freedom in the Middle East. We will consistently challenge the enemies of reform and confront the allies of terror. We will expect a higher standard from our friends in the region, and we will meet our responsibilities in Afghanistan and in Iraq by finishing the work of democracy we have begun.[40]

It was nearly six months since the "shock and awe" of the initial U.S. military assault on Iraq when Bush spoke in London of the new American course, and the first questions had arisen over the war as the WMDs that Saddam Hussein supposedly had hidden remained undiscovered. Beyond rationalizing the failure to find the so-called WMDs, Bush's promise to pursue a "different course" did describe how the shock of 9/11 had begun to alter thinking in the White House. Neoconservatives, many of them former Cold War liberals, uncomfortable with détente in the Nixon-Ford years, now had their footing again. They saw the liberation of Iraq as the beginning of a process that would extend to Cairo—perhaps especially to Cairo, as the cultural leader of the Middle East. Bush did sound a cautionary note about expecting too much too soon: "The movement of history will not come about quickly. Because of our own democratic development—the fact that it was gradual and, at times, turbulent—we must be patient with others. And the Middle East countries have some distance to travel."

It was true, certainly, that after 9/11, Bush policymakers believed the way to advance American interests in the Middle East—which included protecting the oil-producing regions and keeping the Arab-Israeli tension from exploding again—would be to encourage reform. But would it work? Having ignited a fire in Iraq, who could say where it would spread? Mubarak was a cynic about American policy, and he saw Iran as the principal beneficiary of Bush's folly. The WikiLeaks cables show him time and again expressing his frustration about the results of the invasion and the White House's constant chiding about Egyptian politics.

For the "War on Terror," having an aging despot in place turned out to be quite handy. Nevertheless, in June 2005 Secretary of State Rice went to Cairo to deliver a speech at the American University calling upon Egypt to guarantee free elections that fall, as a natural follow-up to a national referendum that changed the constitution to permit multiple candidates in a presidential election. She met with Mubarak before the speech, and after the meeting she said Cairo should start taking steps toward democracy. "The people of Egypt should be at the forefront of this great journey, just as you have led this region through the great journeys of the past."[41]

Rice began her speech with a reference to Bush's second inaugural address that talked about the American mission in spreading democracy to the Middle East. "America will not impose our style of government on the unwilling. Our goal instead is to help others find their own voice, to attain their own freedom, make their own way." Perhaps that was meant to soften more-stringent demands for reform, but it revealed the schizophrenic fault line in American policy. After meeting with the Egyptian president and foreign minister, Rice adopted a lecturing style once more. Egypt was such an important country, she said, that it was essential that those elections be free and fair. "I think our Egyptian friends understand that, and I believe will take their responsibilities seriously. People will watch what happens in Egypt, because this is an important country in the region, a region that is changing very much."

The Egyptian foreign minister replied in mock amazement, "Who would object to fair, transparent elections?" He added, "It will be so, I assure you." The September election was a sham, as everyone expected it would be, and the opposition candidate, Ayman Nour, who supposedly received six hundred thousand votes, was immediately arrested. Nour was charged with turning in falsified petitions containing thousands of names in order to get on the ballot, and was sentenced to five years in prison, while changes in Egyptian law made it unlikely that another challenger could even gain access to the ballot the next time around in 2011. There were no Mubarak visits to Washington during Bush's second term. Rice canceled a second trip to Cairo, and Bush mentioned Nour in a speech—but nothing happened until Obama came into office and Nour was suddenly released, apparently as a gesture to the new administration to stave off more complaints about Egypt's internal affairs.[42]

Mubarak used every opportunity he had to tell every visiting American official as well as the ambassador what he thought of American policy. Egypt's dangerous "neighborhood" had only become more so since the fall of Saddam Hussein, he said to Ambassador Scobey. "Nasty as he was," Saddam had "stood as a wall against Iran." Tehran's hand now moved with ease from the Persian Gulf to Morocco. The Iranians were behind efforts to stir up unrest in Gaza, Yemen, Lebanon, and even the Sinai. They were involved with the Muslim Brotherhood in Egypt. Americans knew the line by heart. Mubarak always emphasized the supposed danger of the Muslim Brotherhood as his prime example of the dangers of pushing democratic reform. American policy, he concluded, threatened to unleash chaos on the Middle East.[43]

Foreign Minister Gheit lamented the recent history of "endless lectures and public quarrels," claiming the trouble stemmed from a lack of understanding of Egypt's circumstances. "We confront many dangers and challenges to stability and progress." The Muslim Brotherhood was at the center of the problem. Look at Gaza, he said, where women were now forced to wear the veil. Would his wife and daughters soon be forced to wear it? The government of Egypt must stop those who produce this incitement. Ambassador Scobey acknowledged the many challenges Cairo faced, but, she said, "human rights would remain a critical component of the U.S.-Egypt dialogue."[44]

Gheit's illustration about the situation in Gaza, nevertheless, was a hit exactly on the fault line of American policy. In an effort to show progress not only in terms of reforms inside Egypt and other countries, Washington had pushed for elections in Lebanon and the Gaza Strip that turned out the wrong way, elevating to power the more-radical Palestinian organization, Hamas. Rice rejected the implication that Washington had misjudged what would happen with the dangerously simplistic approach that elections were a cure-all. But her response seemed abstract and even evasive. "What we're seeing here," she said, "is the growing—the birth pangs of a new Middle East. And whatever we do, we have to be certain that we are pushing forward to the New Middle East, not going back to the old one."[45]

Final Frustration

After the 2006 election in Gaza proved so disappointing, the United States did ease up a bit—actually more than a bit. All the rhetoric of the 2003 Whitehall speech faded away, as the spotlight shifted again in Iraq to straight military concerns about the possibility of losing the war. The American ambassador to Cairo at the time, Frank Ricciardone, even parried questions about Ayman Nour's imprisonment by stating the real question was not what Americans thought about the affair, but what Egyptians believed. "I bet if there are a hundred people, I bet I'd get a hundred different answers." It was a pretty lame response. And he was not finished. "You know if Egyptians are not sure what to make of this, then I hope you will forgive Americans for not understanding the complexity of this case."[46] Then came Bush's speech at the 2008 World Economic Forum, held at the Egyptian Red Sea resort town of Sharm el-Sheikh. According to one of the speechwriters, the speech had started out in a White House draft as a Reagan-like "tear down this wall" demand that Nour be released, but at Sharm el-Sheikh it became instead a mild lecture, with no mention of Nour's name.

At the World Economic Forum, Saudi King Abdullah apparently convinced Bush that Mubarak was holding back the radicals.[47] When Bush brought up the lack of political reform, Mubarak turned the tables with his usual retort that the effort to impose democracy from without could only bring chaos and instability. The main cause of instability in the region, he asserted, was not the political situation within Arab countries, but the unresolved conflict between Israel and the Palestinians. With that statement, the U.S.-Egyptian dia-

logue reverted to issues Washington had hoped to keep out of the
public spotlight, and where the dictator held the advantage in his
home court.[48]

Meanwhile, Assistant Secretary of State David Welch had testified that Egypt had been very helpful in various areas in backing
U.S. foreign policy in the region; for example, in supporting efforts
to call Iran to account for noncompliance with international obligations on its nuclear energy program, in its role in guarding the
Egypt-Gaza border, and in pressing the Hamas-led Palestinian government in Gaza to recognize Israel and renounce violence. Welch
and another State Department aide took turns calling Egypt the
"cornerstone of our foreign policy in the Middle East" and "one of
the pillars of our foreign policy in the Middle East . . . our military
assistance is a key element of that strategic partnership." To those
who might complain about Egypt's attitude about the Iraq War,
Murbarak's aid was actually "invaluable." He gave the U.S. military
free passage through Egypt's airspace and priority for naval vessels
through the Suez Canal. Between 2001 and 2005, according to
American figures, Egypt granted airspace access for 36,553 aircraft.
He was also helping out with reconstruction projects in Afghanistan. And so on.[49]

The failure to persuade Mubarak to halt the human rights violations, let alone open up the political process, indicated both that he
intended to run again for president in 2011 and that he could not
change his policies under any pressures the United States dared to
impose without endangering the "strategic relationship." It was now
widely believed, as well, that his son Gamal, the leader of the National Democratic Party and a proponent of economic liberalism,
was his designated successor. There had already been some concern
in recent years that Mubarak's aspirations for Gamal conflicted with
the military's preference for Omar Suleiman, a man who would keep
in place the economic advantages and special position its officer
corps had enjoyed for so long. A London-trained banker, Gamal had
different ideas about running the economy. However that might be,
a succession struggle was the last thing Washington wanted to see.

Even before the American succession from George W. Bush to
Barack Obama, Washington had moved to damp down tensions
partly in response to such fears, and partly because public diplomacy
was obviously getting nowhere. At the end of December 2008, after
Obama's election, Ambassador Scobey wrote to General David Petraeus, head of Central Command, to brief him on what to expect
from his upcoming visit to Cairo. Her comments on the unsuccessful
efforts to broaden Egyptian thinking about its military mission pretty
much tell the story of the $50 billion gamble: "The United States has
sought to interest the Egyptian military into expanding their mission
in ways that reflect new regional and transnational security threats,
such as piracy, border security, and counterterrorism. Egypt's aging
leadership, however, has resisted our efforts and remains satisfied with
continuing to do what they have done for years: train for force-on-
force warfare with a premium on ground forces and armor."[50]

A retired Egyptian general, Hossam Sweilam, boiled down the
conflict with Washington to its essence. Egypt viewed defense of
the Sinai as the military's core mission, and suspected that American wishes had to do with Israel more than antipiracy or border security. "The U.S.," he said, "should not impose on us reformulating
our military the way it wants, which we think is ultimately what
suits Israel and we don't want to do what suits Israel." Others believed, however, that the core mission of the Egyptian military was
to keep the regime in power—that rhetoric about Israel was like
excuses made not to open the political process out of concern about
the Muslim Brotherhood.[51]

Relations between the two countries badly needed a reset, Ambassador Scobey believed, as Obama had promised in regard to Russia and, possibly, Iran. "U.S. and Egyptian differences over the pace
and direction of political reform have drained the warmth from the
relationship on both sides," Scobey noted. "We believe President
Mubarak would be interested in an early visit to Washington to consult with President Obama, in large part to try to begin repairing
the relationship."[52]

Such an invitation was arranged—but Obama came first to Cairo,
in June 2009. The day after his own inaugural, indeed, Obama

phoned Mubarak. The secretary general of the National Democratic
Party hailed the contact as an initiative "that reflects a change [in
U.S. policy], demonstrating that the new U.S. administration is keen
to listen to the views of the most important country in the Middle
East." It was to be hoped that Obama's gesture signaled as well that
the "double standards" when dealing with Israel and the Arab countries would come to an end.[53]

Obama's speech in Cairo on June 4, 2009, was billed as a message
to the Muslim world. It began with a fulsome reference to the city as
the home of two great institutions of Islamic learning and Egypt's
advancement over the past century. "Together, you represent the
harmony between tradition and progress." This was the theme he
pursued throughout the speech as a refutation that sweeping changes
brought by modernity and globalization should be viewed as "hostile
to the traditions of Islam." He acknowledged the heritage of suspicion that began with long-ago religious wars and Western "colonialism that denied rights and opportunities to many Muslims." He also
acknowledged that during the Cold War "Muslim-majority countries
were too often treated as proxies without regard to their own aspirations."[54]

It was hard to miss here the criticism of American policy as formulated by Dean Acheson and John Foster Dulles in the aftermath
of the 1952 revolution that toppled King Farouk. But then Obama
went on to argue that the accumulation of tensions had been ex-
ploited by "a small but potent minority of Muslims" who carried out
the attacks on September 11, 2001. It was necessary to find a way to
end a situation that empowered "those who sow hatred rather than
peace, and who promote conflict rather than the cooperation that
can help all of our people achieve justice and prosperity." He had
come to Cairo, he went on, to seek a new beginning between the
United States and Muslims around the world.

It was a long speech, which touched on nearly all the issues that
had influenced Washington's decision making in recent years, em-
phasizing that the world could not be separated because of religious
or political beliefs when it came to protecting citizens against terrorism, or defending the rights of women. As the president of the

United States, he said, his first duty was to protect its citizens. Al-Qaeda had killed three thousand Americans on 9/11, and "even now states their determination to kill on a massive scale. They have affiliates in many countries and are trying to expand their reach. These are not opinions to be debated; these are facts to be dealt with." On the other hand, he called the Iraq War a war of choice, while stating his belief that "ultimately" the Iraqi people would be better off without the tyranny of Saddam Hussein. He called for an end to the stalemate in the Israeli-Palestinian peace negotiations. Neither side in that conflict could ever eliminate the other. Privately, he said, many Muslims recognized that Israel would not go away. And many Israelis recognized the need for a Palestinian state. "It is time for us to act on what everyone knows to be true." The speech required a great deal from his audience—near and far. It also required much of Obama that he would find difficult to fulfill:

> And, finally, just as America can never tolerate violence by extremists, we must never alter our principles. 9/11 was an enormous trauma to our country. The fear and anger that it provoked was understandable, but in some cases, it led us to act contrary to our ideals. We are taking concrete actions to change course. I have unequivocally prohibited the use of torture by the United States, and I have ordered the prison at Guantanamo Bay closed by early next year.[55]

In Cairo the speech caused a sensation. The embassy reported that Egyptians were "proud and excited" that Obama had chosen the city as the venue for this remarkable speech "and have been eager to talk about [the] follow-up," even before Air Force One departed on June 4. "It had energized the Egyptian-American dialogue," enthused the ambassador. "The challenge will be to maintain that momentum as we look for practical ways to put the ideas into practice." Scobey listed an impressive number of proposals on the table for assistance to educational resources "focused on the need to improve the quality of Egyptian graduates and to ensure that they play a significant role in economic development." "Ideas on possible U.S.

support for science and technology model high schools have been well received."[56]

Encouraged by all this activity, Scobey put forward a proposal "that could serve to mitigate the inevitable tensions that will accompany the transition of power in Egypt in the post-Mubarak era." The idea was for opening a channel of communication between an American "organization" such as the Carnegie Endowment and a group in Egypt that would include representatives from the National Democratic Party as well as dissidents who demanded changes. "The goals of such a channel of communication would include . . . the creation of a safe environment for Egyptian activists to challenge each other over the direction and content of Egyptian reform," and identifying ways the U.S. government could "support indigenous efforts."[57]

Post-speech euphoria, let alone wishful thinking about the transition period of Egyptian politics, still faced reality in Hosni Mubarak. "No issue [better] demonstrates Mubarak's worldview," Scobey had advised Washington before Obama's visit to Cairo, "than his reaction to demands that he open Egypt to genuine political competition and loosen the pervasive control of the security services. Certainly the 'name and shame' approach in recent years strengthened his determination not to accommodate our views." Scobey offered a character analysis: "[Mubarak] is a tried and true realist, innately cautious and conservative, and has little time for idealistic goals. [He] viewed President Bush as naïve, controlled by subordinates, and totally unprepared for dealing with post-Saddam Iraq, especially the rise of Iran's regional influence." To sum it up, "In Mubarak's mind, it is far better to let a few individuals suffer than risk chaos for society as a whole."[58]

When the Egyptian president traveled to Washington in August 2009, he showered Obama with lavish praise for the speech and for trying to restart Israeli-Palestinian peace talks. "The Islamic world had thought that the U.S. was against Islam, but his great, fantastic address there has removed all those doubts."[59] While the United States continued to try to devise ways to get around Mubarak's attitude that, inevitably, a few must suffer to preserve the safety of the state—knowing full well it was indeed more than just a few—Mubarak had some advice for the United States concerning Afghanistan. Proposals for a second troop "surge" were spreading in Washington. Mubarak suggested that working through local groups and tribes would be better than sending troops, who would face the same problems as the Russians had years earlier. "Tell President Obama that Egypt can help," he told special envoy George Mitchell, as "we know some elements."[60]

Some Other Elements

Given Mubarak's aversion to dealing with the Muslim Brotherhood on any level, one might wonder what he knew about "some elements" in Afghanistan, and how he thought he could help the United States to defeat the Taliban and its allies. In any event, President Obama did not take Mubarak's advice. Instead he sent forty thousand troops to Afghanistan, bringing the number of soldiers sent to the country known as the "graveyard of empires" to one hundred thousand. Obama promised he would start bringing the soldiers home in July 2011. Months before that time came, Mubarak was gone.

The "revolution" that forced Mubarak's resignation on February 11, 2011, actually began in Tunisia on December 17, 2010, when "an unemployed man, Mohammed Bouazizi, distraught when police confiscated his unlicensed produce stand, set himself on fire." Bouazizi finally died three weeks later, on January 3, 2011. His desperate act inspired other youths to attempt suicide as protests spread from the smaller towns to cities across Tunisia—triggering the so-called Jasmine Revolution. Eleven days after Bouazizi died, longtime president Zine el-Abidine Ben Ali, who had headed the "most tightly run ship in the Arab world," was forced to resign. "Is there a more poignant portrayal of what ails the Arab world," wrote Egyptian-born author Mona Eltahawy the day after Ben Ali fell, "than images of its young people killing themselves as their leaders get older and richer?"[61]

"No doubt," she added, "every Arab leader has watched Tunisia's revolt in fear while citizens across the Arab world watch in solidarity, elated at that rarity: open revolution." In Cairo a *Time* magazine reporter doubted the Jasmine Revolution would spread. Egyptian media had made public half a dozen cases of successful or attempted self-immolation in the previous two weeks, she wrote, part of a copycat wave that had swept through "the politically stagnant streets of North Africa." "But in Egypt, it doesn't go much deeper than that." A greater percentage of Egyptians than Tunisians lived below the poverty line, but even with a regime that "knows more about torture than it does about public service," and which swallowed domestic profits before they could reach the lower classes, the dominant feeling "seems to be a kind of political resignation about the efficacy of protests." In Tunisia, at a critical turning point the army joined the protestors, but in Egypt the military was known to stand with Mubarak. There had been a call for a national day of protests on January 25, but no one expected much from it. "It is, Egyptian observers say, a typically lackluster response to what appeared to be a golden opportunity."[62]

Harvard foreign policy expert Stephen Walt also dismissed the idea that what had happened in Tunisia could spread to Egypt or elsewhere. The men who headed the Arab governments had shown themselves capable of deterring or deflecting popular uprisings. "Color me skeptical," he wrote in the journal *Foreign Policy*. "In fact, the history of world revolution suggests that this sort of revolutionary cascade is quite rare, and even when some sort of revolutionary contagion does take place, it happens pretty slowly and is often accompanied by overt foreign invasion."[63]

Egyptians decided otherwise. On January 25, 2011, thousands answered the call for a "day of rage," assembling in Cairo's Tahrir Square. Similar protests took place in other cities, sparking the first clashes between protestors and the police. The interior ministry issued a predictable statement blaming the Muslim Brotherhood. But what had worked in the past was not going to stop things this time. Communications between protest groups quickly spread via Twitter and Facebook, something new, but perhaps not surprising given the demographics of Middle Eastern countries with their high percentages of young people, collectively a group whose most valued possession was often a cell phone. Some would argue, indeed, that what was about to happen across the Middle East surprised skeptics because they underestimated this new force. Vietnam was the first war in color television; Egypt was the first Twitter revolution.

On the second day of protests, White House press secretary Robert Gibbs said that the Egyptian government should "demonstrate its responsiveness to the people" by recognizing their "universal rights." Vice President Joe Biden added that Mubarak needed to "move in the direction" of being responsive "to some . . . of the needs of the people out there." Pressed by Jim Lehrer on PBS's television *NewsHour* to say whether it was time for Mubarak to go, Biden responded with the classic rationale for the $50 billion gamble: "Mubarak has been an ally of ours in a number of things. And he's been very responsible on, relative to geopolitical protest in the region, the Middle East peace efforts; the actions Egypt has taken relative to normalizing relationships with—with Israel. . . . I would not refer to him as a dictator."[64]

Biden and Secretary of State Hillary Clinton both issued appeals for restraint and called for each side to avoid violence. "What we should continue to do," said the vice president, "is to encourage reasonable . . . accommodation and discussion" to resolve peacefully claims "by those who have taken to the street." Those that "are legitimate should be responded to because the economic well-being and the stability of Egypt rests upon the middle class buying into the future of Egypt." One commentator on Biden's statements wondered whether the protestors—if they were paying attention at all to Biden—thought any of their demands were *illegitimate*.[65]

The first few days of the protest saw several of these anodyne comments emanating from Washington. The Obama administration found itself in a quandary. On the one hand, it did not want to intervene and be blamed for attempting to prop up a government that its people had deserted; on the other hand, it did not want to be held responsible for deserting a government that had been a "cornerstone" of U.S. Middle Eastern policy. In the first case there was the risk of losing influence with a new generation of leaders; in the second, the fear of chaos and alienating other powerful allies, especially those in Saudi Arabia, Yemen, and Bahrain—countries that offered oil, opposition to al-Qaeda, and a valuable naval base.

Israel also feared what would happen to the 1979 treaty if Mubarak disappeared. Secretary Clinton, therefore, at first brushed aside suggestions Washington might cut off military aid, and instead praised the Egyptian army for displaying restraint, "trying to differentiate between peaceful protestors—who we support—and potential looters and other criminal elements who are a danger to the Egyptian people." It was something of an equivocal statement reflecting a conviction the United States had the right to pass judgment on the worthiness of the contending forces.[66]

On January 27, the former head of the UN nuclear watchdog agency, Mohamed ElBaradei—who had argued for more time to complete his team's work in Iraq, much to George W. Bush's annoyance before the Iraq War—arrived in Egypt saying he was ready to lead the transition. And once again he criticized Washington, this time not for rushing to take action, but for indecisiveness. On American television, ElBaradei declared, "It is better for President Obama not to appear that he is the last one to say to President Mubarak, 'it's time for you to go.'"[67]

Obama did not tell Mubarak to go—at least not right away. But he did prod the Egyptian president in a thirty-minute telephone call to carry out reforms he had promised in a speech to the protestors in which he announced he was firing his government. "This moment of volatility has to be turned into a moment of promise." There were difficult days ahead, but the United States would stand up for the rights of the Egyptian people "and work with their government in pursuit of a future that is more just, more free and more hopeful." Press Secretary Gibbs hinted at least that Washington might cut off military aid. "This is a warning to the military: You guys be careful; we could pull the plug," said former ambassador Edward Walker. "This is very serious."[68]

As the protests continued to grow, and Tahrir Square became a popular nighttime "reality show" on international television, Mubarak announced additional concessions as he clung to power. He appointed a vice president for the first time in his three decades of power, Omar Suleiman—an unlikely champion of reform. Then he promised that neither he nor his son Gamal would run for the presidency in September. But he refused to step down until then. Suleiman promised a dialogue with protestors but warned that the government could not tolerate the situation continuing. Among the voices in Tahrir Square calling for Mubarak to leave were those of the iconic Egyptian film star Omar Sharif, who, fittingly enough, had starred in *Lawrence of Arabia*, and Khalid Abdel Nasser, the son of the leader who had emerged out of the 1952 revolution, Gamal Abdel Nasser.[69]

Mubarak's speeches mixed self-pity and pride in ways that stirred louder demands he leave at once. "The Hosni Mubarak who speaks to you today," he said, justifying his decision to delay until September his retirement, "is proud of his achievements over the years in serving Egypt and its people. This is my country. This is where I lived, I fought and defended its land, sovereignty and interests, and I will die on its soil." The dictator's latest move, Mohamed ElBaradei declared, was "clearly an act of deception" by a man who refuses to listen to the voice of the people and leave. If he did not heed the call and leave at once, he would be "not only a lame duck president but a dead man walking."[70] Truckloads of hired goons arrived in Tahrir Square, along with others on horseback and even on camels, but the protests continued to gain momentum. It was apparent that a contest between Washington and Mubarak for the Egyptian army's loyalty was under way and would probably determine the outcome of the endgame. President Obama and his aides heaped praise on the army for its restraint in not opening fire on protestors. Perhaps the final payoff of the $50 billion gamble came down to the political "interoperability" the Pentagon hoped it had achieved with the Egyptian military over the three decades of Mubarak's rule. Indeed, this had been the goal since 1952, a postcolonial version of the Arab Legion—not under direct command of a Glubb Pasha (the Arab Legion's British commander), but one coordinated with American objectives.

Getting Egypt to go along with American objectives had never been completely realized, of course, as the WikiLeaks cables showed Washington had been unsuccessful in getting Mubarak to shift focus from his Sinai-centric military strategy to supposed twenty-first-century threats. Appointing Suleiman vice president and taking

Gamal out of the picture might appease a military fearful of losing its central place in Egyptian politics, but that was more than offset by the possible loss of its annual stipend of $1.5 billion. Actually, it was unlikely that the United States could afford to cut off the money under almost any circumstances, for it had paid for too many valuable relationships over the years. Congress had raised questions now and again but never succeeded in forcing the issue of whether the military aid was also connected closely to the regime's domestic policies.

Admiral Mike Mullen, chairman of the Joint Chiefs, spoke frequently with his Egyptian counterpart, a Pentagon spokesman said in an e-mail statement on February 2, 2011, and had "expressed his confidence in the Egyptian military's ability to provide for their country's security, both internally and throughout the Suez Canal area." Already, then, the United States was anticipating the post-Mubarak transition. Two days later the British newspaper the *Guardian* reported that the Obama administration had refused to cut military aid to Egypt, "and instead is working behind the scenes with the commanders of the country's armed forces on how to oust President Hosni Mubarak." Admiral Mullen put it as plain as plain could be: "I recognize that [the money] certainly is a significant investment, but it's an investment that has paid off for a long, long time."[71]

Even though these moves were hardly a secret, the White House continued to say that the final outcome was up to the Egyptians, partly because it feared alienating Saudi Arabia and other Middle East allies, and partly because it did not want to be accused of pursuing "regime change" in the light of Iraq and Afghanistan. But it was impossible to provide words to disguise what was happening, however hard the spin doctors might try. The president, explained a White House press aide, had said now was the time to begin a peaceful, orderly, and meaningful transition, with credible, inclusive negotiations. "We have discussed with the Egyptians a variety of different ways to move that process forward, but all of those decisions must be made by the Egyptian people."[72]

Calls went out to Suleiman from Obama and Biden—as part of that process—asking him to end the thirty-year-old emergency law, under which so many had been imprisoned. He refused in a public statement, declaring that Egyptian society lacked "a culture of democracy" and was not ready for an immediate lifting of the state of emergency. How ironically fitting that was. The CIA's point man for rendition and torture in the War on Terror—fought, Bush had said, to protect America by making space for Middle East democracy—now claimed there was no "culture of democracy" to bring out in Egypt. "I don't think that in any way squares with what those seeking greater opportunity and freedom think is a timetable for progress," White House Press Secretary Robert Gibbs rebuked Suleiman. A greater threat of instability would come from a refusal "to see progress from their government."[73]

Suleiman then reported that Mubarak had named a panel to recommend constitutional amendments. "He gave orders to abstain from prosecuting [arrested protestors]," the vice president said on state television, "and forfeiting their rights to freedom of expression." He had met with opposition leaders to establish a panel to work on other measures as well. These steps toward "national reconciliation" were welcomed by President Mubarak, Suleiman insisted, "assuring that it puts our feet at the beginning of the right path to get out of the current crisis."

On Thursday, February 10, General Hassan al-Roueini, commander of the Cairo district, strode into Tahrir Square and announced "All your demands will be met today." And in Washington, CIA director Leon Panetta told a congressional committee that there was a "strong likelihood that Mubarak may step down this evening." Anticipation ran high that this was "it." But not quite yet. Appearing on television standing next to the Egyptian flag, Mubarak said he had heard the protestors. He would investigate the deaths of an estimated three hundred people during the demonstrations. "I speak to you as a father speaks to his children. I say to you before anything else that the blood of your martyrs will not be in vain and that I will hold perpetrators to account." He was transferring most of his power to Suleiman, but he would stay in office only to see that the next election in September would mark a transition to "free and transparent" elections. Casting himself as a mediator in the national drama, he lashed out at the Obama administration as an unwanted

interloper in the reform process, which, he insisted, he would see
through as head of state. Foreign intervention in Egypt was "shame-
ful." He would never accept it, "whatever the source might be or
whatever the context it came in." In this self-parodying fashion he
went on as if he were Nasser: "We will prove that we are not follow-
ers or puppets of anybody, nor are we receiving orders or dictations
from anybody. No one is making the decisions for us."[74]

The Supreme Military Council, now the de facto ruling authority under Suleiman, declared it approved Mubarak's position, but
also that it would remove the emergency-law restrictions as soon as
the streets were calm. Wherever that advice came from, it was not
sufficient. Throngs of demonstrators across the country, not only in
Tahrir Square, demanded that Mubarak must go at once. In Cairo
crowds rushed at the State Television and Radio Tower and swarmed
around the building. The soldiers stood by and watched as the
crowd chanted, "This is the people's army, not Mubarak's army."[75]

Meanwhile, in Washington, Panetta and his aides sought to explain that the director's comments on Mubarak's stepping down
were not based on anything other than newspaper stories. But why
was the CIA in the dark? In a second round of explanations, Panetta
said that he had received reports, but "We have not gotten specific
word that he, in fact, will do that." Ever since 9/11 the intelligence
services had been under heavy fire for not having been able to
identify and stop the conspirators from attacking the World Trade
Center and the Pentagon. Then there had been the "slam dunk"
assurances George Tenet had given President Bush that Saddam
Hussein had developed an arsenal of WMDs. Panetta insisted that
his agency had, indeed, provided warnings that Egypt's government
could be toppled, even as he acknowledged the agency needed to "do
a better job of spotting specific vulnerabilities for governments and
of monitoring the Internet's role in fomenting protests."[76]

Mubarak's speech brought a quick response from President Obama.
"The Egyptian people have been told that there was a transition of
authority, but it is not yet clear that this transition is immediate,
meaningful or sufficient." For the first time the United States had
issued a direct call for Mubarak's resignation. It reached Suleiman.

According to an anonymous American "official" who spoke to reporters, Obama's statement forced Suleiman to join with the military in demanding Mubarak leave. "He had been trying to walk a
fine line between retaining support for Mubarak while trying to
infuse common sense into the equation," the official said. "By the
end of the day, it was clear the situation was no longer tenable."[77]

At eleven o'clock in the morning in Cairo, an ashen-faced Suleiman stood before television cameras: "President Hosni Mubarak
has decided to step down from the office of president of the republic
and has charged the high council of the armed forces to administer
the affairs of the country. May God help everybody."[78]

"This is not the end of Egypt's transition," said President Obama.
"It is the beginning." It already *was* the beginning of something bigger, and no one could predict the ending.

6

ARAB SPRING

The United States is committed to standing with the people of Egypt and Tunisia as they work to build sustainable democracies that deliver real results for all their citizens, and to supporting the aspirations of people across the region. On this our values and interests converge. History has shown that democracies tend to be more stable, more peaceful, and ultimately, more prosperous. The trick is how we get there.
—Hillary Clinton, speech at the U.S.-Islamic World Forum,
April 12, 2011

Even as Secretary of State Hillary Clinton pondered "how we get there," the first wave of enthusiasm over what had happened at Tahrir Square had begun to recede a bit. The clamor in the United States over who deserved praise for Mubarak's demise quieted down, as threatened upheavals in Bahrain and Yemen forced out into the open the shadowy history of dealings with autocratic presidents, now backed into a corner by protesting crowds emboldened by Egypt's example. The United States had already sent military forces to help try to unseat Libyan tyrant Muammar Gaddafi, but had done little more than shake a finger at the Bahraini king, Hamad bin Isa al-Khalifa. Clinton tried to explain why that was so. "We understand that a one-size-fits-all approach doesn't make sense in such a diverse region at such a fluid time."

Part of this fluidity—which Clinton did not discuss publicly—stemmed from the fear that disturbances in Bahrain would add to American problems with Saudi Arabian nervousness about Iranian influence in the Persian Gulf, and possibly even provoke demands that the U.S. Fifth Fleet leave a port almost indispensable to reassuring its allies. But Clinton did insist that in the long run, principle and power interests coincided: "As I have said before, the United States had a decades-long friendship with Bahrain that we expect to continue long into the future. We have made clear that security alone cannot resolve the challenges facing Bahrain. Violence is not and cannot be the answer. A political process is. We have raised our concerns about the current measures directly with Bahraini officials and will continue to do so."

The long winter of the Arab world, Clinton said, had begun to thaw. Bush loyalists had initially felt a surge of redemption flowing through their veins as they stared out the windows of their think-tank offices pondering the rapidly changing political landscape in the Middle East. Hadn't his administration broken with the realist position that talking about democracy was whistling in the wind? Across the street, liberals in other think tanks speculated about America's future role in guiding revolutionary forces in a proper direction. Senator John Kerry, chairman of the Foreign Relations Committee, cautioned, "I don't think anybody should be getting too carried away with a victory lap today." What would be the response elsewhere, he wondered? The Egyptian military was in charge, but nobody knew if it could handle the kind of transition that would move the process forward. "The question is how do they respond and we need to work with them on how to do so. This is the challenge of the Middle East."[1]

Seizing on the scene in Tehran, where police cracked down on huge pro-Egypt rallies, President Obama found a perfect way to contrast the Iranian regime with where he hoped Cairo would now lead the Middle Eastern countries. "We have sent a strong message to our allies in the region," he told a press conference, "saying, 'Let's look at Egypt's example, as opposed to Iran's example.'" The advances in communications through smart phones and Twitter, he went on, meant rulers must now recognize they had to act with the consent of the people. "Governments in that region are starting to understand this," he said, "and my hope is that they can operate in a way that is responsive to this hunger for change, but always do so in a way that doesn't lead to violence."[2]

As for Egypt itself, Obama responded to fears that supposed radical organizations, such as the Muslim Brotherhood, would use the opportunity to seize control of the transition process. "Egypt's going to require help in building democratic institutions," he said, "for strengthening an economy that's taken a hit as a consequence of what happened. But so far at least, we're seeing the right signals coming out of Egypt." And again, "Obviously there's still a lot of work to be done in Egypt itself." But, he added, "What we've seen so far is positive."

The administration had worked closely with the Egyptian military during the critical days before Mubarak's forced resignation. As John Kerry had said, much depended on the Egyptian military's example, inside and outside Egypt. If the region's unelected leaders did not learn from what happened to Mubarak, they, too, would be swept away. Secretary of Defense Robert Gates and Admiral Mike Mullen had made phone calls to their counterparts almost every day, and these counted for more than Mubarak's orders to disperse the crowds. Gates lavished praise on the Egyptian officers for the military's restraint: "Frankly, they have done everything that we have indicated we would hope that they would do. . . . They have made a contribution to the evolution of democracy and what we're seeing in Egypt." Talking about one-on-one contacts, Pentagon spokesman Geoff Morrell added, "That's just an example of how engaged we are with the Egyptians."[3]

Obviously, everyone in Washington hoped it would stay that way, as the Supreme Military Council took charge. Presided over by Mohamed Hussein Tantawi, Mubarak's longtime defense minister and loyal servant in the past, a courtly figure who had avoided publicity, the council, in its first proclamations, promised an end to the hated thirty-year-old emergency law used to detain political opponents without trial, "as soon as the current circumstances are over," and an amendment to the constitution to "conduct free and fair presidential elections." It would fulfill all these pledges, said the council, "within defined time frames."

John Negroponte, the first director of U.S. national intelligence under Bush and a longtime diplomat under Republicans and Democrats, predicted what Washington would do if the military tried to reverse course. The U.S. government, he said on CNN, will "play a role of holding the military's feet to the fire" to ensure it keeps its promises.[4]

Negroponte's prediction immediately collided with Mohamed Tantawi's determination not to give up any of the military's longtime perks in the Egyptian economy. At first, the purges the Supreme Military Council carried out affected only those who, while advocating more openness in the economy, were actually ripping off the country, such as Mubarak's son Gamal and his big industrialist friends. But others it accused of corruption were highly regarded internationally as economic reformers. "Protecting its businesses from scrutiny and accountability," said Robert Springborg, an expert on the Egyptian military at the Naval Postgraduate School, "is a red line the military will draw. And that means there can be no meaningful civilian oversight."[5]

Questioned about how much American military aid wound up in firms controlled by the Egyptian military, the Pentagon passed the inquiry to the State Department, which provided a gentler version of the Negroponte prophecy. Military aid, it said in an e-mail, "assists Egypt in maintaining a strong and disciplined defense force, which is imperative at this time, and critical to ensuring Egypt's continued role as a regional leader able to act as a moderating influence." Retired Air Force major general Michael A. Collings, however, who was the top military representative in Cairo from 2006 to 2008, said that the Americans were not able to track the "for-profit" arm of the Egyptian army that runs factories, farms, and high-tech corporations, but "I do know that a fair amount goes back to the senior officers that are in charge of these particular factories."[6]

By early April, crowds were back in Tahrir Square, chanting new slogans, among them, "Dictator, dictator, Tantawi is next." This time the troops dragged an unknown number of protestors away, throwing them into police trucks, leading to accusations that while one dictator was gone, the dictatorship was still there in full power. "My opinion is that the military council is a supporter of the old regime," said Sayyid Hozayen, a businessman who attended a rally in the square. "They were a part of it, so they are defending it in every way they can."[7]

After the military used clubs and tear gas, the crowds dispersed, only to return again amid the black smoke from three vehicles, including two troop carriers, and over unused bundles of barbed wire that had been brought out to cordon off the protestors' rallying points. It was not clear who set the vehicles ablaze. "The square is with us again," cheered one protestor. "Thank God," said another, "we resisted them and we are still here."[8]

If it was difficult to see the future shape of Egyptian politics through the smoke of burning troop carriers at these post-Mubarak rallies, it was impossible to see where the Egyptian "lead" would take the Middle East. From the time of the 1952 revolution, American policymakers had urged Cairo to provide an example for others to follow by joining a free-world commonwealth of nations, with a promise of material and military rewards. After Nasser, Sadat gave up on neutralism, a role that his successor Hosni Mubarak fully accepted, albeit on terms that limited American influence on Egyptian internal politics. That Washington eventually became intensely frustrated as it watched Egypt sail closer and closer to the far edges of stability is one of the great revelations of the WikiLeaks diplomatic cables. Yet what could one expect, after all, when the United States made use of Cairo as a central receiving point for CIA-rendered terrorist suspects who could not legally be taken to American interrogation sites?

However one thinks about such contradictions, the new situation facing the United States—the challenge of the Middle East, as John Kerry put it—was suddenly visible in central squares and villages across the region as protests erupted and spread from country to country via digital networks. On the day after Mubarak's resignation, Ben Rhodes, the deputy national security adviser for strategic communication, said that the White House had reached out by phone across the Arab world in recent days, to assure allies that the United States intends "to keep its commitments."[9]

American commitments varied, of course, from place to place, as did the protests. How was it possible to bridge the contradictions in

American policy that the protests had so dramatically revealed? At times the administration appeared tongue-tied in facing threats to the very foundations of its influence throughout the region. "The mystique of America's superpower status has been shattered," said Steve Clemons, a director at the liberal think tank New America Foundation. Clemons had attended two meetings of the National Security Council where Egypt had been discussed, and his pessimism about a future where the United States no longer occupied that untouchable place seemed well warranted after Iraq, ten years of war in Afghanistan, and now the cascade of falling regimes across the region.[10]

Historians are sometimes criticized for not providing precise answers or theories about how to "get there from here." That is probably because we are concerned with "how we got *here*." Think-tank theorists are problem solvers who wish to save the essence of superpower policy by identifying past mistakes and avoiding errors in the future. Their search is for a "usable past." But what if that past is no longer usable? Correcting past mistakes is not at all the same as learning from the past; it is a keyhole operation, not unlike using pinpoint drone attacks to destroy an insurgency that flows like lava down the sides of a volcano.

Egypt had been identified as a target of post–World War II policy— for the opportunities it offered for U.S. influence in the Middle East, as well as for the challenge it posed, given the breakdown of the old colonial order. Policymakers from Dean Acheson to Hillary Clinton have tried to find the proper mix of inducements, advice, and warnings to achieve a stable environment for the burgeoning expansion of U.S. political and economic interests in the region. Early on they believed that the Cold War offered a way to bring into play arguments to overcome resentment about past treatment at the hands of European colonial powers, and, possibly, a way to find reconciliation with the Arab world in its anger at the creation of Israel. Neither of these problems could be resolved, but a pattern was established nonetheless of using military aid to encourage cooperation, or to deny it to governments that did not cooperate. Great-power rivalry was a fact of Middle East life, of course, as it was elsewhere in the third world. The choices U.S. policymakers made were not unreasonable in that re-gard, but the pattern of supporting those who accepted terms proved easy and imposed itself as the template for all future policy. Few questions were raised about whether the danger was a Russian advance into the Middle East militarily, or whether nationalist ambitions were at the heart of American difficulties; and as the years went by, the arms continued to arrive to satisfy a hunger or a demand that had been created by what America offered, and justified at home in Washington by the rhetoric itself. Few questions were asked, there-fore, about whether or how American military aid deterred or delayed Middle East political development and brought us to the "here and now."

In Egypt's specific case, American policy toward Nasser demon-strated to Anwar Sadat that one could not easily find an escape hatch from dependence on the goodwill of the Western superpower. With Hosni Mubarak, that dependence kept him in power for thirty years until it finally became too stifling for the Egyptian people to endure. Yet Tahrir Square was not an anti-American revolution, despite all the fears, and we can learn from it about the oxymoron of seeking to impose self-determination.

Some see the choice facing American policymakers as between "realism" on one hand and a Wilsonian mission to make the world safe for democracy on the other. On April 14, 2011, Secretary of Defense Robert Gates traveled the short distance from the Penta-gon to George Washington's home at Mount Vernon to preside at a groundbreaking ceremony for a new national library for the study of America's first president. He used the occasion to deliver a lecture on the different forces that pulled on policymakers from the very beginning as the United States emerged on the world scene.

George Washington, Gates said, was of the opinion that the United States could not survive if it took the position that it could deal only with nations that subscribed to our ideals:

> In just the past few months [we have] begun to witness an extraordinary story unfolding across the Middle East and North Africa. People across the region have come together to demand

change, and in many cases, a more democratic, responsive government. Yet many of the regimes affected have been longstanding, close allies of the United States, ones we continue to work with as critical partners in the face of common security challenges like Al Qaeda and Iran, even as we urge them to reform and respond to the needs of their people.

An underlying theme of American history going back to Washington is that we are compelled to defend our security and our interests in ways that, in the long run, lead to the spread of democratic values and institutions. . . . When we discuss openly our desire for democratic values to take hold across the globe, we are describing a world that may be many years or decades off.[11]

Gates wishes his fellow countrymen would understand the limits on American power, and the ultimate danger to the national interest posed by those who want to remake the world overnight. It is more difficult to determine what he believes the United States can do to navigate through the revolutions that reverberate through the Middle East today. The Washingtonian realism he inserts in the debate over where to intervene and where to abstain is helpful as a starting point, but it is inadequate if we wish to go very far beyond our current predicament. Before the events in Tahrir Square, for example, Gates would not have supported a reconsideration of American military aid to Hosni Mubarak, the means by which the United States hoped to channel Egyptian nationalism into the American version of a postcolonial world order from the time of the 1952 revolution. Picking and choosing today among revolutions while insisting, as Hillary Clinton and Robert Gates do, that power and principle can ultimately be reconciled, postpones coming to terms with the implications of the road to Tahrir Square.

POSTSCRIPT

*After America's withdrawals from Iraq and Afghanistan and the con-
straint to our strategic reach produced by the revolution in Egypt, a
new definition of American leadership and America's national interest
is inescapable.*

—Henry A. Kissinger,
The Washington Post, June 7, 2011

"Justice has been done," President Obama said in a brief television
appearance near midnight on May 1, 2011. The death of the author of
"the worst attack on the American people in our history" came "after
a fire fight." No Americans were harmed, he assured the nation, and
the Navy SEALs took care to avoid civilian casualties. Then they
took custody of the body and buried it at sea. Almost immediately
questions arose about the circumstances of Osama bin Laden's discovery and killing in his Pakistan hiding spot, but the most important
thing about the dramatic night raid was that it shoved the Egyptian
Revolution and, indeed, the "Arab Spring," into the background.

At least for the moment the American public was enthralled by
the news of how bin Laden had been tracked to his lair and shot to
death by a Special Forces team. However, the reaction in Egypt
sounded a different note. "I want to give you a message to America,"
an Egyptian woman told an interviewer studying the Muslim world.
"I wish America would respect human beings everywhere and try to
save lost human rights all over the world, just as much as it is concerned about bin Laden." She was not alone. A Gallup Poll of Egyptian opinion revealed an "overwhelming tsunami of negative
opinions" about the United States. Slightly more than half of those
questioned opposed any U.S. aid to Egypt, and three-quarters opposed any aid to specific political groups.[1]

These reactions were especially noteworthy because the Egyptian
economy was in a perilous state after the revolution, with the Egyp-

tian pound falling in international currency rates, the unemployment rate rising to above 12 percent, and investors frightened by the "social-ist" turn of the interim military government that had attempted to ameliorate the impact of the crisis by raising wages of public workers and taking other steps. These were seen by new groups of protestors who had returned to Tahrir Square in late May as not nearly enough to fulfill the promise of the revolution to end the years of special privi-leges for the few and increasing poverty for the many. Major General Mahmud Nasr, a member of the Supreme Military Council, openly admitted that the poverty rate could reach 70 percent, leading to fears of a "revolution of the hungry."[2]

So, again, why was there such skepticism about possible American aid? The Gallup Organization's chief analyst of the poll claimed the reason was simple: Egyptians had long perceived U.S. aid to be the reason why Egypt could not make its own decisions politically and why Egyptian "aspirations on the ground are not reflected in the way the country is governed." In addition, he said, opinion would signifi-cantly improve if the United States would pressure Israel to halt settle-ment expansion "in the Palestinian territories." But the main reason was suspicion that American aid only went to perpetuate the condi-tions of the Mubarak years.[3]

The new Egyptian regime was in danger of failing even before the scheduled September elections, where the Moslem Brother-hood, repackaged as the Freedom and Justice Party, now in a coali-tion with an old liberal party, the Wafd Party, would likely have a strong chance of winning control of parliament and the ensuing constitution drafting process. The message had gotten through to Washington, where President Obama announced on May 19, 2011, an aid package that included $1 billion in debt forgiveness, and an-other $1 billion guarantee on Egyptian Eurbonds, designed to re-duce the country's borrowing costs. "The American backing is a complete game changer," said a Boston financier. The changed times from when George H. W. Bush forgave Egypt's debt to encourage Cairo to participate in Gulf War I politically and even militarily (in a small way), was an obvious indicator that fears of a crisis that could influence the entire Middle East was behind the decision.[4]

The message had also gotten through to the IMF, which a few days before the events that triggered the revolution on January 25, 2011, had published a report praising Hosni Mubarak's economic stewardship. Now the fund implicitly admitted it had been out of step with Egyptian opinion, and announced it was offering Cairo a $3 billion deal—without the usual conditions that demanded the sort of austerity measures that it had required years earlier from Anwar Sadat, who jettisoned Nasserite socialism to comply. Sister agency to the IMF, the World Bank added a $2.2 billion loan to assist. "The revolution brought forth many expectations and hopes," said an IMF representative, "And as we can see in Egypt, one of the biggest priorities of the government is indeed social justice . . . then we respect that priority."[5]

The message certainly got through to Saudi Arabia, deeply fearful of the further spread of unrest in the Middle East that could be the result of an Egyptian collapse. Riyadh offered the biggest single sum of $4 billion in economic and budgetary aid, at about the same time as it was raising wages and housing subsidies at home. Even with this "stimulus" package, there were serious doubts about whether it would be enough. Moody's Financial Services had issued a statement on May 24, just before Obama's speech, that said, "Egypt suffers from deep-seated political, socio-economic challenges," including a "chronic high rate of unemployment, elevated inflation, and widespread poverty."[6]

It remained to be seen, furthermore, whether old ways of dealing with Egyptian nationalism since the days of Nasser and his more complaisant successors would still dominant policymakers' thinking as Cairo struggled to find a new balance internally and externally in relations with the outside world. One indication that Washington felt it still had supervisory responsibilities came in a press conference Secretary of State Hillary Clinton gave in Brazil. She announced that the State Department had concerns about the interim government's plans to put Hosni Mubarak on trial. "We are keeping very close watch on events in Egypt," she said, warning that a trial on charges that he had caused the deaths of Tahrir Square protestors would be emotionally charged. It must be con-

ducted with the highest legal standards, she said, adding that the
military government appeared to be cracking down itself on journalists and bloggers, "which we don't think is in keeping with the
direction the Egyptian people were heading when they started out
in Tahrir Square."[7]

More generally, and more indicative of Washington's fears it was
losing leverage in Egypt, Admiral Mike Mullen, the retiring chair
of the Joint Chiefs, expressed concern in an interview with Bloomberg News in New York that U.S. military assistance in Latin
America and Africa could be cut as the Pentagon faced $400 bil-
lion in budget reductions over the next twelve years. "These are
preventative investments," Mullen said. The aid programs avoid
conflicts, he went on, and allowed the United States to better respond in a crisis. American leadership will continue to be "critical,"
but other countries will have to provide help in future situations.
"We're so interconnected and interdependent," and, "it will be more
and more the case that there isn't a single country that can do it
alone." Mullen then explained thirty years of funding Egypt's military, and the returns it had yielded. He had been in frequent contact with his Egyptian counterpart during the days of turmoil, he
said as "the Egyptian military . . . decided how to handle the protests." He had just returned from a visit to Cairo, he concluded, and
had gained more assurances. "He considered U.S. funding for
Egypt's military a 'relatively inexpensive investment.'"[8]

The Obama administration faced challenges in the Middle East
that had escalated into a watershed, and a turning point. Even as it
attempted to extricate itself from a war in Iraq without abandoning
its influence in Baghdad, and to scale down an over-ambitious effort
to shape Afghanistan's future, the situation in Egypt portended far
greater long-term dangers. It remained to be seen if these could be
overcome with some new mix of financial aid without attaching
conditions that would alienate Egyptian sensibilities and without
falling back on the "relatively inexpensive investment" of military
aid to solve Egypt's political problems.

The remarkable admission by Henry Kissinger that the Egyptian revolution requires a new definition of American leadership and American national interest is indeed inescapable.

NOTES

Introduction

1. David D. Kirkpatrick, "In Shift, Egypt Warms to Iran and Hamas, Israel's Foes," *New York Times*, April 28, 2011.

2. See Steven Myers article under the headline quoted at the beginning of the introduction.

1. Prelude: Searching for a Policy

1. See footnote relating to Roosevelt's comment, dated March 3, 1945, Department of State, *Foreign Relations of the United States, 1945: The Near East and Africa*, vol. 8 (Washington, D.C.: Government Printing Office, 1969), 4 (hereafter cited as *FR*).

2. Roosevelt to Hull, January 12, 1944, Papers of Franklin D. Roosevelt, Franklin D. Roosevelt Library (hereafter FDRL), Hyde Park, New York, President's Secretary's File, Iran.

3. See Lloyd C. Gardner, *Economic Aspects of New Deal Diplomacy* (Madison: University of Wisconsin Press, 1964), 220.

4. William A. Eddy to Secretary of State, March 3, 1945, *FR, 1945*, 8:9.

5. George F. Kennan, "Review of Current Trends in U.S. Foreign Policy," February 24, 1948, *FR, 1948*, vol. 1, pt. 2, 510–29.

6. Ibid.

7. Lewis Douglas to Secretary of State, May 1, 1947, *FR, 1947*, 5:769–70.

8. S. Pinckney Tuck to Secretary George Marshall, May 14, 1948, *FR, 1948*, 5:991; Jefferson Caffery to Secretary Dean Acheson, October 12, 1949, ibid., 223.

9. Holmes to Secretary of State, January 7, 1949, ibid., 6:187.

10. "King Ibn Saud," undated memorandum, Harry Hopkins Papers, box 170, FDRL; Edward Stettinius to Roosevelt, January 9, 1945, Roosevelt Papers, President's Secretary's File, Arabia, FDRL.

11. "Memorandum of Conversation Between the King of Saudi Arabia and President Roosevelt," February 14, 1945, *FR, 1945*, 8:2–3.

12. Gordon Merriam, Chief, Division of Near Eastern Affairs, Department of State, Memorandum to Jonathan Daniels, March 17, 1945, and Daniels's note on the

memorandum, with clipping from *New York Herald Tribune*, March 17, 1945, Roosevelt Papers, FDRL.

13. Summary of Correspondence with Prince Abdul Ilah, March 10, April 2, April 10, and April 12, 1945, Roosevelt Papers, OF 3500, FDRL.

14. Stettinius to Truman, April 18, 1945, FR, 1945, 8:704–5.

15. Stettinius to the General Counsel at Jerusalem, August 18, 1945, ibid., 722.

16. Loy Henderson, Memorandum of Conversation, August 17, 1945, ibid., 721.

17. Henderson to Acheson, October 1, 1945, ibid., 751–53.

18. Henderson, Memorandum of Conversation, October 3, 1945, ibid., 756–58.

19. Henderson, Memorandum of Conversation, October 12, 1945, ibid., 766–69.

20. Press Conference, October 18, 1945.

21. William Roger Louis, *British Empire in the Middle East, 1945–1951* (Oxford: Clarendon Press, 1984), 428–29.

22. The complicated 1945 deliberations and correspondence can be followed in *FR, 1945*, 8:679–844.

23. "Memorandum by the Minister to Saudi Arabia. . . ." October 26, 1945, ibid., 790–91.

24. "Memorandum by the Director of the Office of Near Eastern and African Affairs," November 13, 1945, ibid., 11–18.

25. John Keay, *Sowing the Wind: The Seeds of Conflict in the Middle East* (New York: W.W. Norton, 2003), 340.

26. Secretary of State Byrnes to the Ambassador in the United Kingdom, July 23, 1946, FR, 1946, 7:650.

27. The Chargé in Egypt to Secretary of State, August 2, 1946, ibid., 676–77.

28. Memorandum by Major General John H. Hildring, September 24, 1947, FR, 147, 5:1162–64.

29. Ilan Pappé, *The Making of the Arab-Israeli Conflict, 1947–1951* (New York: I.B. Tauris, 2001), 24–25.

30. Tom Segev, *One Palestine, Complete: Jews and Arabs Under the British Mandate*, trans. Haim Watzman (New York: Henry Holt, 2001), 158–59; Simha Flappan, *The Birth of Israel: Myth and Realities* (New York: Pantheon, 1987), 38–39.

31. Tuck to Secretary of State, December 3, 1947, FR, 1947, 5:1295–97.

32. Memorandum of Conversation, May 12, 1948, ibid., 972–76.

33. Truman, *Memoirs*, vol. 2, *Years of Trial and Hope* (Garden City, N.Y.: Doubleday, 1956), 168–69.

34. Read by Clifford at the White House Meeting, May 12, 1948, FR, 1948, 5:977–78.

35. Ritchie Ovendale, *The Origins of the Arab-Israeli Wars* (London: Longman, 1984), 123–24, 130.

36. Robert Lovett, Memorandum of Conversation, December 17, 1948, FR, 1948, 5:1672–74.

37. See FR, 1949, 6:1436.

38. Report by the National Security Council, October 17, 1949, ibid., 1430–40.

39. Memorandum of Conversation, January 31, 1950, FR, 1950, 5:712–15.

40. Elath to Acheson, February 13, 1950, and George McGhee to Acheson, March 25, 1950, ibid., 736–41, 816–17.

41. Footnote 6, ibid., 135.

42. Miles Copeland, The Game of Nations: The Amorality of Power Politics (New York: Simon & Schuster, 1969), 58.

43. Caffery to Secretary of State, November 22, 1950, FR, 1950, 5:322–23.

44. Caffery to Department of State, April 1, 1951, FR, 1951, 5:352–55.

45. Ibid.

46. Caffery to Department of State, October 9, 1951, FR, 1951, 5:392–95.

47. Interview with Gaddis Smith, "Mr. Acheson Answers Some Questions," October 12, 1969, www.nytimes.com/books/98/08.

48. Acheson to Caffery, October 16, 1951, FR, 1951, 5:226–27.

49. New York Times, November 21, 1951.

2. The Nasser Gamble Fails

1. Memorandum by Felix Belair Jr., April 29, 1946, Papers of Arthur Krock, Seeley G. Mudd Manuscript Library, Princeton University, Princeton, New Jersey, box 1.

2. James Reston, "Truman Asks Aid to Greece; British Unable to Bear Cost," New York Times, February 28, 1947.

3. Memorandum for the Secretary of State, May 19, 1952, FR, 1952–1954, vol. 9, pt. 2, 1804–7.

4. Kennett Love, Suez: The Twice-Fought War (New York: McGraw-Hill, 1969), 170–71.

5. Ibid., 173.

6. Ibid., 177.

7. Donald Neff, Warriors at Suez: Eisenhower Takes America into the Middle East (New York: Simon & Schuster, 1981), 68–69; Love, Suez, 180–81.

8. Barry Rubin, "America and the Egyptian Revolution, 1950–1957," Political Science Quarterly 97, no. 1 (Spring 1982): 73–90; Memorandum of Telephone Conversation, January 27, 1952, FR, 1952–1954, vol. 9, pt. 2, 1756–57.

9. Minutes of Ministerial Talks in London, June 24, 1952, FR, 1952–1954, vol. 9, pt. 2, 1813–19.

10. Rubin, "America and the Egyptian Revolution."

11. Caffery to Department of State, August 20, 1952, FR, 1952–1954, 9:1851.

12. Caffery to Secretary of State, September 18, 1952, ibid., 1861–62.

13. Secretary of State to Caffery, September 30, 1952, ibid., 1863–65.

14. Mohamed Heikal, *Cutting the Lion's Tail: Suez Through Egyptian Eyes* (New York: Arbor House, 1987), 34–35.

15. Caffery to Department of State, November 25, 1952, *FR, 1952–1954*, vol. 9, pt. 2, 1894–95.

16. Love, *Suez*, 265; Dulles to Eisenhower, June 13, 1953, Papers of John Foster Dulles, Seeley G. Mudd Manuscript Library, Princeton University, Princeton, New Jersey, White House Memos, box 1.

17. Memorandum of Conversation, May 11, 1953, *FR, 1952–1954*, vol. 9, pt. 1, 8–18.

18. Ibid.

19. Ibid. Emphasis in original.

20. Mohamed Heikal, *The Cairo Documents: The Inside Story of Nasser and His Relationship with World Leaders, Rebels, and Statesmen* (Garden City, N.Y.: Doubleday, 1973), 32.

21. Ibid., 40–41.

22. Ibid.

23. Memorandum of Conversation, May 12, 1953, *FR, 1952–1954*, vol. 9, pt. 2; Heikal, *Cairo Documents*, 19–25.

24. Meeting with Congressional Leaders, March 9, 1953, Papers of Dwight D. Eisenhower, Dwight D. Eisenhower Presidential Library, Abilene, Kansas, Legislative Series, box 1; Dulles, "Conclusions on Trip," undated, May 1953, Dulles Papers, box 475.

25. Dulles, "Conclusions," May 1953.

26. See Lloyd C. Gardner, *Three Kings: The Rise of an American Empire in the Middle East After World War II* (New York: The New Press, 2009), chap. 4, "The Iran Oil Crisis," 85–134; Said K. Aburish, *Nasser: The Last Arab* (New York: St. Martin's Press, 2004), 43, 76.

27. Copeland, *Game of Nations*, 101–2.

28. "Dulles Says U.S. Aim Is to Gain Friends," *New York Times*, June 2, 1953.

29. "Cairo Sees Gains in Dulles' Report," ibid., June 3, 1953; "Israel Asks Dulles to Clarify Report," ibid., June 9, 1953; Dana Adams Schmidt, "Sensitive Israelis Concerned Over Shifts in World Opinion," ibid., June 28, 1953.

30. Dulles Testimony, June 3, 1953, in U.S. Congress, Senate Foreign Relations Committee, *Executive Sessions of the Senate Foreign Relations Committee (Historical Series)*, vol. 5, 1953, 83rd Congress, 1st sess. (Washington, D.C.: Government Printing Office, 1977), 439–41. I have changed the order of the quotations in order to summarize Dulles's main points.

31. Ibid.

32. Churchill to Eisenhower, June 21, 1954, *FR, 1952–1954*, vol. 9, pt. 2, 2275.

33. Memorandum by the Deputy Assistant Secretary of State, September 28, 1954, *FR, 1952–1954*, vol. 9, pt. 2, 2305–6.

34. Memorandum of Discussion, June 1, 1953, ibid., pt. 1, 378–86.

35. William J. Burns, *Economic Aid and American Policy Toward Egypt, 1955–1981* (Albany: State University of New York Press, 1985), 26–27.

36. "'Byroadeism' Held Blow at Zionism," *New York Times*, June 24, 1954.

37. Henry Byroade to Department of State, March 1, 1955, *FR, 1955–1957*, 14:78–79.

38. Love, *Suez*, 200–202.

39. Townsend Hoopes, *The Devil and John Foster Dulles* (Boston: Atlantic–Little Brown, 1973), 320–23; Love, *Suez*, 88.

40. Caffery to Department of State, December 11, 1952, *FR, 1952–1954*, vol. 9, pt. 2, 1908.

41. "Points of Agreement in London Discussion of Arab-Israeli Settlement," March 10, 1955, *FR, 1955–1957*, 14:98–107.

42. "Memorandum of Conversation," Economic Sanctions Against Israel and Related Matters Affecting US-Israel Relations, October 25, 1953, Dulles Papers.

43. Byroade to Department of State, April 14, 1955, *FR, 1955–1957*, 14:151–53.

44. Hoopes, *Devil and John Foster Dulles*, 315–17.

45. Heikal, *Cutting the Lion's Tail*, 69.

46. Love, *Suez*, 241.

47. Steven Z. Freiberger, *Dawn over Suez: The Rise of American Power in the Middle East, 1953–1957* (Chicago: Ivan R. Dee, 1992), 122–24.

48. Byroade to Department of State, September 21, 1955, *FR, 1955–1957*, 14:497–98.

49. Freiberger, *Dawn over Suez*, 124.

50. Ibid.

51. Ibid.

52. Rubin, "America and the Egyptian Revolution, 85; Anthony Eden to Eisenhower, November 27, 1955, and Herbert Hoover to Dulles, November 28, 1955, *FR, 1955*, 14:808–10.

53. Byroade to Department of State, November 17, 1955, *FR, 1955*, 14:781–83.

54. Hoover to Cairo, January 31, 1956, *FR, 1955–1957*, 15:117.

55. "Message to Washington," January 24, 1956, ibid., 60–63.

56. Memorandum of Conversation with the President, July 13, 1956, Dulles Papers, White House Memoranda Series, box 4.

57. George Allen to Dulles, July 13, 1956, and July 17, 1956, both in *FR, 1955–1957*, 15:828–30, 849–51.

58. Byroade to Department of State, July 13, 1956, ibid., 832–35.

59. Memorandum of a Conversation, July 19, 1956, ibid., 863–64.

60. Memorandum of a Conversation, July 19, 1956, 4:10–5:07 P.M., ibid., 867–73.

61. Dana Adams Schmidt, "Aswan Decision Marks a Turn in U.S. Policy," *New York Times*, July 22, 1956; Osgood Caruthers, "Nasser Says U.S. Lied in Explaining Bar to Aswan Aid," *New York Times*, July 24, 1956; Love, *Suez*, 345–53.

62. Memorandum of Conversation with the President, August 14, 1956, Dulles Papers, White House Memoranda Series, box 5.

63. Memorandum of Conversation with Secretary-General Hammarskjöld, August 10, 1956, ibid., Memos of Conversations, box 1.

64. Memorandum of Conversation with Selwyn Lloyd, August 24, 1956, ibid., Dulles-Eisenhower Correspondence, box 1.

65. Freiberger, *Dawn over Suez*, 171–75.

66. Ibid., 178–85.

67. Dulles, Memorandum of Conversation with Mr. Harold Macmillan, September 25, 1956, Dulles-Eisenhower Correspondence, box 1; Dulles, Memorandum of Conversation with the President, Meetings with the President, box 4.

68. Memoranda of Conferences with the President, October 29, 1956, 7:15 P.M., and 8:15 P.M., ibid., Meetings with the President, box 7.

69. Diary Notes, October 26–November 6, 1956, Emmett John Hughes Papers, Seeley G. Mudd Manuscript Library, Princeton University, Princeton, New Jersey, box 1.

70. Neff, *Warriors at Suez*, 375–76.

71. Diane Kunz, *The Economic Diplomacy of the Suez Crisis* (Chapel Hill: University of North Carolina Press, 1991), 135, 146–47.

72. Heikal, *Cairo Documents*, 119–20.

73. Memorandum of Conversation, September 6, 1956, Subject Series, box 1.

3. Eisenhower Doctrine to Six Days of War

1. "Kennan Disputes U.S. Policy in U.N.," *New York Times*, November 4, 1956.

2. U.S. Congress, Senate Foreign Relations Committee, *Executive Sessions of the Senate Foreign Relations Committee*, vol. 9, 85th Congress, 1st sess., 1957 (Washington, D.C.: Government Printing Office, 1970), 159–74.

3. William J. Burns, *Economic Aid and American Policy Toward Egypt, 1955–1981* (Albany: State University of New York Press, 1985), 108.

4. Copeland, *Game of Nations*, 202–3.

5. *Executive Sessions*, 19.

6. Robert Vitalis, *America's Kingdom: Mythmaking on the Saudi Oil Frontier* (Stanford, Calif.: Stanford University Press, 2007), 184–88.

7. Draft Communiqué, February 8, 1957, Dulles Papers, Dulles/Eisenhower, Subject Series, box 5.

8. Dulles, Memorandum of Conversation with the British Ambassador, February 7, 1957, ibid., Memos of Conversation, box 1; Salim Yaqub, *Containing Arab Nationalism: The Eisenhower Doctrine and the Middle East* (Chapel Hill: University of North Carolina Press, 2004), 102.

9. Yaqub, *Containing Arab Nationalism*, 103.

10. Dulles, Memorandum of a Conversation at the Mid-Ocean Club, March 20, 1957, Dulles Papers, Memoranda of Conversations, box 1.

11. Yaqub, *Containing Arab Nationalism*, 162; Vitalis, *America's Kingdom*, 186–93; Ben Fenton, "Macmillan Backed Syria Assassination Plot," *Guardian*, September 27, 2003.

12. Vitalis, *America's Kingdom*, 191; Dulles, Memorandum of Conversation, October 6, 1957, Dulles Papers, Memoranda of Conversations, box 1.

13. Aburish, *Nasser: The Last Arab*, 156–61.

14. Memorandum to the President, February 8, 1958, *FR, 1958–1960*, 13:421–22.

15. Hare to Department of State, April 26, 1958, ibid., 446–49.

16. Ibid.

17. Ibid.

18. Yaqub, *Containing Arab Nationalism*, 205–15; Dulles, Memorandum of Conversation with Prime Minister Daud, June 25, 1958, Dulles Papers, Memoranda of Conversations, box 1.

19. H.W. Brands, *Into the Labyrinth: The United States and the Middle East, 1945–1993* (New York: McGraw-Hill, 1994), 76–77.

20. Copeland, *Game of Nations*, 235–43.

21. Dulles, Memorandum of Conversation, January 19, 1959, Dulles Papers, Memoranda of Conversations, box 1.

22. "The Dissembler," *Time*, April 13, 1959, www.time.com/printout/0,8816,810960.00.html.

23. Sergei N. Khrushchev, *Nikita Khrushchev and the Creation of a Superpower*, trans. Shirley Benson (University Park: Pennsylvania State University Press, 2000), 290–91.

24. Nikita Khrushchev, *Khrushchev Remembers*, trans. Strobe Talbott, with introduction, commentary, and notes by Edward Crankshaw (Boston: Little, Brown, 1970), 438.

25. Sandra Mackey, *The Reckoning: Iraq and the Legacy of Saddam Hussein* (New York: W.W. Norton, 2002), 181.

26. Joe Stork, *Middle East Oil and the Energy Crisis* (New York: Monthly Review Press, 1975), 102–8.

27. Ibid.

28. Unsigned State Department Paper, "The Situation in Iraq," April 15, 1959, *FR, 1958–1960*, 12:414–22.

29. Burns, *Economic Aid*, 113–14; Hare to Department of State, November 29, 1958, *FR, 1958–1960*, 13:500–502; Dana Adams Schmidt, "Tense Mideast Focuses on Jordan and Iraq," *New York Times*, November 9, 1958.

30. Memorandum of a Conference, December 23, 1958, *FR, 1958–1960*, 13:507–9.

31. Memorandum of Discussion, April 2, 1959, *FR, 1958–1960*, 12:402–6.

32. Memorandum of Discussion, April 17, 1959, ibid., 423–37.

33. Ibid.

34. Special Committee on Iraq, Memoranda for Record, April 27 and December 8, 1959, CP Iraq (Philip Halla Files), National Security Council Staff Papers, 1953–1961, box 5, Papers of Dwight D. Eisenhower, Dwight D. Eisenhower Library, Abilene, Kansas.

35. Said K. Aburish, A *Brutal Friendship: The West and the Arab Elite* (New York: St. Martin's Press, 1998), 138–42.

36. Aburish, *Nasser: The Last Arab*, 213–14.

37. Memorandum of a Conversation, September 26, 1960, *FR, 1958–1960*, 13:600–607.

38. Robert Komer, "Memorandum for the Record," November 14, 1963, *FR, 1962–1963*, 18:779–86.

39. Department of State to the Embassy in the United Arab Republic, December 24, 1962, ibid. 275–76.

40. Ibid.

41. Memorandum of Conversation, December 27, 1962, ibid., 276–83.

42. Ibid.

43. The Hawk missile rationale and sale are explored in Warren Bass, *Support Any Friend: Kennedy's Middle East and the Making of the U.S.-Israel Alliance* (New York: Oxford University Press, 2003), 180–85.

44. Ibid., 178–79.

45. Walt Rostow, "Memorandum for the President: Our Policy Toward the UAR," April 14, 1964, encl. Polk to Rostow, "Our Policy Toward the UAR," April 7, 1964, Papers of Lyndon B. Johnson, Lyndon B. Johnson Library, Austin, Texas, National Security File, Country File, Turkey, UAR, box 158.

46. Polk, "Our Policy," ibid. The remainder of this discussion is taken from Polk's memorandum.

47. Heikal, *Cairo Documents,2* 28–32.

48. Ibid., 229.

49. Ibid., 237.

50. Ibid.

51. "Memorandum of Conversation," February 23, 1966, *FR, 1964–1968*, 18:557–60.

52. Rufus Taylor, "Memorandum for Record," June 1, 1967, ibid., 19:223–25.

53. Ibid.

54. Briefing Note for Helms, May 23, 1967, *FR, 1964–1968*, 19:272–77.

55. Memorandum of Conversation, May 26, 1967, *FR, 1964–1968*, 19:140–46.

56. Ibid.

57. Memorandum to Johnson, June 4, 1967, ibid., 272–77.

58. Rostow, Memorandum for the Record, November 17, 1968, ibid., 287–92.

59. Robert Anderson to Secretary of State and the President, November 3, 1967, ibid., 973–81.

60. U.S. Senate, Foreign Relations Committee, *Executive Sessions of the Senate Foreign Relations Committee (Historical Series)*, vol. 9, 85th Congress, 1st. sess., 1957 (Washington, D.C.: Government Printing Office, 1979), 140–43.

4. Life with Anwar Sadat: Or a Story of Empire by Invitation

1. Lance Morrow, "Sadat: Murder of a Man of Peace," *Time*, October 19, 1981, www.time.com/time/magazine/article/0,9171,924939,00.html#ixzz1G7vh7Rp.

2. James MacManus, "President Sadat Assassinated at Army Parade," *Guardian*, October 7, 1981, www.guardian.co.uk/theguardian/2010/oct/07/archive-president-sadat -assassinated.

3. Bob Woodward, *Veil: The Secret Wars of the CIA* (New York: Simon & Schuster, 1987), 168–69, 312–13.

4. Henry Kissinger, *Years of Upheaval* (Boston: Little, Brown, 1982), 460.

5. Dean Rusk and Richard Rusk, *As I Saw It* (New York: Penguin Books, 1991), 389.

6. Anwar el-Sadat, *In Search of Identity: An Autobiography* (New York: Harper & Row, 1977), 276.

7. Seymour M. Hersh, *The Price of Power: Kissinger in the Nixon White House* (New York: Summit Books, 1983), 219–20.

8. Sadat, *In Search of Identity*, 198.

9. Ibid., 217.

10. Sadat, *In Search of Identity*, 280.

11. Ibid., 285.

12. White House Situation Room, "Memorandum for Dr. Kissinger," June 1, 1971, Declassified Documents Reference System (hereafter DDRS).

13. Quoted in Hersh, *Price of Power*, 404.

14. Summary of a Telephone Call, Sisco/Kissinger, February 28, 1871, DDRS.

15. Sadat, *In Search of Identity*, 229.

16. Ibid.

17. Ibid., 287.

18. Burns, *Economic Aid*, 176.

19. Sadat, *In Search of Identity*, 213–14.

20. Ibid.

21. Rostow, "Memorandum for the President: Our Policy Toward the UAR," April 14, 1964, encl. Polk to Rostow, "Our Policy Toward the UAR," April 7, 1964, Papers of Lyndon B. Johnson, Lyndon B. Johnson Library, Austin, Texas, National Security File, Country File, Turkey, UAR, box 158.

22. Burns, *Economic Aid*, 177.

23. Tito to Nixon, January 27, 1973, DDRS.

24. Mohamed Heikal, *The Road to Ramadan* (New York: Ballantine Books, 1975), 204–8. Unless otherwise noted, the discussion that follows is based largely on Heikal's account taken apparently from Egyptian notes.

25. Brent Scowcroft's handwritten notes of the Nixon/Ismail Meeting, February 23, 1973, Gerald Ford Presidential Library, Ann Arbor, Michigan.

26. Ibid.

27. Heikal, *Road to Ramadan*, 207.

28. Ibid., 208.

29. William B. Quandt, *Peace Process: American Diplomacy and the Arab-Israeli Conflict Since 1967*, 3rd ed. (Washington, D.C.: Brookings Institution Press, 2005), 102–3.

30. Kissinger to Nixon, June 2, 1973, DDRS.

31. Heikal, *Road to Ramadan*, 210.

32. David Hirst and Irene Beeson, *Sadat* (London: Faber and Faber, 1981), 155.

33. Quandt, *Peace Process*, 104.

34. *New York Times*, October 8, 1973.

35. Donald Neff, *Warriors Against Israel: How Israel Won the Battle to Become America's Ally, 1973* (Brattleboro, Vt.: Amana Books, 1988), 228–29.

36. Kissinger, *Years of Upheaval*, 712.

37. Quandt, *Peace Process*, 124.

38. Hirst and Beeson, *Sadat*, 176.

39. Ibid., 174.

40. Sadat, *In Search of Identity*, 267; Walter Isaacson, *Kissinger: A Biography* (New York: Simon & Schuster, 1992), 539.

41. Mohamed Heikal, *Autumn of Fury: The Assassination of Sadat* (New York: Random House, 1983), 68.

42. Ibid., 69.

43. Kissinger, *Years of Upheaval*, 768.

44. Kissinger, Background Memorandum, October 31, 1973, DDRS.

45. "Meeting between Secretary Kissinger and Egyptian Ambassador," December 7, 1973, Anwar Sadat Archive, College Park, Maryland, sadat.umd.edu/archives.

46. Nixon to Sadat, December 27, 1973, ibid.

47. Memorandum of a Conversation, April 30, 1974, ibid.

48. Memorandum of a Conversation, April 18, 1974, ibid.

49. Memorandum of Conversation, May 1, 1974, ibid.

50. Ibid.

51. Burns, *Economic Aid*, 180–81.

52. Memorandum of Conversation, November 6, 1974, Sadat Archive.

53. Ibid.

54. Quandt, *Peace Process*, 175–76; "Middle East: The Eleventh Shuttle: Is Peace at Hand?" August 25, 1975, www.time.com/time/magazine/article/0,9171,913418,00.html.

55. Heikal, *Autumn of Fury*, 71.

56. Kissinger to Ford, October 27, 1975, DDRS.

57. Burns, *Economic Aid*, 188.

58. Ibid., 188–89.

59. Memorandum of Conversation, October 14, 1976, DDRS.

60. Heikal, *Autumn of Fury*, 98.

61. "Middle East: Sadat's Sacred Mission," *Time*, November 28, 1977, www.time.com/time/magazine/article/0,9171,919150-1,00.html. The account of the meeting is largely taken from this source.

62. Ibid.

63. Quandt, *Peace Process*, 192–93.

64. A succinct account of these negotiations and their outcome is found in Scott Kaufman, *Plans Unraveled: The Foreign Policy of the Carter Administration* (DeKalb: Northern Illinois University Press, 2008), 78–85.

65. Ibid., 85.

66. Memorandum for the President, November 20, 1978, and Memorandum for the President, January 23, 1979, DDRS.

67. news.bbc.co.uk/onthisday/hi/dates/stories/ . . . /2806245.stm.

68. William Shawcross, *The Shah's Last Ride* (New York: Simon & Schuster, 1988), 380, 385.

69. William E. Farrell, "Sadat Assassinated at Army Parade. . . ." *New York Times*, October 6, 1981.

5. The $50 Billion Gamble: Thirty Years of Egyptian-American Co-Dependence

1. Lloyd C. Gardner, *The Long Road to Baghdad: A History of U.S. Foreign Policy from the 1970s to the Present* (New York: The New Press, 2008), 59–60, 68–70.

2. This is not the place for a long discussion of Iran-Contra, but see ibid., 66–67, and Theodore Draper, *A Very Thin Line: The Iran-Contra Affairs* (New York: Hill & Wang, 1991).

3. See, for example, Ambassador Margaret Scobey to Secretary of State, February 2, 2010, WikiLeaks Cable Viewer, http://213.251.145.96/cable/2010/02/.

4. Lawrence Wright, *The Looming Tower: Al-Qaeda and the Road to 9/11* (New York: Alfred A. Knopf, 2006), 50–51; Alexander Haig to South African Foreign Minister, October 11, 1981, DDRS.

5. William B. Quandt, *Peace Process: American Diplomacy and the Arab-Israeli Conflict Since 1967*, 3rd ed. (Berkeley: University of California Press, 2005), 250–54.

6. Reagan to Mubarak, August 30, 1982, DDRS.

7. Quandt, *Peace Process*, 257.

8. Associated Press, "King Hussein Backs Plan for Dialogue: Endorses Mubarak's Request for Talks by U.S., Palestine," *Los Angeles Times*, March 6, 1985, http://articles.latimes.com/1985-03-06.

9. Norman Kempster, "Reagan Doesn't Back Mubarak Call for Talks," *Los Angeles Times*, March 13, 1985, http://articles.latimes.come/1985-03-13; Quandt, *Peace Process*, 263–65.

10. Quandt, *Peace Process*, 266–67.

11. Wright, *Looming Tower*, 33–37.

12. Ibid., 39.

13. Ibid., 48–49.

14. Andrew Higgins and Alan Cullison, "Saga of Dr. Zawahri Sheds Light on the Roots of al Qaeda Terror," *Wall Street Journal*, July 2, 2002; Wright, *Looming Tower*, 214–20.

15. Scobey to Washington, May 19, 2009, "Scenesetter: President Mubarak's Visit to Washington," WikiLeaks release, reprinted in *Guardian*, December 9, 2010, www.guardian.co.uk/world/us-embassy-cables-documents/207723.

16. Ibid.

17. Tarek Osman, *Egypt on the Brink: From Nasser to Mubarak* (New Haven, Conn.: Yale University Press, 2010), 179.

18. Gardner, *Long Road to Baghdad*, 74–75.

19. Ibid., 75–76.

20. Ibid., 77.

21. Majid Khadduri and Edmund Ghareeb, *War in the Gulf, 1990–91: The Iraq-Kuwait Conflict and Its Implications* (New York: Oxford University Press, 1997), 127–28.

22. Ibid.

23. George Bush and Brent Scowcroft, *A World Transformed* (New York: Alfred A. Knopf, 1998), 363, 374.

24. Gardner, *Long Road to Baghdad*, 95.

25. Ibid., 113.

26. David Remnick, "Letter from Cairo: Going Nowhere: In Mubarak's Egypt, Democracy Is an Idea Whose Time Has Not Yet Come," *New Yorker*, July 12, 2004, www.newyorker.com/archive/2004/07/12/040712fa_fact1.

27. Ibid.

28. Stephen Grey, *Ghost Plane: The True Story of the CIA Torture Program* (New York: St. Martin's Press, 2006), 42.

29. DCM Stuart Jones, "Scenesetter for Deputy Secretary Zoellick's Visit to Egypt," May 14, 2006, WikiLeaks Cable Viewer, http://213.251.145.96/cable/2006/05; and see, for example, Jane Mayer, *The Dark Side: The Inside Story of How the War on Terror Turned into a War on American Ideals* (New York: Doubleday, 2008), 113.

30. Dana Priest, "CIA Holds Terror Suspects in Secret Prisons," *Washington Post*, November 2, 2005.

31. Scobey to Senator George Mitchell, January 23, 2009, WikiLeaks Cable Viewer, http://213.251.145.96/cable/2009/01.

32. Mary Beth Sheridan and Joby Warrick, "Mubarak Resignation Throws into Question U.S.-Egyptian Counterterrorism Work," *Washington Post*, February 13, 2011.

33. Mark Mazzetti and Scott Shane, "Old Arab Ties May Harm New Ones," *New York Times*, March 17, 2011, www.nytimes.com/2011/03/18/world/africa/18cia.html.

34. Hillel Frisch, "Guns and Butter in the Egyptian Army," *Middle East Review of International Affairs*, June 2001, http://meria.idc.ac.il/JOURNAL/2001/issue2/frisch .pdf.

35. Charles Levinson, "$50 Billion Later, Taking Stock of US Aid to Egypt," *Christian Science Monitor*, April 12, 2004, www.csmonitor.com/2004/0412.

36. Fawaz A. Gerges, *The Far Enemy: Why Jihad Went Global*, 2nd ed. (New York: Cambridge University Press, 2009), 139–45.

37. Levinson, "$50 Billion Later."

38. Charles Feldman and Stan Wilson, "Ex-CIA Director: U.S. Faces 'World War IV,'" CNN.com, April 3, 2003, http://articles.cnn.com/2003-04-03/us/sprj.irq.woolsey .world.war_1_woolsey-world-war-iv-cold-war?_s=PM:US.

39. Lee Smith, "Egypt After Mubarak: Beware the Trust-fundamentalists," *Slate*, July 9, 2004, www.slate.com/id/2103651/.

40. George W. Bush, "Address at Whitehall Palace," London, November 19, 2003, www.presidentialrhetoric.com/speeches/11.19.03.html.

41. "Rice Speech Promotes Democracy in Egypt," CNN.com, June 21, 2005, http:// articles.cnn.com/2005-06-20/world/mideast.rice_1_sharm-presidential-election-rice -speech?_s=PM:WORLD.

42. Michael Slackman, "Egyptian Political Dissident, Imprisoned for Years, Is Suddenly Released," *New York Times*, February 18, 2009.

43. Margaret Scobey, "Scenesetter for FBI Director Mueller," February 9, 2010, WikiLeaks Cable Viewer, http://213.251.145.96/cable/2010/02.

44. Scobey to Secretary of State, August 4, 2009, ibid., http://213.251.145.96/cable/ 2009/08/.

45. Gardner, *Long Road to Baghdad*, 257–58.

46. Eli Lake, "Déjà Vu in Cairo," *New Republic*, February 1, 2011, www.tnr.com/ article/world/82456/egypt-riots-bush-mubarak.

47. Matt Latimer, "When Bush Caved to Egypt," *Daily Beast*, January 30, 2011, www.thedailybeast.com/blogs-and-stories/2011-01-30/president-bush-pulled-his -punches-on-egypts-mubarak-too/.

48. "Jibes Highlight Bush-Mubarak Rift," May 20, 2008, BBC News, http://news .bbc.co.uk/go/pr/fr/-/2/hi/middle_east/7410669.stm.

49. Rick Kelly, "Bush Administration Defends US Military Aid to Egypt," World Socialist Web site, May 22, 2006, www.wsws.org/articles/2006/may2006/egyp-m22 .shtml.

50. Scobey to Petraeus, December 21, 2008, WikiLeaks Cable Viewer, http://wikileaks.ch/cable/2008/12/08.

51. "U.S. Said Frustrated with Egypt Military," CBS News, December 31, 2010, www.cbsnews.com/stories/2010/12/31/world/main7199741.shtml.

52. Scobey to Petraeus, December 21, 2008, WikiLeaks Cable Viewer.

53. Scobey to Pascual, January 27, 2009, WikiLeaks Cable Viewer, http://213.251.145.96/cable/2009/01.

54. Text of Obama's speech, *New York Times*, June 4, 2009.

55. Ibid.

56. Scobey to Department of State, July 22, 2009, WikiLeaks Cable Viewer, http://213.251.145.96/cable/2009/07.

57. Scobey to Department of State, July 2, 2009, ibid.

58. Scobey to Department of State, May 17, 2009, ibid., http://213.251.145.96/cable/2009/05.

59. Steven R. Hurst, "Obama, Mubarak Meet to Repair Relations After Bush," *Huffpost World*, August 18, 2009, www.huffingtonpost.com/2009/08/18/obama-mubarak-meet-to-rep_n_262194.html.

60. Scobey to Secretary of State, September 17, 2009, WikiLeaks Cable Viewer.

61. Mona Eltahawy, "Tunisia's Jasmine Revolution," *Washington Post*, January 15, 2011.

62. Abigail Hauslohner, "After Tunisia: Why Egypt Isn't Ready to Have Its Own Revolution," *Time*, January 20, 2011, www.time.com/time/world/article/0,8599,2043497,00.html.

63. Stephen M. Walt, "Why the Tunisian Revolution Won't Spread," *Foreign Policy*, http://walt.foreignpolicy.com/posts/2011/01/15/why_the_tunisian_revolution_wont_spread.

64. Dan Murphy, "Joe Biden Says Egypt's Mubarak No Dictator, He Shouldn't Step Down. . . ." *Christian Science Monitor*, January 27, 2011, www.csmonitor.com/World/Backchannels/2011/0127/Joe-Biden-says-Egypt-s-Mubarak-no-dictator-he-shouldn-t-step-down.

65. Ibid.

66. Kevin Dolak, "Hillary Clinton on the Crisis in Cairo: 'We Want to See Reforms,'" ABC News, January 30, 2011, http://abcnews.go.com/Politics/hillary-clinton-crisis-egypt-reforms/story?id=12797571.

67. "ElBaradei: Cut US Mubarak Support," *Al Jazeera*, January 30, 2011, http://english.aljazeera.net/news/middleeast/2011/01/201113020265198814.html.

68. Paul Richter and David S. Cloud, "Obama Pushes Mubarak to Fulfill Reform Pledge," *Los Angeles Times*, January 28, 2011, http://articles.latimes.com/2011/jan/28/world/la-fg-us-egypt-20110129.

69. "Timeline: Egypt's Revolution," *Al Jazeera*, February 14, 2011, http://english.aljazeera.net/news/middleeast/2011/01/201112515334871490.html.

70. Anthony Shadid, "Obama Urges Faster Shift of Power in Egypt," *New York Times*, February 1, 2011; "Baredi Says Mubarak Must Go," Reuters, February 1, 2011, www.reuters.com/article/2011/02/01/us-egypt-elbaredi-idUSTRE7109UH20110201.

71. Viola Gienger, "Three Decades with Egypt's Military Keep U.S. in Loop," Bloomberg.com, February 2, 2011, www.bloomberg.com/news/2011-02-02/three-decades-of-missions-weapons-training-for-egypt-keep-u-s-in-loop.html; Ewen MacAskill, "Egypt Protests: US Resists Calls to Cut Military Aid," *Guardian*, February 4, 2011, www.guardian.co.uk/world/2011/feb/04/egypt-protests-us-military-aid.

72. MacAskill, "Egypt Protests."

73. Leila Fadel, "Opposition: Mubarak Must Act Now or Risk 'Complete Chaos,'" *Washington Post*, February 9, 2011.

74. David D. Kirpatrick, Kareem Fahim, and Alan Cowell, "Protests Swell in Rejection of Egypt's Limited Reforms," *New York Times*, February 8, 2011; Scott Wilson, "Mubarak Defense Puts U.S. on Defensive," *Washington Post*, February 10, 2011.

75. Craig Whitlock, Ernesto Londono, and Leila Fadel, "Huge Demonstrations Across Egypt; Crowds Reject Mubarak's Stance," *Washington Post*, February 11, 2011.

76. Greg Miller, "Comments by Panetta Stoke Unmet Expectations," *Washington Post*, February 11, 2011.

77. Joby Warrick, "In Mubarak's Final Hours, Defiance Surprises U.S. and Threatens to Unleash Chaos," *Washington Post*, February 12, 2011.

78. Ibid.

6. Arab Spring

1. Scott Wilson, "Mubarak Resignation Creates Political Vacuum for U.S. in Middle East," *Washington Post*, February 12, 2011.

2. Tom Raum, "Obama Calls for Peaceful Response in Middle East," *Washington Post*, February 15, 2011.

3. Tom Curry, "U.S.-Egypt Military Links Come Under Stress," NBC Connecticut, February 11, 2011, www.nbcconnecticut.com/news/politics/U_S_-Egypt_military_links_come_under_stress-115878029.html.

4. Leila Fadel, "Mubarak Loyalists Change Stripes to Fit into the New Egypt," *Washington Post*, February 14, 2011; Viola Gienger, "U.S. Connects to Egypt's Army with Private Calls, Public Praise," *Bloomberg Businessweek*, February 13, 2011, www.businessweek.com/news/2011-02-13/u-s-connects-to-egypt-s-army-with-private-calls-public-praise.html.

5. David D. Kirkpatrick, "Egyptians Say Military Discourages an Open Economy," *New York Times*, February 17, 2011.

6. Aram Roston and David Rohde, "Business Side of Egypt's Army Blurs Lines of Aid from U.S.," *New York Times*, March 5, 2011.

7. Mona El-Naggar and Michael Blackman, "Hero of Egypt's Revolution, Military Now Faces Critics," *New York Times*, April 8, 2011.

8. MSNBC, "2 Killed After Egypt Army Cracks Down on Rally," April 9, 2011, www.msnbc.msn.com/id/42506738/ns/world_news-mideast/n_africa/.

9. Wilson, "Mubarak Resignation Creates Political Vacuum for U.S. in Middle East."

10. Adam Entous and Jay Solomon, "Crisis Flummoxes White House," *Wall Street Journal*, February 11, 2011, http://online.wsj.com/article/SB10001424052748703745704576136743649012416.html.

11. Robert M. Gates, "National Library for the Study of George Washington Groundbreaking Ceremony," Mount Vernon, Virginia, April 14, 2011, www.defense.gov/Speeches/Speech.aspx?SpeechID=1555.

Postscript

1. Emily Badger, "Why Are the World's Muslims So Mad at America?" Miller-McCune Journalism, May 19, 2011, www.miller-mccune.com/culture; Sarah Burke, "Poll Finds Deep Skepticism of U.S. in Egypt," *ABC News*, June 7, 2011, http://blogs.abcnews.com/thenote/2011.

2. Robert Tait, "Egypt Staves Off 'Revolution of the Hungry,'" *Radio Free Europe*, June 7, 2011, www.rferl.org/articleprintview/.

3. Burke, "Poll Finds Deep Skepticism of U.S. in Egypt."

4. Alan Shahine and Ahmed A. Namatalia, "Egypt Debt Buoyed by Obama Guarantee for $1 Billion Eurobonds: Arab Credit," June 13, 2011, www.bloomberg.com/news/print.

5. Tait, "Egypt Staves Off 'Revolution of the Hungry.'"

6. Shahine and Namatalia, "Egypt Debt Buoyed by Obama Guarantee."

7. David Gollust, "Clinton: NATO Committed to Reducing Afghan Civilian Deaths," June 1, 2011, VA News.com, www.printhis.clickability.com/.

8. Viola Glenger, "Pentagon's Foreign Military Aid May Face Cuts, Mullen Says," June 13, 2011, www.bloomberg.com/news/2011.

INDEX